NEXT TIME ROUND IN TUSCANY

Also by Ian Norrie

Non-fiction

Next Time Round in Provence
Next Time Round in the Dordogne
Sabbatical: Doing Europe for Pleasure
A Celebration of London (photographs by Dorothy Bohm)
Hampstead: London Hill Town (photographs by Dorothy Bohm)
The Book of Hampstead (Editor, with Mavis Norrie)
The Book of the City (Editor)
The Book of Westminster (Editor)
The Heathside Book of Hampstead and Highgate (Editor)
Writers and Hampstead (Compiler)
Hampstead, Highgate and Kenwood: A Short Guide

Publishing and Bookselling (with Frank A. Mumby)
Publishing and Bookselling in the Twentieth Century
Sixty Precarious Years: A Short History of the National Book
League, 1925–1985
A Hampstead Memoir: High Hill Bookshop, 1957–1988

Novels

Hackles Rise and Fall
Quentin and the Bogomils
Plum's Grand Tour

NEXT TIME ROUND IN TUSCANY

IAN NORRIE

with drawings by Michael Floyd

Aurum Press

First published in Great Britain 1998
by Aurum Press Ltd, 25 Bedford Avenue, London WC1B 3AT

Text copyright © 1998 by Ian Norrie
Illustrations copyright © 1998 by Michael Floyd

A catalogue record for this book is available from the British Library.

ISBN 1 85410 541 8

Design and maps by Don Macpherson
Typeset in Palatino
Printed and bound in Great Britain by MPG Book Division

For Michael, Rosalyn, Jonathan and Robert

In the hope that they will come to find
Tuscany as exhilarating as their grandparents do

List of Drawings

Contents

'My' Tuscany

My introduction to Tuscany, travelling in a cramped Ford Escort during a June heatwave, was via the coastal road from the naval port of La Spezia. It was not an auspicious start and has led to a lifelong antipathy to the resorts of the Italian Riviera. On this first visit my companions and I so disliked what we saw that, although on a direct route to Pisa, where we had made reservations, at Viareggio we turned inland to seek relief from the monotony of beaches backed by anonymous villas and hotels set amongst endless pine woods. We made for the walled city of Lucca and there the enchantment began.

On that initial visit we concentrated, as is usual and not unreasonable, on Pisa, Florence, San Gimignano, Siena, Fiesole, and they, between them, make a good recipe for cultural indigestion when you have only a fortnight.

First time rounders familiarize themselves at Pisa with the leaning tower, the cathedral complex and a view of the Arno, and try to ignore the souvenir stalls. At Florence (as we must call the beautifully named Firenze because that is the fashion in the English-speaking world) they will marvel at the dome of the cathedral, the carved doors of the baptistery, the Uffizi, the Ponte Vecchio, the Boboli Gardens, Michelangelo's *David*. They will stand in the Piazza della Signoria dazed by the effrontery of the seemingly incomparable tower rising above them, not at that moment knowing that a similar experience awaits them across Chianti country, when they make their way through gloomy Sienese streets to the Piazza del Campo. En route between these rival cities of the Renaissance they may well detour to San Gimignano through undulating countryside excitingly bristling with vines. There, in another walled town, they will observe the remaining twelfth–fourteenth-century towers of the medieval merchants who built them for defence and/or prestige.

When the heat of crowded Florence becomes intolerable the first timer, if he is permitted to act independently of a tour operator, or finds himself in the care of an enlightened one, will take the increasingly

9

steep hill northwards to the ancient Etruscan city of Fiesole, where the manifold delights on offer range from an excavated Roman theatre and baths, through an entrancing church and cloister, to a particularly exhilarating town hall and square.

But my theme is, what comes next? I had already been commissioned to write about Provence when Mavis and I thought up the next-time-round approach, as a guide to those places in a region where you go when you have done their Taj Mahals and Statues of Liberty, their Prados and their Horse Guards.

Now, having written and published Provence and the Dordogne, it is the turn of Tuscany, a formidably different task from either of its predecessors. The official area it covers (22,990 sq.km) is much larger than the two departments of Provence I chose, themselves more than twice the size of the single department of the Dordogne to which I all but confined myself.

Having cut 'my' Tuscany down to what I term the centre of the region it is still necessary to be more specific. I have omitted a whole chunk of the south, including the Maremma and Elba; I have cut off the north-west, the Apuan Alps and Garfagnana where the marble quarries of Carrara lie; I have been ruthless about the resorts on the Ligurian Sea because they are basically the same anywhere on the Mediterranean, indeed, anywhere in the world. I can tolerate sandy beaches for an hour or two but there is nothing I wish to write about them, even disparagingly.

'My' Tuscany is for the inquisitive who have already been to the places I have named, although every time round in this delectable region you must be drawn to Florence because it was the birthplace of the Renaissance and has immeasurable attractions on offer. Fourth, fifth, sixth time rounders will still swarm to the Medici capital. Florence may not be the most ravishingly beautiful city in the world but it has its own magnetism. In considering the structure of this book, it quickly came to me that I must spend more time on Florence than I had originally planned because, although I thought I was acquainted with its greatest treasures, I found a quite unexpected number of only slightly lesser ones that I had missed on earlier visits.

So 'next time round' does not mean neglecting favourite places. I will take you again to Pisa, Lucca, San Gimignano, Fiesole, Arezzo, Siena, to record familiar features, but I will concentrate more on the others. And we will delve into the countryside to see towns and villages which do not fill the colourful pages of most travel brochures.

The history of Italy as a whole is as complicated as that of most European states; that of Tuscany is marginally simpler because it was not

10

always dominated by the powers which occupied territories to its north and south. It is necessary, however, for a better understanding of Tuscany to think of Italy first and to view it geographically and historically at the same time. It is the most vulnerable of countries, with a long coastline which has attracted invasions by the Greeks, Normans, Germans, French and Spanish, plus the Allies of World War Two. Even from the north it has proved far from impregnable. Hannibal, Attila, Barbarossa, Napoleon and others made the Alps their highway. What is extraordinary is that the Italians in general, and the Tuscans in particular, developed and preserved a singular identity despite the fact that, until the unification of 1860, Italy was at no time one nation, although it had been part of both the Roman empire and also of Charlemagne's. But it must be remembered that the peninsula had enjoyed a common language for nearly six hundred years before achieving nationhood, since the time that the Tuscan dialect became Italian, thanks to the writings of Dante, Petrarch, Boccaccio and others.

Possibly the earliest arrivals, over the Alps in about 1000 BC, were the Villanovans, whose descendants seem to have been the Etruscans. For long, on the evidence of Herodotus, it was supposed that the Etruscans had come from the eastern Mediterranean, partly because they worshipped the same gods as the Greeks and developed an Aegean style of painting. This is no longer the received opinion, although derivation from the Villanovan culture does not explain the Greek influence. Wherever they came from, it is certain that the Etruscans worked minerals, built castles and walls, and were obsessed by funerary rites. They left behind them numerous burial grounds and tombs, along with much sculpture in and beyond the territory to which they have given their name. For a few centuries they were the dominant power in central Italy and the western Mediterranean. They formed a loose confederation of twelve cities including, under earlier names, Volterra, Arezzo, Cortona and Fiesole, and spread southwards to found a settlement on the site of Rome. Briefly, they ruled Rome.

Federation was not a recipe for prolonged rule and the Etruscans were no match for the Romans in the long run. All Italy and much of Europe and beyond was to become part of the Roman empire until the inevitable decline when, first, the Lombards (whose forebears had also made their way across the Alps) fought and pillaged their way towards Rome, ravaging Tuscany *en route*. Charlemagne, most militant of Christians, conquered the Lombards and became their king as well as Holy Roman Emperor, a title assumed and proudly maintained by a series of German princes who marched their forces into (and sometimes out of) the peninsula. In their time came the origin of the Guelph and Ghibelline factions, leading to a prolonged and often bloody feud symptomatic of the

11

Christian religion at its worst. The Guelphs supported the popes, the Ghibellines the emperors because, by now, the gratitude which the Christians of Rome had felt at being liberated by Charlemagne had become a bitter struggle for power between the spiritual and temporal contenders. Inevitably this became more complicated when Guelphs, in Florence, split into two camps, and when Ghibellines and Guelphs changed sides.

In the fourteenth century the Black Death, which killed up to fifty per cent of the population, effectively put paid to this fracas. Whilst it raged, and after it had abated, the church settled down to its own schisms (the popes went off to Avignon for most of the century) and individual city states in Tuscany which had already begun to organize and prosper sought to dominate each other.

In medieval times Pisa was the most powerful city. Lucca always contrived to remain aloof and independent. Siena and Volterra ruled over expanded territories but gradually it was Florence which came to be almost all powerful.

Scarperia: the road to La Concia

In Florence the Renaissance was born. In Florence, despite an interlude when the puritanical priest Savonarola exercised an authority which ended only with his burning, the Medicis came to rule for several centuries. They were tough administrators, formidable businessmen, generous art patrons. At least one of them became pope. When their line ended the Austrians, by the Treaty of Utrecht (1713), had replaced the Spaniards and the French as the chief foreign presence in Italy. The Holy Roman Empire had long since degenerated into a struggle for pre-eminence between the Spanish, who had infiltrated the centre and south (leaving the papal enclave of the Vatican intact), and the French, occupying the north. Tuscany sandwiched between them, enjoyed its Medicean independence, although it was not immune from territorial violation, or outright attack. Yet the arts continued to flourish in the aftermath of the Renaissance; so did commerce, banking, learning. It was as though the spirit of the Italian people was determined to prevail despite war and the machinations of kings and politicians.

The Treaty of Utrecht awarded the Grand Duchy of Tuscany to the French House of Lorraine, with which it had ties of marriage. Then, nearly one century later, Napoleon Bonaparte strode across the Alps, drove the Austrians out of Lombardy, occupied Venice (which he also plundered), turned his attention to Tuscany, appointing Elisa, his sister, Grand Duchess and had himself proclaimed king of the entire country, little knowing that within a few years he would be exiled to Elba.

After Napoleon's empire had disintegrated, the Congress of Vienna decreed that the Austrians should have their Italian territories restored. They held them until the movement for Italian independence, the Risorgimento, under Garibaldi, Cavour, Mazzini, was successful. In 1861 Victor Emmanuele II became king (the first Victor Emmanuele was king of Sardinia only), with his capital first at Turin; then, from 1865 to 1870, at Florence.

In World War One Italy was on the side of the Allies; in the second, thanks to having submitted to the dictatorship of Mussolini, she was, from 1940 to 1943, part of the Axis. This led to two grim years during which much of Italy, and almost all of Tuscany, was fought over by the retreating Germans and the slowly advancing Allies. Evidence of the widespread destruction wrought at that time will be found in many of the places to be visited in these pages, although much of it has been concealed by subtly effective restoration.

It is astonishing, in view of the havoc imposed upon town and countryside in this and previous centuries, that so much of the urban content particularly is still markedly medieval. Arezzo, Siena, central Florence, are still cities out of the Middle Ages. Pienza, Sinalunga, Poppi,

13

Montepulciano, Montalcino, Cortona and numerous others today have electricity, efficient plumbing, underground car-parks and all mod cons. They are into microwaving, faxing, e-mail, the internet. They bleep and whirr with the most advanced technological neuroses of our time. Yet, visually, they are five hundred years out of date. In all the towns and villages I visited whilst fieldworking this book I sought for something contemporary for Michael Floyd to draw. All I can remember is a bank outside the walls of San Casciano in Val di Pesa, a decent enough building in its own right, despite its function, but nothing to rank beside the hundreds of castles, Medici palaces, piazzas, churches, abbeys, farmhouses, courtyards, Gothic terraces and palazzi pretori/comunale, not to mention the hill towns, hill villages, hill hamlets, and the cellars, crypts, cloisters, undercrofts, canopied ways, loggias, arched over passages and streets with amazing gradients, lined with houses which ought to have crumbled away centuries ago. All these features I vividly recall but I cannot put a face on any twentieth-century edifice standing in its own right apart from that bank, the church at Castellina in Chianti (a Romanesque revival job) and the sprucely dull hillside of small villas overhanging the valley at Gaiole.

This exemplifies the paradox of modern Italy. So do the ingeniously constructed motorways which burrow through rock and are carried above deep ravines on bridges built on stilts, perpetuating a native genius for engineering handed down from Roman times. Once away from these impressive highways you are on your own in country lanes where the most frequent feature is a hairpin bend. For the most part you are architecturally well into the past, although high-rise building has, of course, encroached in Florence and other cities, and, in most towns, there are housing estates with blocks of 'workers' flats' looming over contemporary shops and villas. But, visually, they are no more photogenic than Gaiole; and the modern settlements, perched on, or spreading over, a neighbouring hillside are invariably apart from the medieval centre.

In the ancient parts, rebuilding and restoration have followed old street plans, steep, straight, cobbled or roughly paved thoroughfares leading from gated walls to a main piazza and cathedral. They are criss-crossed by concentric rings of other streets now forming an ingenious one-way system for the traffic. This has become essential because the narrow streets can take nothing wider or longer than the municipal dustcart. (This last comment does not apply to those 'new towns' of the thirteenth century laid out on the grid system, like French bastides. The designers of that age foresaw what eluded the planners of the early twentieth century.)

Medieval architecture in the cities can be oppressive. High six- to eight-storeyed buildings with overhanging eaves are a blessing in strong southern sunlight in June but on rainy days – and 'sunny Italy' gets a lot of

14

rain – they are gloomy, even sinister. The effect is lessened in the smaller urban centres just because of their size. Light is usually there at the end of the tunnel, the actual countryside probably being visible, making a pleasing backdrop to the vistas. And it is the countryside which is one of the three greatest glories of Tuscany. The other two are the art and the architecture.

Some of Tuscany is mountainous, the Apennine chain marking its northern and eastern boundaries. Much more is hilly. Comparatively little is flat. There is a plain through which the Arno flows westwards from Florence to the Ligurian Sea and here there is a centre of industry. Inevitably this is the least attractive part of the region. In the other direction from Florence the course of the Arno moves roughly south-south-east between the undulations of the wine-growing Chianti country on its western side, and the higher Pratomagno range to the east. Then, when Arezzo on the range's southern peak is already in view, it turns briefly towards the Adriatic, before rejecting that direction for the north, with the Pratomagno now on its western side. It rises above Stia, on the border with Romagna, in the Benedetto Alps.

The Chianti country, regarded by many as quintessentially Tuscan, lies between the valleys of the Arno and the Elsa, with Florence at its northern limit, Siena at its southern. It is dotted with small hill towns surrounded by vineyards, thick woods, olive groves, chestnut plantations, rows of cypresses picking out ridges, and partially hidden castles and abbeys. Some land is spared for cereal farming; dairy farming is not in evidence. There are few straight roads and a minimum of flat ones.

South of Siena the landscape – called Le Crete – changes abruptly, with greater sweeps of unwooded country and many volcanic peaks. The valleys of the Orcia and Chiana are wider than those of the Elsa and upper Arno, and they are dominated by the highest peak of the region, Monte Amiata. At all levels, towns and villages cling to the hillsides overlooking, or overlooked by, others. To the west of the Elsa there are more dramatic volcanic peaks than elsewhere; to the north of Florence, in the Mugello, the foothills of the Apennines prevail.

Much of Tuscany can be reached only by using country roads. Motorways do not, as yet, connect all the principal places and, even when they do, there will still be many communities accessible solely by secondary roads. Some of these plunge into deep valleys or snake up tree-clad hillsides and over mountains. Almost everywhere the views are ravishing. I shall try not to comment on them too often but you may expect, unless you are curiously unresponsive to natural beauty, to give vent to much ooh-ing, and even more aah-ing, at what you observe as this bend is rounded and that hilltop scaled. Very little of the terrain is savage. This is a land

15

that has been lived in and worked for more than two millennia, apart from periods when malarial marshes made habitation impractical. Few, if any, parts of Tuscany are unknown, although some forests are so vast and deep that they cannot have been much explored, except in wartime. Many sections of it are still truly off the beaten track, despite official Italian Tourist Board signposts encouraging visitors to remote churches and archaeological sites. If the overall response attracts coach parties it will become necessary either to ban them or to strip lush greenery to make parking spaces. At venues such as the monastery of La Verna this has already happened. I can only absolve myself of guilty feelings for mentioning some of these remote places by adding the recommendation that you should travel to them on foot, by bike or in the smallest available Fiat. (As I did not.)

Between five and six hundred years ago Florence became the centre of the Renaissance, the term given to the rebirth of classical art and architecture which Giotto had heralded a century earlier. In painting, this gave the world Masaccio, Fra Angelico, Piero della Francesca, Botticelli, Leonardo, Michelangelo, the Lippis, the della Robbias, as well as Duccio and Raphael, who do not come into the Tuscany story. In architecture, there were Michelozzo, Brunelleschi, the Sangallos, Sansovino, Vasari, Michelangelo again – all these and many others. It was the end of the church's stranglehold on creativity. Even religious subjects were allowed secular backgrounds and non-religious ones became tolerated. The Middle Ages were over.

It is the work of the men I have mentioned, and of others, in the Sienese and Pisan schools, for instance, that are to be appreciated in the cities and galleries of Tuscany, in the cathedrals, churches, Medici villas, town halls. You can become punch drunk from the paintings after overexposure to countless annunciations, depositions, nativities, assumptions, crucifixions, last suppers, pietàs and maestàs. Saturation level can be reached quite quickly, but above all the fifth- and sixth-rate representations of adoring magi, kneeling supplicants, apostles and madonnas stand out the works of those masters who illustrated the familiar themes with their own touch of genius, introducing notes of secularity, even profanity, into their work. Much of this output can still be appreciated without the visitor having to become part of a seething tourist throng. This applies even in Florence and Siena, and certainly in Arezzo, Sansepolcro, Cortona and other places on my itineraries. In Florence, alas, there is a serious problem and, short of issuing limited numbers of visas to visit the city, I don't know how it is to be resolved. I count myself lucky to have been many times to the Uffizi in the days when you did not have to queue for hours to gain admission. I doubt I will ever step inside it again unless regulated entry by

16

advance booking is introduced.

The same problem applies to the architectural riches, particularly, again, those of Florence, and also of Pisa, but there is still much that can be appreciated without becoming a victim of overcrowding.

The Romans were, of course, in Tuscany. Sufficient of an excavated theatre is there in Fiesole for the visitor to test the acoustics; the vestigial remains of an amphitheatre can be seen in Arezzo and statuary can be found in various museums, but there is nothing as spectacular as you will find in Rome, Verona, Arles, Bath or on Hadrian's Wall. The Etruscans are much more extensively represented, particularly in their tombs, several thousands of which may be viewed *in situ* or in museums. As for Renaissance architecture, it is the very soul of many of the places we shall visit, and I find it endlessly fascinating and rewarding to study the palazzi pretori (town halls) and castles where outer walls are often emblazoned with crests and medallions of the families who ruled over, and probably tyrannized, the communities they administered. These emblems are irregularly positioned, affixed to the nearest convenient vacant space. Some are gaily coloured, some dull and grey. They relate history in terms that can be easily understood. I love them. Michael Floyd's drawings include a selection; they are a theme of the book.

As in my previous volumes on Provence and the Dordogne, I have suggested itineraries. This is as much for the convenience of the writer as the reader. Some pattern must be imposed for the sake of coherence but I do not suppose that anyone will slavishly follow my routes. For one thing, wherever you stay, some of each day's undertaking will involve you in travel between one high spot and the next; for another, you will not wish to fall victim to cultural or touristic dyspepsia. Do not attempt to take in too many sights or sites at one go. They will all be there next year, as J.G. Links, author of the best travel guide ever, *Venice for Pleasure*, would say, earthquakes and other acts of God permitting. Enjoy at leisure all the riveting things that there are to be seen. Do not, while at Colle di Val d'Elsa, walking the tightrope of this hill town perched upon a ridge, be fretting for San Gimignano or Volterra, and wondering if you have time to take in both of them. And when you do reach one or other of them, don't enquire anxiously of your companions, 'Will there be time for San Miniato, too, today?' Instead, sit down opposite the cathedral, at either place, preferably at a restaurant with an awning against the sun, and enjoy a three-course lunch, washed down with litres of the local wine. When replete, arise and explore. That is how travel should be.

I do not give opening times or quote prices of admission unless they call for comment for other reasons; nor, with a few exceptions, do I recommend hotels and restaurants. Owners and chefs change, so do meal

17

Volterra: skyline

and ticket prices. For the most up-to-date information always consult the Michelin Red and Green Guides. They are indispensable, although I hope to take you to places that they do not include.

For long, one of the curses of touring in Italy was to find that the particular museum, castle, archaeological site that you intended to visit was closed because of a strike or for lack of staff. When this was so the cost of admission was probably insufficient to pay for printing the ticket and nowhere, if you were of pensionable age, were you charged. Today few places make concessions to pensioners, although groups sometimes qualify for a discount, and admission prices are more realistic, anything from three to ten thousand lire. This is not because there is any greater stability of government in Italy than of yore (the average life of an administration is eight months) but because someone in authority somewhere makes this attractive country function, even though anarchy and inflation seem rampant. I cannot say whether it is the Mafia, the Roman Catholic Church (always an influential presence) or a handful of level-headed civil servants who enforce decisions which they or others have made, but work it does, in my experience. Shops are well stocked, hotels are efficiently run, the trains and buses keep to advertised schedules, the banks change Eurocheques without demur, more and more businesses accept credit cards and it is even known for postcards to reach their foreign destinations before the sender arrives home.

One reform that would prove a blessing, for all visitors at least, would be for the lira to lose two noughts. For a British person, in the 1990s, wishing to have roughly £100 in cash, around one quarter of a million lire must be purchased, but at least small change is no longer given in individually wrapped fruit drops. Instead, rounding up, or even down, is the policy.

Perhaps the most reassuring aspect you will find on revisiting Tuscany is that it is still different. Despite the efforts of some

18

Euro-bureaucrats to impose uniformity in as many directions as they can detect on the compass, Tuscany and Italy are still very much abroad. *Not* everyone speaks English, most shops close on Sundays (unlike Britain), almost everyone uses per favore and grazie for every exchange of information and business, salt has still not been introduced into breadmaking and it is impossible to make an Italian understand that a teabag should be immersed in water at the moment of boiling.

On our first visit to Italy, forty years ago, the friend who drove us there burst into an aria as we crossed the border. 'Everyone in Italy,' proclaimed Martyn, 'down to the youngest butcher's boy, whistles or sings Puccini all the time.' I cannot recall actually encountering a butcher's boy, let alone hearing one whistle themes from opera, but I believe it is not too exaggerated to state that, in this land where natural disasters alternate with economic catastrophes and where the countryside has all too often heard the sound of the invaders' marching feet, it is rare for the visitor to confront a native who lacks innate charm. From nearly everyone you meet you can expect a sparkling smile, a wide-faced grin, a willingness to help. For me, the feel-good factor in Tuscany is almost always apparent. Even on hairpin bends.

Note

On all my journeys I was accompanied by my ever helpful friend, Christopher Wade, and on some also by my wife. They are referred to in the text, without further explanation as 'Christopher' and 'Mavis'. I am most grateful to Christopher and to Martyn Goff, for reading my typescript, pointing out errors and making constructive suggestions, and also to Julia MacRae, who removed some howlers at proof stage.

My dear friend, Michael Floyd, who illustrated this book and previous ones in the series, died on 6 December 1997. He was the most amiable and untemperamental of collaborators. Pat, his wife, Christopher, Mavis and I enjoyed what was to be our final fieldwork lunch together at a restaurant in Fiesole overlooking the subject of the drawing on p. 34.

The full names and dates of birth and death (where known) of painters, architects, sculptors etc., referred to in the text are included in the Index. Italian words and phrases have not been italicized because almost all those I use have become incorporated into current English and have entries in our dictionaries. The few which do not fall into this category are defined when they first appear unless their meaning is obvious.

1   The Mugello

Bosco ai Frati; Cafaggiolo; San Piero a Sieve; Scarperia; Borgo San Lorenzo; Vicchio; Monte Senario; Settignano; Fiesole; Pratolino; Sesto Fiorentino

If you come to Tuscany by air you will probably fly to Pisa international airport, where you will hire a car; there is also a smaller terminal at Florence. If you come by train, again Pisa or Florence are your obvious setting-down points. But if you bring your car you have a choice of Alpine passes, or you can take the thunderous autostrada, which is a continuation of the French A8, and pass the time counting the number of tunnels and viaducts, and guessing which will notch up a century first. I prefer to use the Mont Cenis pass. Not from any wish to follow in the footsteps of Napoleon, this being the route by which he descended upon the plains of Lombardy, arriving at the foothill town of Susa, as Hannibal and others had before him, but because I enjoy the drive over the Mont Cenis.

After Susa a fast and efficient autostrada, entirely lacking tunnels and bridges until after Bologna, gets you speedily to Tuscany. Some way before Florence you leave the motorway to enter the wondrous countryside which you have been passing by and over since the scenically dull Lombardy plain ended. You take the Barberino exit when you are still in wild, mountainous terrain, having noticed little by way of inhabited land for miles. Nor is there much when you pay your toll and take signs to Borgo San Lorenzo. Here, you are in mid but not spectacularly high Apennine territory, although you will soon come to the Mugello valley through which the River Sieve flows.

You are privileged to arrive on the northern doorstep of Florence in better shape, and by a better road, than Barbarossa's army tramped along in the twelfth century. Nor, with any luck, will you suffer the pestilence that decimated his troops. Other invaders used other valleys, one bringing them, via the once heavily fortified town of Firenzuola (whither I am not taking you), to Scarperia, which is very much next time round and will repay your attention. We have twice stayed in an old farm building in its environs.

Although it was at Lucca that our enchantment with Tuscany began, it was on a wooded hilltop close to Scarperia that Mavis and I first pierced its skin and began to probe its subtleties. Since then we have stayed, on several occasions, well off the beaten track, down unmade roads leading to and from remote mills, farmhouses, solid and not-so-solid second homes. It was at Scarperia, during our five months' sabbatical in 1982, when we toured Europe from Amsterdam to Istanbul and back to Paris, via Greece, Italy and Iberia, that we had the blissful experience of spending eight nights at La Concia, a converted stone barn where, astonishingly, both electricity and water were supplied. The shower was often merely a trickle, the voltage was low, but we found ourselves in a demi-paradise where Mavis was amazed to observe that I didn't mind having hens pecking away an inch from my feet as I lay reading in the tiny garden. I even became acclimatized to the Pavlovian barking of Coma, the alsatian, so cleverly leashed that it was safe for those who lived in our part of the barn to pass by him unscarred. The young couple who occupied the upper part of the building lived there only in the summer months. For the rest of the year, when it is often bitingly cold, they had an apartment in Scarperia, from which the signor set off each morning to make his calls, as a commercial traveller, to places as far distant as Milan. Like many people living in towns they had a summer residence to mitigate the effects of intense heat.

From La Concia we had planned to make regular trips to Florence and Fiesole. In the event, during those eight days, and during another stay two years later, we seldom ventured beyond Scarperia. We immersed ourselves in the placidity of the setting, the only tensions arising, in my case, not from hen-pecking, but from having to drive daily to town to fetch provisions, along a singularly rutted and tortuous lane. There was no freezer and in any case Italian bread is horrific enough on the day of baking without making it last longer. It is extraordinary that in the total of fifteen days that we stayed there I never met another vehicle on this imitation, narrow, ancient Roman road. But it is only by staying somewhere as isolated as La Concia that you can begin to enjoy the true flavour of Tuscany.

Barberino, to which you are soon signed after leaving the motorway, was once a Florentine border fortress against Bologna. One guide offered a fifteenth-century palazzo pretorio and a thirteenth-century Medici villa. We could find neither and both a priest and a municipal official denied all knowledge of them. The main square is pleasant but unexceptional. Beside a teatro comunale stood a group of villainous-looking layabouts. Christopher and I made our way to a *badia* (abbey) standing, with an ugly, peeling frontage, attached to a short terrace of houses. My advice is to stay on the road which bypasses Barberino and, instead, watch for a turning to Bosco ai Frati. From it a superior track leads through farm and woodland to a Franciscan chapel, part of a monastery, which Cosimo the Elder commissioned Michelozzo to rebuild early in the fifteenth century. The Medici emblem of six balls can be seen on pillars above the portico. In the chapter room of the church, which will almost certainly be locked, is a wooden crucifix by Donatello. The most remarkable feature, however, can be seen just below the eaves on the outside of the nave. Here, part of the cornice which is decorated with a honeycomb pattern continuing round the five-bay apse, has been replaced by an actual honeycomb. You will see bees entering and leaving it. Which came first, the bees or the decoration?

The church has a nave but no aisles. The single bell tower is enclosed between the apse and the nave, with one side becoming part of the outer wall of the whole church. The frontage, above the portico, looks like modern stone-cladding; in it is a rose window. At right angles to the facade is a house where, if you are fortunate, you may obtain the key to the church.

From the church you can continue along the track, parts of which are not badly surfaced, directly to Scarperia, but my route takes you back to the main road because, further along, in the direction of Borgo San Lorenzo is a Medici fortress which the same Michelozzo converted into a country home for Cosimo. The Medicis hailed from these parts and had many homes built for themselves in their native countryside. There is another, also by Michelozzo, at nearby Trebbio, but let us settle for Cafaggiolo. It, like Trebbio, is private property so there is no visitors' car-park but you can pull into the driveway, or find a space by the post office of the so-called town. (I counted all of six houses visible from the road but perhaps there is more of it lurking out of view. It is said to be known for its majolica ware, but I did not see any of that either.) Nevertheless, it is worth stopping to ogle the Medici complex through the railings. Michelozzo may have converted the fortress into something domesticated by fifteenth-century standards, but to me it looks like a very finely preserved and moderately impregnable castle. There is a formidable gatehouse, with a rusticated, rounded doorway. This reaches two storeys higher than the bulk of the building. High crenellations run round the entire edifice and the top floor, once open battlements, is enclosed with low windows under an overhanging roof. It does, I have to say, look just a little like a prison. This effect is toned down by two giant cedars on the lawn and a pretty, half-timbered free-standing annexe, at an angle of 45 degrees, one of Michelozzo's innovations. It has a ground floor and mezzanine and could have been stables. Michelozzo was a pupil of Brunelleschi and worked for the Medicis in many places. He was one of the most renowned architects of his time. Lorenzo (later to be dubbed the Magnificent) and his brother, Giuliano, spent some of their childhood here. One guide says that the fine interior is now used for storing hay, adding that it may be visited by appointment. There is no sign on the spot to suggest this but you could always ask at the post office.

Soon after turning in the Scarperia direction you reach San Piero a Sieve, a little town on the hillside overlooking the river. The Medicis were here too but they employed a younger architect than Michelozzo, one Bernardo Buontalenti, to run them up a fortress for defensive purposes, in 1569. Two centuries later it was turned into a farmhouse. Its name is San Martino and it stands on a wooded hillside but it was closed for repairs when we were there. What made our stop worthwhile was the Villa Adami, a splendidly maintained town house coloured in a rich yellow wash, with a little wrought-iron balcony above the round top door, both symmetrically placed, with three bays on either side. Late sixteenth–early seventeenth century, at a guess, it is now used as a social centre, and municipal library, with function rooms. The caretaker delayed her lunch to allow us in. She took us up two flights of stairs to a small back entrance, off a narrow alley, leading by steep steps to an overgrown public garden for the use of the elderly. I didn't see any takers.

Over the door of one functions room there is a sculpture, on the pediment, of a lion ravenously demolishing a cow. The door is off an inner courtyard lit by street lamps fixed to the walls. Another carving, of a much larger lion (the symbol of Florence) faces the villa across the forecourt. The way up to San Martino is beside it.

The drab parish church of unrendered brick has grass growing from the roof of the nave and faces an equally battered-looking Oratorio della Misericordia of the thirteenth century. The church is said to have a fifteenth-century font by one of the della Robbias, much of whose work we shall see all over Tuscany. I missed this one. The church looked not so much closed as abandoned.

The road climbs from San Piero to Scarperia, a handsome, almost compact, town with a modest grid system and an outstanding palazzo pretorio, modelled on Florence's Palazzo Vecchio. If your architect is in imitative mood, what finer example could he choose? The frontage has over one hundred emblems and plaques fixed to it. It overpowers the thin main street, running north–south, but opposite is a small piazza where you can stand back to admire its massive presence. It was built in the early 1300s to accommodate the deputies of the Mugello region who conferred here, and the attached palace was the home of the military governor. Scarperia was an important link in the defence system protecting the northern borders of Florentine territory. The palazzo is an exciting yet simple building with its battlemented tower and adjoining frontage dotted as irregularly with windows as it is with plaques. Inside there are frescoes to be seen and exhibitions are held. From the piazza, the size is deceptive,

Scarperia: Palazzo Pretorio

concealing from view a formidable mass of palace and townhall behind the facade.

In the piazza are two churches, one of them a Gothic oratory with a shrine by Jacopo del Casentino. The other has a Madonna and Child by Benedetto da Maiano, whose mentor was Michelozzo, and another painting of the same subject by Taddeo Gaddi. (I shall not mention all the madonnas and babies that are to be seen in Tuscany – just a few hundred for good measure.) In the Oratorio there is another, said to be by Filippo Lippi.

The main street has all the necessary shops on two sides but parking only on one. At the foot of the 'high street' is a shady public garden with fish pond and children's playground, and down a side street from it is Il Torrino di Scarperia Collacchioni, boasting another fourteenth-century tower. This also is municipally owned and is used for sculpture exhibitions. It overshadows a strange building with many chimneys and

25

another with a large pigeon house. Below the gardens is an establishment proclaiming itself Moulin Rouge – Music Hall.

In different vein, at 3.5 km, is the Mugello race track, built in 1974 for motor cyclists. More to my taste, on a road parallel to the west of the town, is the poignant entrance to the hillside where we stayed at La Concia, preluded by a lane through flat fields with cypresses, alone or in small groups, standing as elegant sentinels. Silhouetted against sky and distant mountains they symbolize Tuscany for me. (See drawing, p. 72.)

On the outskirts of the town there are nowadays more signs of industrialization than when I first knew it, although long before that it was celebrated for the manufacture of cutlery. To get to Borgo San Lorenzo there is a main road back through San Piero or another, winding across farm land, which adds variety to the journey.

Borgo is more industrial than Scarperia and much larger. It is a centre of agriculture as well as commerce and has a reputation for earthquakes, one of which, in 1919, wrought terrible havoc. It has a small, old centre into which are crammed church, town hall, market square and a few medieval streets and gateways. Outside the walls, the Piazza Dante has wide avenues of trees over gravel paths used in the passeggiata (the evening promenade). There is also an outsize war memorial and, as a change from Garibaldi, a statue of a hound named Fido, said to have been a symbol of fidelity. Parking is free and, since we are talking of cars, it was here that a woman driver stopped for me, voluntarily, on a pedestrian crossing.

The church, whose frontage appears to have been rebuilt, following the earthquake, with breeze blocks of varying hues, is of no special interest apart from its campanile which is on top of the actual apse and, for that reason, is shaped like a crescent. This makes it a collectors' piece. Some books, erroneously, refer to it as hexagonal, which it certainly is not from what is visible on the outside. It is said to be thirteenth century but the actual church dates from the twelfth, although it suffered from imposed baroquery in the sixteenth. The interior has a Madonna and Child, possibly by Taddeo Gaddi, and it is claimed that the face of the virgin on the reredos is by Giotto. Beside the frontage is a statue of St Francis, with badges and emblems of all the churches for which he is named decorating both sides, a variation on the pennant theme popular on the rear windows of cars. The town's own emblems are inside the rebuilt hall, on what may once have been its outer wall. Or is it a replica? Old and rehabilitated old merge in a country devastated by war and earthquake but what matters, as with the face which may or may not have been painted by Giotto, is, do they arrest you, give you an authentic sense of the past? Often, as here, they do.

Within sight of the church are the governor's palace and the

26

Borgo San Lorenzo: clock tower

clock tower which survived the last earthquake and is a favourite with young painters. This is understandable because it is like a rather grotesque modern sculpture, an elongated abstract with a high, pointed arch between its 'legs', and with its 'arms' clutching at the roofs of two lower buildings. There is something faintly suggestive about it, although the view between its 'legs' is of a demure old street, perfectly framed.

The shops in Borgo indulge in leisurely closing for the siesta. Many remained open up until 13.30, by which time Christopher and I were having problems finding a restaurant. Eventually we located one, off the Piazza Romagnoli, with an inner courtyard under an awning rife with vines and roses. The Ristorante Birreria degli Artisti claims to have the ambience of an English pub but that can mean anything. It specializes in its own pastas and Christopher indulged in potato-filled ravioli. I opted for typically dry lamb chops with herbs clinging to them like lichen. The Italians are not always strong on sauces with their meats. But the after-taste was good and so was the white wine of the house. While waiting to be served I became intrigued watching a man living high above the courtyard who was having problems keeping pigeons out of his penthouse.

Borgo has a Porta Fiorentina of the fourteenth century, part of the surviving walls of the town.

At Vicchio, farther down the valley of the Sieve, east of Borgo, name-dropping could become endemic. Fra Angelico was born here, so, stretching a parish, was Giotto. Benvenuto Cellini spent his final twelve years in the town and close by, for good reason, there is a Ponte Cimabue, although Giotto's precursor was actually born in Florence.

Fra Angelico's credentials vis-à-vis Vicchio are impeccable. There is a plaque on the site of the house where he was born, in the Via Garibaldi, a museum is named for him on the Piazzetta Don Milani and a school also commemorates him. Fra Angelico, known also as Beato Angelico, became a Dominican monk near Fiesole (see below) and was so intrinsically devout that it is recorded he prayed on every occasion for inspiration before taking up his brush. On the routes I have chosen his work will be encountered many times, though not in the house at Vicchio where the major exhibit is an Andrea della Robbia of St John the Baptist. Angelico gets a statue there in which he is depicted wearing monk's clothing and clasping a palette to his chest. I have this only from hearsay; museums in Tuscany, like churches, have a tendency to be closed when I am in the offing.

Nor did I see anything more than the exterior of the house where Cellini died. He was a braggart and a cheat, but also a superb sculptor, engraver, goldsmith, silversmith (the salt cellar reached a peak of perfection in the sixteenth century, thanks to him) and he wrote a masterpiece

28

of autobiography. The house where he ended his days is unremarkable but made less than humdrum by the adornment of a plaque. A road is named after him and, at one end of it, the original town walls are incorporated into contemporary housing. Close by is a medieval tower, next to a Renaissance loggia. You might imagine the tower to be part of the adjacent church but when you enter through an open doorway you are confronted by private post boxes. It has become an apartment block.

I confess that, in poor weather, the charm can quickly wear off old Italian stone buildings and I'm not averse to spending my nights in comfortable modern hotels, but it is the picturesque that beckons us to Italy and the tower at Vicchio comes into that category whatever the living conditions may be like inside it.

Giotto was born (probably) in the next-door hamlet of Vespignano but he has a statue in Vicchio in an agreeable piazza where a pale yellowish-cream church in one corner has a muted, unobtrusive presence.

The birthplace is well signed off the Borgo–Vicchio road and here there are many artefacts relating to his life and work. Vasari states that the artist was the son of a poor peasant farmer who gave him the name of Giotto instead of his own, which was Bondone. Set to tend sheep, the young Giotto spent his time in the fields sketching and it was while he was thus engaged that Cimabue, on a visit from Florence, came across him and was so impressed that he asked permission to take the child to his studio. Father Bondone agreed and, no doubt, that is why the bridge is called Cimabue. It marks the spot where the two early masters met.

The Casa di Giotto may, or may not, be authentic. It certainly doesn't look seven hundred years old, but it is reasonable to suppose that over the centuries there have been necessary renovations and a few new roofs. Its presence, however, and that of the statue at Vicchio, allow visitors to concentrate their minds on this great painter who, aided by the example and teaching of Cimabue, kick-started Renaissance painting, substantiated the school, and gave us all that stunning work at Assisi, Padua and elsewhere. And if some of the paintings are only 'school of' in the estimation of art historians, then Giotto had some talented pupils; but never mind whose hand held the brush, what is the effect on you, the viewer? The more you are exposed to painting the more likely you are to become discerning. Even though you lack the expertise of a Berenson or a Clark you will very likely come to detect genius, or lack of it, and begin to form your own judgement. There will be plenty of opportunity to test this theory, if you need to, when you visit the galleries and churches included in this book.

Return to Borgo San Lorenzo, perhaps turning from the main road briefly to take a respectful look at the Ponte Cimabue, then embark on

29

a slightly tortuous route to reach the highest point of this tour, the monastery of Monte Senario. There is a main road to Olmo, also a minor one which joins the first half-way. Both go through luscious country. Just before Olmo double back on your tracks, again on a minor road, to reach the monastery which, inexplicably, is omitted from so many books about the region.

Senario was built in the 1230s for the Order of the Servants of Mary. Its founding saints were seven high-born Florentines who renounced their wealth and material goods, and retired to this summit, over 800 metres high. At first the approach, after a drive through quite bland countryside, is sinister, with a particularly thick fir wood on either side of a steep ascent, the Way of Silence. Then the trees thin and you see the actual monastery (rebuilt in the seventeenth–eighteenth centuries) ahead of you, up a straight, wide avenue of deciduous trees. There are car-parks, a picnic area, with an enormous slab of rock for a table, bottle banks, dustbins, toilets, a bus stop. Two rows of steps lead to the somewhat gaunt chapel which has a baroque interior. However, the main motive for the visit is to perambulate on the terrace around the monastery and take in the truly panoramic views which, some claim, are the finest in the whole region. They are sensational from all sides and while you are experiencing them I doubt you will wish to dispute the claim. There is an atmosphere of total tranquillity. This emanates as much from what you observe of sweeping folds in the hills and mountains, of valleys, rivers, fields and woods encompassing little by way of habitation, as from the holiness within. The air is pure. Drink it in. Rejoice a while in the stillness of it all and reflect, perhaps, how wise those thirteenth-century Florentine nobles were. From the approach road there is a private drive to the cave of one of them, St Alexis, and the fountain of another, St Filippo Benizzi.

Descend through the dense woods to the winding small town of Bivigliano where no two houses are on the same level. Most of them are of recent construction, some are second homes for less than saintly modern Florentines, others are let to visitors. I can think of few places more delectable to make your centre for a tour of the Mugello.

Six kilometres or so to the south, past Caselline, is the Parc Demidoff, on the edge of Pratolino, a small town of little if any antiquity.

There was once a Medici villa here but since its demolition in the nineteenth century Demidoff has become the name of a planned garden with grottoes, fountains, ponds, avenues of trees, statuary – all set in entrancing country. Montaigne, who came here soon after the villa was built, is said to have been moved to raptures by the setting. The gardens are open for part of the week only.

Another route from Bivigliano rejoins the main road we left

before Olmo and leads to Fiesole, but first we will wander off it again to make a vertiginous descent, through more woods and olive groves to Settignano, and the Villa Gamberaia, and to pay homage to various great men. There is a link with no less a genius than Michelangelo who was placed here with a wet nurse and later spent part of his boyhood living among the stone cutters working the greyish-blue rock featured in many Florentine buildings. Michelangelo's father and brother lived here in the latter part of their lives. Other architects and sculptors of distinction were born here, or in nearby Maiano. Settignano was also popular with the Florentine upper crust, some of whom are described by Boccaccio in the *Decameron* as taking refuge here from the plague. In the same fourteenth century the Benedictine monks erected a monastery slightly to the east of the town and cultivated land around it. The Villa Gamberaia now stands on this spot.

In the nineteenth century the British streamed in, followed by the American Bernard Berenson who spent much of the remainder of his life at the villa I Tatti, becoming the foremost authority on Italian Renaissance painting. He formulated the tactile approach to authenticating canvases and was the acknowledged expert who decided which master-piece was the work of which master. His method should not be followed too literally or you may set alarm bells ringing. Berenson was often the cen-tre of controversy in the art world. The experience of living and working with him is entertainingly recorded in Kenneth Clark's first volume of autobiography. The Berensons and I Tatti feature also in many accounts of Tuscan life among the expatriate British and American communities. He certainly chose his venue well. From Settignano you look down and over the whole of Florence, with views of it surpassed only by those from Fiesole. The poet-statesman Gabriele d'Annunzio was a short-term resident and gave his name to a long avenue leading down to the Medici city. Here he celebrated his affair with the great tragedienne Eleonora Duse. It was in Settignano, also, that Mark Twain is said to have written *Puddn'head Wilson*.

In the town itself, which has one of the steepest straight streets I have encountered, and which you enter after passing through a stretch of country where the young lady in Forster's *A Room with a View* was, or was not, kissed in a meadow, is the church of Santa Maria. Here there is a Madonna and Child with two angels by Andrea della Robbia and a pulpit by Buontalenti. On another road, in the Florence direction, is San Martino a Mensola where, according to one writer, the body of the Scottish St Andrew lies.

The main object of your visit, unless you are going to I Tatti, now a centre of Renaissance studies, administered by Harvard University, is the Villa Gamberaia. The monastery where the Benedictines once worked and prayed was converted into a villa modelled on Pliny's description of his Tuscan home, with gardens inspired by Leon Alberti's 'ideal garden'. The road leading to it, out of Settignano, is narrow and becomes narrower. The entrance to the villa, immediately before a tunnel in the hillside, has room for all of four cars to park.

The Gamberaia, privately owned, is on two floors. All you will see of the interior is the hall where you pay for admission. You are then directed into the gardens, to roam at will. They are formal, impeccably maintained and trance-inducing in their quietness. The walled garden has statues of dogs and lions, and much foliage. There are two ponds in what you might fancifully dub the nave and a third, in the ambulatory, covered in lilies and overhung by cypresses and yews. At one end of a grassy terrace beside the house is an immaculate umbrella pine standing handsomely apart from the other trees. Facing the house on two sides is a formal high hedge to trim which the gardeners have to climb elaborate platform ladders. Beyond it is a rough olive grove that comes as something of a relief after so much rigid geometrical layout. On the east side of the house is an enclosure of grottoes and mosaics. The entire garden was destroyed in World War Two, since when it has been lovingly restored under the direction of Marcello Marchi, then by the present owners, Antonio and Pier Capponi, all with expert assistance.

After a day spent tramping around Florence a spell at the Villa Gamberaia is particularly acceptable. From the west terrace you can see down to where you have been and rejoice in the absence of motor scooters and other polluting agents. The admission price of 12,000 lire (slightly more than £5 in 1997) is well worth it. I hope, by recommending it, I shall not cause a traffic jam in the so-called car-park. When a fifth visitor left his vehicle there he was summoned to remove it so that a tractor could gain access to the olive grove. It seems almost criminal to disturb the solitude of the villa but it is advertised as being open to the public.

If you have to live and work in London the ideal place for a home is on the northern heights, at Hampstead or Highgate; if you must be close to your business in Florence you will probably aim to live in or around Fiesole, if you can afford to. But, whereas London pre-dates its most desirable suburbs, Fiesole was a centre of civilization long before Florence and in the range of what it has to offer today it is superior to its English counterparts. It is, in fact, one of Tuscany's prime attractions and access is relatively difficult because the motorway doesn't come near it on any side.

One reason for Fiesole's long dominance of Florence was geographical. Whereas Florence is a mere 49 m above sea level, Fiesole is 295.

In the sixth and seventh centuries, when the Etruscans founded the latter place, the Arno basin on which Florence stands was marshy and mosquito-ridden. Fiesole on its eminence was an obvious location for one of the cities of the Etruscan federation. Scarcely anything of what was built then remains outside of museums because the Romans made a thorough job of creating their own settlement in their traditional image. Much of their theatre, set against the northern hillside, has been excavated and the ruins of the baths, and of a temple, may be inspected when you go 'backstage'. On the same site, sections of Etruscan wall have been preserved but the Roman dictator Sulla was responsible for replacing their temple with the said theatre. He also downgraded Faesulae to the status of colony, from that of allied state, because the citizens dared to take the side of Marius against him.

In the early fifth century the Goths devastated the Roman city; just over one hundred years later the Lombards conquered it; in the Dark Ages it held a bishopric. A Roman temple, on the acropolis, was the site of a Christian church in the sixth century and, in the ninth, the Basilica di Sant'Alessandro was erected there. A convent of nuns replaced it but that was taken over by Franciscan monks in 1407, according to a plaque which states that here 'at the CHURCH and CONVENT of SAN FRANCESCO stood the city's ancient fortress which was destroyed in 1010'. All the books I have consulted say that the Florentines razed Fiesole to the ground, apart from the cathedral and the Bishop's palace, in 1125, after which Fiesole became a political backwater – as desirable a status as many citizens might have wished for at the time.

Nowadays the image is more that of a country town than of a city. You may still park in the Piazza Mino da Fiesole, in the triangular area below the prettiest of town halls. This faces the former Bishop's palace, now an austere-looking hospital standing next to the start of a particularly steep passage leading to the Franciscan church. At a right angle is the cathedral with a fine, thin crenellated tower that overlooks both piazza and Roman theatre. In front of the town hall are the equestrian statues of Garibaldi and Victor Emmanuele II, meeting on 26 October 1860, the day of Italy's independence. The through-road on one side of the square is tree-lined and bordered by several restaurants where you can eat alfresco at rickety tables placed on a sloping surface.

The town hall is coloured a rich yellow and has a first-floor balcony bedecked with flowers for part of its width. The rest is enclosed and bears plaques. No official edifice could look less pompously municipal. Adjoining it is the church of Santa Maria Primerana, late sixteenth century and in classical style.

The cathedral of San Romolo is plain inside and out. The west door is in a small courtyard facing a handsome buff-coloured house reached up a dual outside staircase. A palm tree stands at one end of its terrace. At the other is a small cloister attached to the duomo. Inside the cathedral, largely a nineteenth-century restoration, the nave has simple columns with a leaf motif on the capitals. From the crossing the altar is raised to reveal a sub-mezzanine crypt.

Rest on a pew in the cathedral before making the gruelling ascent to San Francesco. As you pant your way up, all Florence and beyond fans out before you. Near the top, sit again, on a wall with railings and pick out the landmarks. Note, also, the green belt starting immediately below you and effectively maintained on the higher ground. Unfortunately, lower down, the city has been permitted to spread both upstream and down. Try to climb to this eminence in daylight and again at dusk. It offers a thrilling

Fiesole: Garibaldi meets the King

experience compared with which a visit to the monastery and attendant cloister is relatively tame. But they are there and should be seen, along with the adjoining museum which, curiously, is mostly devoted to Buddhas and other orientalia. Next to the entrance to the church is another door leading, up narrow stairs, to the friars' cells. These are tiny, with a wooden plank along one wall as a bed, a hard chair and a desk beneath a window. The accommodation contrasts markedly with that in the charterhouses of Pisa and Galluzzo which are five star in comparison.

Below this complex on its hallowed site are somewhat dingy public gardens where there is a statue of an unidentified person who was much loathed. The graffiti daubed and scrawled upon it use such words as 'bastardi' and 'merde'. The pigeons have also targeted it. Monks wander meditatively in these gardens which overlook the archaeological site where the seats of the Roman theatre face another wondrous view. When you gaze up at it you will surely sympathize with the actors who had to perform against such a backdrop, or was the proscenium high enough to mask it from the audience? There is nothing today to impede your view and you will recognize Monte Senario commandingly upstaging all else in nature.

Admission to the archaeological zone includes the museum where artefacts found on site are well displayed in an uncluttered interior on two floors. There are examples of black Etruscan ware from the earliest days of occupation and there is a Roman cista, a lead water carrier that earns a glass cabinet to itself. I forget what else is there, from which you may deduce that this worthy museum did not grab me. Christopher, a retired curator himself, didn't linger there long either.

There are two other museums, the Bandini, with many minor paintings, and the Antiquarium Constantini which specializes in Greek and Etruscan vases. I would not return to Fiesole for the sake of its museums but would always go back to savour its unique ambience, its settings, its views, its exquisite town hall. I first visited all of them, with Mavis, from the Pensione Bencista, a hotel situated down the hill to San Domenico, where we have stayed many times.

The Bencista is a converted villa which was used as an emergency hospital during World War Two. When we first visited there was still a large red cross painted on an outside wall. Perhaps that secured its survival; more likely it was due to haphazard targeting. This 'mural', however, brought home to us how little consideration the military of either side were able to give to preserving anything of historic and cultural value. It is probably idiotic to imagine that they could.

At the Bencista there are terraces with wistaria and roses rioting. They face Florence above the olive trees at the bottom of the sloping garden. The approach to the hotel is down a twisting gravel drive to a field where, if you return late at night, you are required to leave your car so that the slumber of other guests is not disturbed. The interior of the pensione is all elegant stone and wrought iron. There are wide, short stairways and plush drawing rooms. There is a library of English books by novelists popular in early Edwardian times.

The Simonis have owned and managed the Bencista for more than forty years. The Signora speaks several languages, adapting continually to the needs of her clientele, but the Simonis lay down the rules. No credit cards, dinner sharp at 19.30 and no second sitting while, until recently, no bedroom had a key. Now, the Signor told me last year, regretfully, the insurers have insisted. That apart, you stay at the Bencista on the Simonis' terms and you like it. We always have. The postal address is actually San Domenico, not Fiesole, but it lies between the two.

In San Domenico there is a fifteenth-century church attached to a monastery where Fra Angelico lived. In a side chapel close to the door is a Virgin and Angels of his. Vasari describes the painting in some detail, complaining that the altarpiece suffered from being re-worked by other artists, one of whom was probably Lorenzo di Credi. There is some confusion, though, about how many Fra Angelicos are, or were, here.

Close to San Domenico is the Badia di Fiesole, a monastery on the site of a cathedral which was replaced by San Romolo further up the hill. The present building, erected at the command of Cosimo the Elder, is today the home of the European University Institute. This Cosimo had a villa at Fiesole designed by Michelozzo. It has finely terraced gardens, so I am told, but is not open to the public.

North-west of Fiesole is Sesto Fiorentino which can be reached through a maze of greater Florentine streets, or by a scenic route from Pratolino. It is questionable how much Sesto rates a visit but the road from Pratolino, at least as far as Monte Morello certainly does. The highest point (609 m) is named the Piazza Leonardo da Vinci. Here there is a hotel-restaurant and, emerging from the woods behind it, a radar tower. The view is spectacular, though there is a gentler one from Cappello de Ceppeto where there are several places to eat, also a ranch and a tiny oblong chapel without adornments. From Ceppeto you have a glimpse of rolling country with cypresses, firs, olive groves, some meadows, a little cultivated land, a village or two, a hilltown here and there, and behind it all, range after range of mountains – a veritable microcosm of Tuscany.

The chief point of interest in Sesto Fiorentino is a porcelain factory started in 1735 in the Villa di Doccia near Florence. It was founded by the Marquis Carlo Ginori and remained in his family until an Englishman, Augustus Richard, merged it with his own company. Richard-Ginori now employs 1065 people in a factory complex covering 105,000 sq.m. In an admin block, down a drive between lawns, is a permanent exhibition of 250 years of porcelain. The exhibits are sparingly displayed in glass cases with something to suit most tastes. I particularly liked a large decorated urn of 1898 with a white background on which cherubs, mermaids, fish and dragons cavort happily. (It stands beside Case 50.) Inevitably, religion intrudes but, for the record, I don't recall seeing even one Madonna and Child. Most exhibits are both secular and functional.

VIA VALFONDA **25**
VIA 22 APRILE
23 SAN MARCO
24 SANT' APOLLONIA
PIAZZA DONATELLO **22**
VIA GUELFA
PIAZZA D'ANNUNZIATA
19
MUSEO ARCHEOLOGICO
20 **21**
OSPEDALE DEGLI INNOCENTI
P.ZA STAZIONE
1 SANTA MARIA NOVELLA
P.ZA UNITA D'ITALIA
VIA DELLA COLONNA
2 PHARMACY
MUSEO DELL'OPERA DEL DUOMO
18
CHIESA OGNISSANTI
7 MUSEO MARINO MARINI
P.ZA DEL DUOMO
PALAZZO RUCELLAI **3**
4 **5** PALAZZO DAVANZATI
PIAZZA DELLA REPUBBLICA
17 CASA DANTE
15 **16** ORSANMICHELE
6 PALAZZO STROZZI
CASA BUONAROTTI
14 BADIA **13**
BORGO S. FREDIANO
PIAZZA DEL CARMINE
8 SANTA MARIA DEL CARMINE
SANTO SPIRITO
9 **12** MUSEO HORNE
CASA GUIDI **10**
VIA LUNG. TORRIGIANI
11 MUSEO BARDINI
BORGO SAN
26 PIAZZALE MICHELANGIOLO
27 SAN MINIATO

38

2   Florence

Only Pisa's leaning tower is more first time round as a Tuscan attraction than the city of Florence. Taken as a whole, the capital of the region has been a target for visitors for several centuries so I shall not attempt more than a brief summary of a dozen or so famous features which few people will have overlooked on their initial trip. If you are already familiar with them you are fortunate, because no place I can think of has been more ruined by tourism than Florence.

Despite pedestrianization and, paradoxically, partly because of it, the centre of the city has become a nightmare of churning groups of visitors, surging round their voice-strained leaders, desperate to experience the wonders of the birthplace of the Renaissance. Their eager flow is impeded at many points by pavements jam-packed with motor scooters. All four-wheeled vehicles, apart from taxis and horse-drawn open carriages, have been banned, so the workforce uses mopeds and vespas by the thousand instead and leaves them where the pedestrians might suppose they had prior rights. It is bad enough while their owners are at work, but at lunch time and in the early evening anarchy reigns. One solution would be a total ban on all wheeled vehicles apart from invalid chairs during the hours of daylight, but native ingenuity might take advantage of that. Florence could become a city of 'the disabled', all exceeding the speed limit.

The fact is that too many people wish to be in the centre for too much of the day and at most times of the year, and many of them wish specifically to be at one of half a dozen places – the cathedral, the Medici chapel, the church of Santa Croce, the Uffizi, in the Piazza della Signoria, or on the Ponte Vecchio. Short of reintroducing the Black Death, what will deter them?

And it is entirely understandable that, if you have just arrived from Yokohama, Denver, Johannesburg or even East Grinstead, keen for a major cultural encounter, you will not countenance denial. Even so, you may have to face it, because unless a quota system is devised, or intending entrants to the city become required to flourish art history diplomas at the

39

frontier, this hallowed spot will seize up. Until a solution is found I seriously suggest that newcomers should experience the most popular attractions vicariously on video, while next time rounders follow my mostly devious route.

An introductory video would relate something of the history of Florence. It would note the Etruscan presence on the heights of Fiesole for centuries before Julius Caesar founded a Roman outpost at a crossing over the Arno in 59 BC. Thus the route from Rome to Gaul, at this particular stage, became a settlement that grew into the medieval city. This was ruled, c.1077–1115, by the devout Catholic Countess Matilda, who kept the Holy Roman Emperor, Henry IV, at bay. It would relate the rise of the banking and commercial community and tell of the temporary eclipse of the Medicis when the monk Savonarola urged the citizens to repent their sins and burn their finery, even their paintings. His reign was brief and you will see the precise spot (if five hundred other tourists aren't seething around it) where he was burned like a witch. (If you miss it, read *Romola* by George Eliot in recompense.)

The Medicis returned and, long after, Napoleon proclaimed the kingdom of Etruria with Florence its principal city, a status it retained during the short-lived republic of the Arno. Then came greater glory, albeit briefly again, when it was the capital of all Italy from 1865-70. For more than a century since it has remained one of Italy's foremost cities, culturally on a par with Rome and Venice.

I will deal summarily with the major attractions mentioned above, before embarking on my itinerary for next time round.

The first architect of the cathedral was Arnolfo di Cambio. Work on it began in 1296. The massive dome, by Brunelleschi, is the city's central landmark. It, the campanile, designed by Giotto and completed well after his death, and the baptistery, also freestanding, are superb architecturally, with intense ornamentation covering most surfaces. The three bronze doors of the baptistery, two of them by Ghiberti, are a miracle of carving. The entire complex is as near perfection as makes no difference, but what detracts from it is the actual setting. Never mind the crowds, it is impossible to enjoy it visually, as a whole, because, like so many great churches, it is too hemmed in by other buildings. That is a problem we shall face many times in this book and it is an aesthetic one which probably did not much concern the original builders. When they were erected these edifices were an integral part of city life which went on largely within protective walls; today they are predominantly tourist attractions and art galleries.

The Piazza della Signoria appeals more to my need for space. It is just large enough not to be totally overwhelmed by the Palazzo Vecchio, one of the most striking buildings in all Europe. Its beautiful redbrick walls rise to crenellations, then sprout into a fortified tower which doesn't know when to stop, even when further battlements are reached. Its final flourish skywards is to an elegant temple topped by a spire, within yet another parapet. It is emphatically superior to those deadening, rusticated palaces which loom forbiddingly over too much of inner Florence.

The Palazzo Vecchio looks four-square but is a bulge of a building, its ground plan like a spatula, though none the worse for that. It was built as a city hall, became a Medici palace, was the centre of government during the Savonarola republic and has had numerous functions since. In contrast to the cathedral, and most of the churches, it is plain. I love its simplicity. Outside it is one of the several copies to be found in the city of Michelangelo's *David*. Between the Piazza della Signoria and the river is the Uffizi, one of the world's most prestigious art galleries, where room after room after crowded room is hung with masterpieces and lesser paintings. The greatest of Botticellis are here – the *Primavera* and the *Venus* – there are rooms devoted to Leonardo, Caravaggio, Raphael, Uccello. In days when it thronged less with visitors than now it was a joy to wander from room to room, detaching oneself eventually from the *Primavera*, the Cranach *Adam and Eve*, the Michelangelo tondo and other favourites, to explore, perhaps discovering Pontormo's *Cosimo I* in a rich, red robe, and many canvases of equally dazzling merit that have not made the top ten. It was good, too, to rest awhile on a bench in one of the long connecting galleries and allow one's gaze to fall on a miniature adorning a pillar or embellishing a ceiling. That is no longer possible but the video will have its consolations and may prove a positive improvement when you get to the second most famous gallery, the Palatine, usually called the Pitti, after the palace in which it is housed.

The Pitti is possibly the worst-hung gallery in Europe, worse even than the Wallace Collection, and tiresome for the same reason. The pictures are placed haphazardly, and without any semblance of artistry, wherever there happened to be room for them when they arrived. This was the custom of the time when the princes of the House of Medici and, later, that of Lorraine, acquired masterpieces by Raphael, Titian, Van Dyck et al., and chose not to make a conscious museum of their mansions. The advantage of this, to the contemporary visitor, is that it is much less of a draw than the Uffizi so you can take time seeking the gems, and even more in looking at them. You might even dare to photograph some of them (I have) without detection.

At the Accademia, back across the Arno, it was always something of a crush because, housed there is the original Michelangelo *David*, in a kind of temple of its own. There are notable unfinished masterpieces from the same hand in the passage leading to it and also some Botticellis. The whole collection is about to be moved to larger premises. When I last passed by an unruly kind of queue blocked part of the roadway.

The other first-time gallery is the Bargello, housed in a smaller version of the Palazzo Vecchio and showing Donatello's *David* (compare and contrast with Michelangelo's) and works by Cellini and Sansovino, amongst others.

The most popular churches for first time rounders are Santa Croce and San Lorenzo. Santa Croce is famed for its cloisters, its Pazzi Chapel, its museum, and for its vast open nave surrounded by tombs and statuary. Rossini and Michelangelo are amongst those buried here. Machiavelli gets a statue and there are frescoes by Giotto in one of the many chapels. Not to mention a sculptured Annunciation by Donatello and a carved pulpit by Bernardo di Maiano. Santa Croce is almost an Uffizi in itself in another sense too. Last time I was there I was depressed to see a slowly moving queue entering, like figures on a treadmill, by one west door, balanced by another emerging jerkily, like automatons, from a second.

Santa Croce: Pazzi Chapel

There is a separate entrance to the Pazzi Chapel, which does not attract large crowds. (You have to pay.) It is reached up a long path, bordered by lawns (on one of them is Henry Moore's sculpture of a warrior) giving way to a double cloister with rose beds. The chapel is perfectly proportioned, with Brunelleschi's dome its chief feature. The interior has plaques of the apostles, by Luca della Robbia, but most of it is plainly decorated. Next to the cloister is the Santa Croce Museum where the major exhibit is a crucifixion by Cimabue. This was badly damaged in the disastrous flood of 1966 but has been restored so far as this was possible. There is also a somewhat faded fresco of the Last Supper by Gaddi (thirteenth century).

San Lorenzo was the Medicis' church (it is also, in the first place, by Brunelleschi) and commands attention with its magnificence of pillars, marbled floors and lavishly ornate ceilings. Attached to it are cloisters, an imposing and rather intimidating library (by Michelangelo) and the Medici chapels. Of these latter, the Princes' Chapel is a horror, all in dark shades of marble with statues of the various Medicis in niches. It rises to a dome. I find it repellent. Nor is the Michelangelo sacristy appealing, despite some inevitably first-rate sculpture. At my last visit the entire complex was teeming with visitors, agog at the marvels acquired or inspired by the Medicis. I don't think I would recommend it, even first time round, because it is screamingly vulgar, but it is on the tourist itinerary, as is the Palazzo Medici-Riccardi, the town fortress that Michelozzo ran up for his patron and friend, Cosimo I.

On the first floor is the chapel painted by Benozzo Gozzoli, with a great mural on four walls of the Journey of the Magi. A multitude, many on horseback, proceed through volcanic terrain expectant, as well they might be, and well pleased with themselves. Visitors are restricted to fifteen at one time; we stood in a crush of twenty-five to admire this superb narrative painting.

The first-time traveller, already culture shocked, will by now be longing for something green. The answer lies across the endearing Ponte Vecchio, the only bridge the retreating Germans did not dynamite in 1944 and the one which also survived the 1966 torrent. It is 650 years old and has houses and jewellers' shops on both sides. From it, and past the arid frontage of the Pitti, you find an entrance to the Boboli Gardens.

The Medicis were not entirely single-minded in pursuing wealth; they were also friendly to the arts and Cosimo I, for one, liked greenery. The Boboli Gardens, with formal and informal areas, plus an amphitheatre, were his idea. That was in the mid sixteenth century. It has survived to become inner Florence's only open space, a sanctuary to be enjoyed by weary tourists and workers alike.

If, on a first visit, you can take in all these places and maintain your verve you will have done well. For the remainder of this chapter I will direct you, without video, to others where you can almost always avoid the crowds, yet stay close to the centre.

What I have chosen does not by any means amount to a comprehensive catalogue of all the marvellous things that are on offer in Florence which, like any other cultural storehouse, needs six weeks at the very least, at the rate of six days per week, to experience its galleries, museums, churches and fine houses. So I will conduct you on an intricate meander that will take in about a score of them.

We will start at the railway station, or the bus terminus next door to it. Do not think of driving into this city. You will be a pest. Emerging from either terminal, the most striking building is the church of Santa Maria Novella with its simple, elegant, brick bell tower. Here you have a rear view. You will see the wide, geometrically ornamented frontage across the piazza of the same name when you leave the narrow Via della Scala, down which we will walk first to absorb some of the true flavour of the unspectacular aspect of Florence. The street is lined with small hotels and shops, but it is also worth a visit for the sake of the pharmacy, founded in 1221 by the Dominican monks of Santa Maria. It is now housed in a fourteenth-century chapel where you may buy herbs, liqueurs, perfumes and confectionery. It is one of several havens of peace to be found in this city and should be valued as such. From the herbal room there a view of the Santa Maria cloister. In the square central chamber of the pharmacy the following message is recorded on the walls in Latin, Italian, French and English. In our language it reads:

TO THE MAGNIFICENT MONUMENTS EXISTING IN SANTA MARIA NOVELLA THIS PERHAPS NOT THE LEAST HAS BEEN ERECTED BY FRIAR DAMIANUS BENI DRUGGIST IN THE YEAR 1848.

Well said. You will not find sweeter-scented air than this in all of Florence.

Where you enter the Piazza Santa Maria Novella there is a grand loggia (with a plaque showing how high the water rose at various times of flood) facing the church which we will visit at the end of the tour – if we have a mind to. At this juncture we turn away from it into a maze of small streets. In another church (San Pancrazio), deconsecrated nearly two hundred years ago, is a museum devoted to the works of Marino Marini. He died in 1980 and his sculpture and painting will make a change from the ever-present, at times overpowering, Renaissance ambience, although you do not need to be an art historian to note Marini's influences. When

44

you enter the museum you can see much of what is on display from the lobby so, if you decide it is not for you there is no need to pay the admission price. Immediately you leave the museum you are taken back four or five centuries, firstly at the Palazzo Rucellai. The facade of this town house, built for a family of merchants who traded with the Orient, is unremittingly austere. On the two upper storeys eight Gothic windows, interlarded with classical columns, impose a similar rigidity on the ground floor which has two doors, symmetrically held between more pillars, and heavy rustication beneath cell-like square windows. It is easy to discern in it a forerunner of the glass-box approach to architecture. Equally formal, though less forbidding, is the Palazzo Davanzati, built one century earlier. I reached it by way of the Via Purgatorio, the Via dell'Inferno and the Via Limbo, which was appropriate because at the time I was searching (in the wrong district) for the Casa di Dante. The Davanzati, housing a museum of furniture, lace etc., has been preserved as an example of a rich medieval merchant's dwelling. It is splendidly sumptuous and the exterior is humanized by a rooftop loggia, with five openings, added in the sixteenth century.

While in this district retrace your steps (with the aid of the diagram at the start of the chapter) to look at the Palazzo Strozzi, rather later in date than either of the other mansions mentioned. It stands on a site almost large enough for a duomo, is overpoweringly impressive at first glance, then quickly becomes tedious. On one side there are nine bays on each of two storeys above a heavily arched doorway which has four small grilled windows to left and right. There are ponderous overhangs above the top floor. On the Via degli Strozzi side there are thirteen bays on each storey, three of them blind. It is an edifice seemingly celebrating the megalomania of the Medicis but in fact was built for their rivals, the Strozzi, who employed a series of eminent architects including Giuliano Sangallo.

Nowadays antique fairs are held at the Strozzi. Opposite this monster is a cheese wedge of a building between the Via delle Spada and Via della Vigna Nuova, and facing the Via de Tornabuoni. It has but minimal aspirations to grandiosity. There is no loggia, for instance, but at the end of the first floor is an open balcony and beneath it is a little carving of a cherub, watched by other putti, pulling aside a canopy to reveal a Victorian-style street light. It is an extremely decorative vignette lovely to experience amongst such surrounding splendour.

But we are going the wrong way. Forgetting Dante until later, we should be making for the Lungarno Amerigo Vespucci where, standing well back from the quayside, across a small square, is the church of all Saints, or Ognissanti. It is flanked by the Grand Hotel and the French Institute (in a splendid merchant's mansion) on one side, and the Hotel

Florence: the cupid balcony

Excelsior on the other. It was almost entirely rebuilt in the seventeenth century. Only the clock tower survived the baroque treatment but the interior is by no means the gaudiest I know. It is moderately subdued but not too dark. Immediately on the right are two frescoes by Ghirlandaio – *Madonna della Misericordia* and *Compianto* (Deposition) in pastel colours. The first actually depicts the Virgin protecting the family of Vespucci, a Florentine who became a naturalized Spaniard and who helped to finance Columbus's expeditions to the New World. (Rather unfairly, and perhaps due to the whim of a cartographer, America was named after Vespucci and not after Columbus.) On the same wall of the nave is an unusual Botticelli of Sant'Agostino, seated at a desk looking anguished, his right hand spread across his breast. Botticelli was buried here. In a chapel in the transept a circle with the name Filippo on it marks the spot.

Cross the Arno by the Ponte alla Carraia, where a statue of Goldoni faces the bridge, and make your way to the church of Santa Maria del Carmine, a brute of a building occupying much of one side of an uninteresting piazza. Within is the Brancacci Chapel, named after a family of merchants for whom it was built. Fortunately it escaped a disastrous fire in the eighteenth century because on its walls are a striking series of frescoes considered by many to be among the crowning achievements of Renaissance painting. They were begun in the 1420s by Masolino, continued by his assistant, Masaccio, and finished thirty years later by Filippino Lippi. The subjects are Adam and Eve, and the lives of St Peter and St John.

In the *Companion Guide to Florence* Eve Borsook wrote that Masaccio 'discerned virtue in the commonplace ... recognised what made men dignified and humane'. Study the figures in the *Lame Man healed by the Shadow of St Peter*, and in the *Rendering of the Tribute Money*, particularly, for confirmation of this.

Berenson illustrated his tactile theory by commenting on Masaccio's work – 'I felt that I could touch every figure, that it would yield a definite resistance to my touch, that I should have to expend thus much effort to displace it, that I could walk around it.' Then, on facing pages he shows Masaccio's *Expulsion from Paradise* and Michelangelo's. Michelangelo's Adam and Eve are agonized giants performing a grand exit; Masaccio's are two young people overcome by remorse, almost too anguished to be able to walk away.

A few shabby blocks away across the Piazza Santo Spirito is the church of the same name, a massive, plain, yellow hulk with a dome by Brunelleschi. Inside, the immediate impression is of a Victorian municipal art gallery where the paintings are hung sparingly, each huge canvas commanding its own territory. The effect palls when you become aware of a highly ornamented baldacchino, and of stands of flickering candles. Some

47

of the paintings are masked by holy statuettes. None of them is labelled. To ascertain which Madonna and Child was by Filippo Lippi I had to buy a postcard in the sacristy. I liked it but preferred another by an unknown artist. Another anonymous one bearing the date, in Roman numerals, 1482, has a particularly beautiful Mary and a charming, overdressed and completely upright bambino. It is a lovely composition, richly coloured, too.

The ceiling of the nave of Santo Spirito is painted in serried rows of simple, identical medallions. Very effective.

This part of Florence is only intermittently picturesque. As elsewhere, the streets are too narrow, the buildings too high, the pavements almost non-existent and you are approaching a pocket of high-density tourism. All the more reason to ring the bell of the Casa Guidi, just within sight of the Pitti Palace but lying back on the Via Maggio. This is where the Robert Brownings lived from 1848 to 1861, and it is where Elizabeth died. Also, where their son, 'Pen', was born. (For a fictional account of their lives read Margaret Forster's excellent *Lady's Maid*, written from the point of view of the formidable young Yorkshirewoman who accompanied the Brownings to Italy and also became an émigré.) While waiting to be admitted to the house note, on the door, that other present-day occupants are named Botticelli and Vivaldi.

Christopher and I were received by a charming young custodian who led us to the first floor, where the bedroom is not always on show because the flat is still occupied by a tenant of the Browning Institute of New York. The suite of rooms includes Robert's study, a living room, a bedroom and, across the landing, the kitchen and maid's quarters. Pen's nursery was upstairs. It is a sympathetic apartment, but slightly dowdy and unluxurious because the Brownings were not wealthy. There is a library of works by and about them, plus a shelf of novels of their time. The flat was once part of a palace, has high ceilings and is furnished in a heavy Victorian style. Elizabeth Barrett Browning maintained that she and Robert transformed it into a home and it became, for a visiting American writer, 'a proper and especial haunt for poets'. Another death occurred here: that of Elizabeth's spaniel, Flush, the subject of an entire book by Virginia Woolf. You will enjoy the quiet of this historic abode, especially as, when you leave, you must make your way past the Pitti and Vasari's corridor leading to the Uffizi, to the crowded Ponte Vecchio. Don't cross it. Turn right instead along the left bank of the Arno, until you reach the turning for the Museo Bardini.

It is easy to walk past this museum, even when you get to it, because the only indication of its presence are small carved letters on a dark-grey stone wall, reading MVSEO BARDINI. The administrators are obviously not into marketing and that in itself is as refreshing as the

48

museum, which I number high among the peaceful havens open to the public in Florence.

Bardini was a dealer in antiques who came, in the mid nineteenth century, from near Arezzo, to study painting. He achieved success as an art dealer and restorer of other people's work. He arranged the sale of antiques and old masters, and was well regarded by Berenson. He bought a church, with monastery attached, and filled it with treasures. He opened branches, held sales and supplied museums and private collectors worldwide. In his last years he decided to leave his still sizeable collection to the city of Florence 'to show his devotion to [its] artistic heritage'. The city repaid his gratitude by rationalizing the bequest into coherent historical order, against Bardini's expressed wishes. In so doing they have achieved a permanent exhibition, sparingly displayed, in premises with lofty rooms, and beamed and painted ceilings. I do not know what may be lying unseen in dark cellars but it adds to the pleasure, for me, not to have the feeling of being in a junk yard, which is the impression you gain in some of the more eccentric museums.

Even so, there is sufficient masonry to have kept a small quarry in business, including enormous chimney-pieces and several tombs. There is much weaponry, several walls hung with carpets, and, when it comes to paintings, the mother-and-child count is alarmingly high. One of them, behind glass and difficult to see, is by Donatello, an unusual treatment because the bambino is lying back, as though falling, and is grasping at his mother. On a mantelpiece in another room is a very cheerful baby, playing with a pair of cherubs who are romping around Mary's skirts. Better than either is a freestanding Virgin, wearing a simple gown with a flower pattern and holding a book in her left hand. It is described as 'Arte Senese Della Prima, XV CENTURY', in polychrome. (Notes in English are supplied by the museum.) In a different vein, don't miss the case of musical instruments, including three serpentini, which are seventeenth-century horns.

Now cross the Arno, by the Ponte alle Grazie, into the Via de' Benci, where you will find another demi-palace which was transformed by an Englishman, Herbert Horne, into what he saw as a Renaissance-style gentleman's mansion furnished and hung with treasures he amassed while living in Florence. He was an architect and scholar, wrote a book about Botticelli, and settled in the city in 1900, remaining there for the final sixteen years of his life. His collection includes an exquisite Giotto of San Stefano (which one I cannot say; there are five in my *Dictionary of Saints*) a pietà by Simone Martini and a triptych of three saints (unidentified) by Pietro Lorenzetti. There is, too, a Filippo Lippi of *La Regina*, standing at the gates of Susa with the right half of the canvas entirely taken up by mountains and trees. (Again, I cannot identify which queen.) The collection also

49

has a wide variety of sculptures, ceramics, cutlery, furniture, playing cards, bric-à-brac, and on the third floor is an old kitchen range with one of those extremely shallow sinks designed to chastise the washer-up. On the ground floor there is a small chapel from which hymns, such as *Abide with Me*, are played loudly on tape.

The Via de' Benci leads into the Piazza Santa Croce. Take any turning off the north side to reach the Via Ghibellina on which stands the Casa Buonarroti. In all probability, Michelangelo didn't actually live here, but he bought several houses and may have dwelt for a while in one of them. When he went to Rome he sold them – or gave them – to his nephew who transformed this house into a family shrine. It was sold in the nineteenth century to the city council.

You enter through a small, open courtyard and climb to a mezzanine floor where there is a tondo by the great man, of a Mother and Child, the first really blissful-looking infant Christ that I can remember seeing. Above, there is more of his work, but mostly it is family memorabilia that is on display. Several rooms are painted – I would say, overpainted – with scenes from the life of the artist.

One room is devoted to a four-wall mural of eminent Florentines – poets and painters, astronomers, mathematicians, navigators, physicians, herbalists, historians, philosophers, theologians, all vigorously discussing weighty matters. Collectively, they are Renaissance Man, so they are a proper subject for celebration here. Elsewhere there are Roman and Etruscan artefacts. In this house, once again, you are off the beaten track, though not for long if you follow me westwards, along the Ghibellina, to reach the badia, or abbey, facing the massive Bargello Museum, already categorized as first time round.

The abbey was founded by the Benedictines well over one thousand years ago. The church has been rebuilt at least twice and, in the course of one such operation, frescoes by Giotto were lost. It has a splendid bell tower and there are fine paintings, notably a Filippo Lippi of St Bernard receiving a visitation. This introduces members of the painter's family in holy guise. Also there are tombs carved by Mino da Fiesole and a wooden ceiling of great delicacy.

Here we are close to another secular shrine, the Casa di Dante, where I was met by a beaming American lady with an unusually soft speaking voice. She greeted me as though welcoming me to her own home. Dante didn't actually live here – the family house was round the corner – but you feel as though he had. The museum is well laid out on three floors. Some captions are in English and there is a guide in several languages. The walls are lined with reproductions of many paintings of famous Dante scenes, from the Bargello, the Pitti, the Walker Art Gallery in Liverpool,

50

Florence: Casa di Dante

51

amongst others. There is a plastic model of Florence in the thirteenth century, a wall map from the *Geography* of Ptolemy and a diorama of the Battle of Campaldino, showing the Ghibelline cavalry charging the Guelphs. Dante, in his role of military man and political activist as well as poet, is seen on the fifth horse of the second line defending the Papal interests. He was later expelled by the Black Guelphs because he had become a White Guelph, factional matters temporarily taking precedence over fighting the Ghibellines.

Amongst the pictures on display is a copy painting of Dante in exile, in red ear cap and robes, standing on a sea cliff; nearby is another of him introducing a dashingly handsome Giotto to Guido da Ravenna, an elderly Florentine worthy. (The originals are in the Pitti.) Another copy is of Henry Holiday's celebrated narrative painting of the poet meeting Beatrice near the Ponte Vecchio.

Possibly the most unexpected exhibit is a single sheet of paper on which is printed the entire text of *The Divine Comedy*, plus an index of characters. It is framed, glass-fronted and of astonishingly small proportions. (Copies are available at the bookstall.) In a top room you can watch a video with commentary, in not-so-soft American, about the various paintings; at an open window there is a good view of the Palazzo Vecchio enabling you to enjoy it without craning your neck, as you so often must at street level.

Close to Dante's house is the eponymous chapel, a small rectangle, where I listened to piped music sounding like Gluck. It certainly wasn't Gregorian chant, nor, mercifully, *Abide with Me*.

On the wall of the church is a list of the incumbents dating back to 1286. There is also a plaque placed there in 1991, the 700th anniversary of the death of Beatrice Portinari. A touching gesture. Dante himself died at Ravenna.

Whilst in mid-most Florence let us potter along to the Via Calzaiuoli, through the crowds, to the restored Orsanmichele. This high, fortress-like church was, for much of its existence, a grain store, but men of genius have worked on it. It has great Gothic windows on all four sides, above statues gleamingly newly cleaned. There are predellas showing craftsmen at work; one is aiming his mallet at a cherub. The detail may well absorb you for so long it will wreck your itinerary. Inside there are two wide rectangular naves, one leading to an elaborate tabernacle enclosing a painting of Madonna and Child. It was designed by Andrea Orcagna who started work on it in 1349. Carvings along the bottom depict the life of the Virgin, but it is difficult to see much because it is partly hidden behind an outer framework of metal. At the end of the other aisle is a large altar surmounted by a carving of Mary looking away from the baby she is holding

52

and reading a book. A mournful St Anne looks on.

The interior of Orsanmichele, where concerts are now held, is vividly painted on columns, ceilings, walls, with abstract designs and figures of saints. From one side of this singular building you can walk into the Piazza della Repubblica, a posh square with a Savoy Hotel of its own.

It is worth lingering a while here, having a drink at one of the cafés with outside tables under awnings and watching the world go by. Despite the hotels and its centrality, the piazza is a slice of real Florence. In an hour spent here you will see genuine Florentine kids fighting each other to feed bread to genuine Florentine pigeons who will probably be beaten to the spoils by genuine Florentine sparrows. People who stop and gossip in the square are almost certainly residents, not tourists; the person making notes as he sips coffee at the table next to yours is probably a businessman or lecturer. I felt more attuned to Florence here than ever I did in the piazzas of Santa Croce or della Signoria, and there wasn't a Renaissance masterpiece in sight, apart from the top of Giotto's bell tower peeping over the Savoy.

Following this interlude, to reach more next-time-round places, it will be necessary to cut a furrow through the throngs around the cathedral complex, perhaps reminding ourselves of that section of Dante's Inferno where the lost souls swirl endlessly round and round. If you have your Walkman handy you might even play Tchaikovsky's *Francesca da Rimini* music as you make your way past the cathedral and into its museum, where there are many items removed from the great church. They include a pietà by Michelangelo and two choirs, one by Donatello, the other the work of Luca della Robbia. Donatello's lives in its joyous carvings, a polychrome statue of Mary Magdalene stands below its stone, shimmering: della Robbia's is lifeless. There are model frontages for the cathedral on display, by Buontalenti and others, and a carved Madonna and Child by Arnolfo di Cambio, architect of the duomo, both figures looking electrified with fear. Brunelleschi's death mask is here, so are the originals of the baptistery doors by Ghiberti, but the crowds are absent.

From the cathedral take the Via dei Servi leading to the Piazza d'Annunziata.

To examine this piazza, and all that surrounds it, you will need at least a whole morning, possibly a day. There is the church itself, facing you, Brunelleschi's foundling hospital on your right and, beyond that, the archaeological museum; while on your left is the confraternity of the Order of the Servants of Mary (now a hotel!). There are three high porticoes, the one in front of the hospital decorated with Andrea della Robbia medallions against a Wedgwood-blue background. In the centre of the square is a statue of Ferdinando I (presumably the Medici one, although there were two others at least, one of whom was a Holy Roman Emperor, another a king of the Two Sicilies). There are also some extravagantly baroque fountains which are fun.

The church was founded by one of those saints from Monte Senario, San Filippo Benizzi, about 1250, but Michelozzo rebuilt it two centuries later, by which time cloisters had been added. The church suffered more restoration in the seventeenth century and, indeed, architects and artists seldom left this piazza and its buildings alone for long. The frescoes, few and large, are by various hands and most of them are fading, especially the Pontormo and the Rosso Fiorentino. Andrea del Sarto's *Birth of the Virgin Mary* makes a change as a subject; Baldovinetti's *Nativity* has a great expanse of country which is refreshing.

The Ospedale degli Innocenti, or foundling hospital, has a similar portico to the homes of the Servants of Mary. It includes a courtyard from which a shady garden can be observed and a gallery on each of two levels. One of them, up many steps, is long and thin, and is used for musical recitals. There are about twenty paintings – a Filippo Lippi, a Ghirlandaio and a Neri di Bicci among them, but the one that captured my attention was a deposition by Battista Naldini, in soft colours, tenderly drawn. There is part of a pietà of his also. On the stairs is a pleasing cherub sticking out of the wall, a welcoming figure to the abandoned babies for whom the hospital catered. The Ghirlandaio is a large Adoration of the Magi, richly coloured.

The Archaeological Museum stands behind a long walled garden. The Egyptians are well represented, so are the Etruscans, Greeks and Romans. A truly remarkable exhibit is the three-headed chimera from Arezzo, cast in bronze, a fearsome creature whose tail turns into a snake's head which is eating the horn of a goat's head rising from the spinal chord of a lion. These aberrations apart, this Etruscan monster is basically normal, with four legs and a handsome body.

Not far from here is the 'English Cemetery' which was described for me by Christopher as being 'appropriately in the middle of a trafficky roundabout at the Piazza Donatello'. It is, in fact, a Protestant or non-Catholic graveyard used by Germans, Russians and other nationalities. The star tomb is that of Elizabeth Barrett Browning which bears merely her initials and date of death (1861). It was restored in 1990. Other graves include Walter Savage Landor (with verses by Swinburne), Arthur Clough (verses by Mathew Arnold) and – a real find for Christopher, this one – Claude Shakespeare Glench, described as the 'last discendente of William Shakespeare'.

To return to the Piazza d'Annunziata, on leaving walk into the next square – the Piazza San Marco – which is dominated by the

Dominican monastery of the same name. Not only a monastery, but a museum which some will have made a first-time-round event because of the paintings. The names of Cosimo the Elder, Michelozzo and Fra Angelico are all indelibly linked with it. Behind the frontage is a superb cloister with frescoes in every recess. Off the cloister – wide-arched with simple capitals – are rooms with fabulous paintings. In the Ospizia are many Fra Angelicos, one of them a Mother and Child in which the names of the attendant saints are actually written on their haloes; another is a scene in Paradise in which every saint is prettily dressed and engaged in dancing a stately minuet. A third I particularly like depicts the laying out of two saints – Cosmo and Damiano – while a dromedary enters from the top right. Elsewhere there are Fra Bartolomeos (he was also a monk here), Ghirlandaios and lots of Last Suppers from various hands. Note the contrasting backgrounds and the differing attitudes of Christ and the apostles.

Go upstairs and, at the turn of a steep flight, you are confronted by yet another Fra Angelico, an Annunciation in which the angel's wings are as exotically beautiful as a peacock's feathers. On this floor the numerous cells of the monks are adorned with individually painted crucifixions. Savonarola had the largest cell, with three rooms now cluttered with souvenirs offset by a Fra Angelico portrait. The best is Cosimo Medici's which, in its upper apartment, has a fresco by the same master, of the Adoration of the Magi. It is set like Gozzoli's, in mountainous terrain, with formalized hills and, behind the wise men, a trail of others, each of them a positive individual, and one who is a wide-boy. You can see him calculating the potential cash value of this remarkable carry-on.

At ground level, as the museum reaches another cloister, it suddenly becomes the Museum of Old Florence with a vast number of exhibits in stone – friezes, stelae, window frames, pediments, columns, archways, decorative panels, shields, plaques.

Since this is a day for collecting Last Suppers we should now proceed to Sant'Apollonia's refectory where the subject is treated masterfully by Andrea del Castagno, although the first impression is of a white line drawn across the canvas. This, in fact, is the tablecloth against which the figure of Judas stands out. St John has fallen on the arm of Jesus and all the other apostles appear withdrawn, reflective, sensing disaster. Judas stares at John. In contrast to all this drama the panels above the table are abstract squares of different designs in marble.

This ex-refectory of the Benedictines became a military storehouse, then part of the university, until assuming its present role. Before deciding upon a visit check the opening days. A sensible system of ensuring that not all galleries and churches are closed on the same day of the week has led to staggering, so that one group will open on alternate

Mondays and another on alternate Tuesdays. Understandably the publishers of guides are finding it difficult to record this, especially as the schedules are liable to change without notice.

On your foot-weary return to the bus or train terminus note, in the Via Valfonda, a plaque on a house where Shelley stayed in 1819–20, and where 'L'ode al vento occidentale' was written. On either side of the present entrance are a naked cherub and a shepherd boy playing a pipe.

Once again you are confronting Santa Maria Novella from the rear. If you have energy left you should go into this famous church if only to see the Ghirlandaio frescoes, but I shall take it as first time round and wait for you at an adjacent café. The last time I stood in the huge nave of Santa Maria it was akin to being in the railway station named after it. Hundreds of people were milling about me, guides harangued small mobs in various tongues and I couldn't get a view of the frescoes. Perhaps one should go before breakfast, or even during a service.

You should also make a separate journey beyond the old city walls to the south, to visit the Piazzale Michelangiolo and the church of San Miniato high above it.

The piazzale, laid out in honour of Michelangelo, has a memorial to him that includes models of some of his works, including *David*. From it the city is laid out before you and is astonishingly close. It is like a stage set as seen from a good dress circle seat and you have the pleasure of piecing together some of the jigsaw in which you have been walking. It is an arduous climb from here up to San Miniato and, even when you think you have arrived, there is worse to come – a wide and uncompromisingly long flight of stone steps.

St Minias was persecuted by the Romans in the third century. After decapitation, down by the river, he walked up here with his head beneath his arm to the spot where he had been a hermit. A Benedictine monastery was later built where there had already been erected a Romanesque church in his memory. This has a frontage of five symmetrical bays, with rounded arches between pillars. Below it is an enlarged gable prettily decorated with geometrical shapes and a vivid mosaic of Christ, Mary and St Minias. It is surmounted by two tiny crenellated towers and an eagle with outspread wings. Next door is the battlemented Bishop's palace on one side and Michelangelo's uncompleted clock tower on the other, hovering over an extension of the cemetery. (Michelangelo was here helping to build defences for the siege of Florence in 1527, against the Germans and Spanish.)

The exterior of San Miniato benefits from its setting; the interior does not let it down. The spacious nave soars up to a fine, beamed roof and, above the altar, another mosaic, of Christ the Pantocrator. The layout is similar to that of the cathedral at Fiesole, with the crypt forming a lower mezzanine level starting at the crossing. This places the apse, and the pulpit, far above the nave. Conducting services from this height must give the preacher a great feeling of power, or of remoteness.

In the sacristy are the Giotto-style frescoes by Aretino which have been well restored. From a door beside it a cloister is visible. At the end of the nave is a strange little temple built to house one small relic. Throughout the church which, like Florence cathedral, is in green and white marble, are many different motifs, mostly abstract, although there are occasional birds painted on pillars including two eagles on a bale of wool, a reference to the use of the church by woolmakers.

Here, the city far below is viewed as from the back of the gallery. Detail is blurred but you can spot Fiesole's cathedral tower on an even higher hill, and there is a panorama which takes in Fort Belvedere, built inside the walls behind the Pitti, the Boboli Gardens and a small spread of green belt which must infuriate all property developers. Long may it survive.

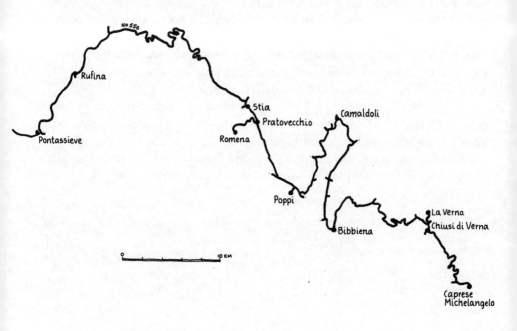

No 556

Rufina

Pontassieve

Stia
Pratovecchio
Romena

Camaldoli

Poppi

Bibbiena

La Verna
Chiusi di Verna

Caprese
Michelangelo

0   10 KM

3   The Casentino

Stia; Romena; Poppi; Camaldoli; Bibbiena; La Verna; Caprese Michelangelo

If we were to follow the Arno from Florence to its source, we would need to go south-eastwards, past Chianti country, then round the southern end of the Pratomagno, before heading north up a valley through the Casentino country to Stia. Instead we will go due east from Florence, making for the foothills of the Apennines through the busy town of Pontassieve which takes the last part of its name from the river we met in the Mugello. Here it joins the Arno and we leave both at this commercial centre of the wine industry to go on, first north, then east again, on a minor road up and over more hills. This is a gently rewarding experience bringing home to the traveller just how much terrain is still all but unpopulated, yet not at all wild. The descent to Stia, lying beneath Monte Falterona (1658 m), on the slopes of which the Arno rises, is through benign country unrolling without menace around you.

Stia is a place where climbers and hikers gather, and from which you can take a lonely drive over the Benedetto Alps into Romagna, a journey Mavis and I made in the opposite direction early in the eighties when we travelled for thirty miles without seeing a soul. When we reached Stia, and the first petrol pump of the morning, we were compelled to picnic in a dull square for ninety minutes while the attendant had his lunch break. In 1996 Christopher and I, after visiting a more sympathetic piazza, had an agreeable restaurant lunch in a town as deserted as our mountain road. Stia was closing down as we arrived, but the church of Santa Maria Assunta, in the Piazza Bernardo Tanucci, was open, though not inviting. It is a church which prides itself on its art collection. Some of it is so badly in need of cleaning that it is hard to make out anything but grey murkiness, even with the aid of two working forty-watt bulbs. There is an Annunciation by Bicci di Lorenzo and some typical della Robbias but a canvas, or panel, attributed to Cimabue was covered over. (The attribution is extremely unlikely, given the rarity of authenticated works by that painter.)

Outside, on an archway, is an Annigoni – and there is no doubt about that one – of St Francis, encased in glass, making it difficult to see

Stia: Piazza Bernardo Tanucci

because of reflection. So we concentrated on the decorated capitals of the twelve columns in the nave and Christopher identified a mermaid and a lamb. He is a great one for decorated, and better still historiated, capitals, so I drew his attention to a wolf-like creature with villainous talons and a double-jointed neck, one up, I reckoned on the chimera in the archaeological museum at Florence.

The Piazza Bernardo Tanucci is shaped like a banana lying on an incline; the steep road beyond it takes to the hills where the Guidis, who owned most of the Casentino, built many castles.

At Porciano the renovated and inhabited remains of a medieval village lie below the pock-marked keep of the early eleventh-century fortress where a small museum of country art may be visited on summer Sundays. We were there on a weekday, and contented ourselves strolling about the village, where we came upon a resident who stated, with satisfaction, that the only restaurant was closed.

Another castle, often associated with Stia, is off a road up the valley. It is called Castello Castagnaia and houses a museum of contemporary art. A ruined Roman temple is nearby.

Following the Arno southwards we come to Pratovecchio, the birthplace of Paolo Uccello who has a square named for him. Leave it by a minor road to the west to Romena to reach an exquisite Romanesque church, part of which was lost irretrievably in an earthquake long ago. So the facade is seventeenth century, but step into the nave, where there is no trace of baroquery, and admire the beamed, chessboard roof and capitals carved by the same craftsman who worked at Stia. The apse is perfect, in the Pisan style, two-tiered with some blind arches on the upper level, and almost entirely blocked in between columns at the lower. The church is built on a site where the Etruscans had a temple and where earlier Christian places of worship stood. If it is closed the key can be obtained from a farmhouse which is also an office belonging to an agricultural agency.

At Romena the church is overlooked by another Guidi castle, approached up an avenue of cypresses that are in themselves worth coming to see. The castle has Dante connections. He sheltered there when his sect of Guelphs was thrown out of Florence and that is strange because the Guidi were Ghibellines. The poet mentions the castle in *The Divine Comedy* in relation to a counterfeiter of coins employed by the Guidi. When the wretched man was caught at his forgery he was burned at the stake. As for the castle, the site is all. Admire the views up, down, across the valley, note the three, out of fourteen, towers remaining. Probably you can see all you wish to without waking the guide.

The other places on this route offer more meat. First comes Poppi which begins unpromisingly as a tatty, busy settlement on a main road. Once over the Arno, however, and you are in a different world. Drive up and round umbrageous lower slopes, enter by a gated wall and you are into a well-nigh perfect hill town. A thirteenth-century castle, facing formal gardens, is now the town hall and museum, dominating churches, houses and streets where shops lurk behind formidable arcades.

61

Admission to the castle is through a small gatehouse displaying a plaque or two. Above the portal of the fortress itself is a carving of that ubiquitous Florentine lion who could scarcely look more disapproving, but press on to find yourself in yet another Guidi residence, one built for them by Arnolfo di Cambio, architect of Florence cathedral, who you might have supposed had Guelph affiliations. The Guidi, being Ghibelline, met defeat at the battle of Campaldino, where Dante fought against them, on a plain to the north-west of Poppi. The Guidi influence here and in all of Casentino ceased, but the province continued to be ruled from their former castle, which was given a curtain wall in the Guelph style.

Inside is a spacious courtyard open to the sky behind an imposing door by Baldassare Turriani who also built the staircases (late fifteenth century). Look up, when you enter, to three floors behind wooden balconies. At mezzanine level are the chambers now housing the town hall, behind a wall smothered with crests and plaques. At the next level is a library of medieval works and manuscripts piled up to the ceiling, plus a grand hall. On the top floor is a heavily decorated room, once a chapel, opening on to another where there are paintings that may be by Giotto's pupil Taddeo Gaddi. There is also a magnificent chimney-piece.

At the top of the highest staircase is the carved figure of Guidi di Battifolle who is said to haunt the castle. He is also intended, caryatid fashion, to hold up the roof, but a gap left between his slightly bent body and a pillar has been infilled with stone. There are numerous chambers, dingy and otherwise, lying off and below the ground-floor courtyard, where exhibitions are mounted.

In the town is the Oratorio Madonna del Morbo, a circular church said to have been designed by the man who invented blood transfusion, Francesco Folli da Poppi. It is charmingly sited where the road divides, one way leading up to the castle, the other along to a small market square with stone benches and a café named Charlie's. The Oratorio has three baroque altars, two of them in side chapels, so far as a round building can be said to have such a feature. The engaging exterior faces a long street, at the end of which is another church, San Fidele, where the works of art are well signed, on display boards, thanks to a society dedicated to promoting appreciation of art. This church, built by the monks of Vallombrosa in the thirteenth century, is something of a barn, with arches decorated in licorice allsorts style. The organ is up above the altar (as at Sinalunga see p. 100). On the roof of the nave there is a painted crucifix.

Across the valley from Poppi a minor road through dense woods goes to the monastery of Camaldoli, and to a hermitage about two miles above it. On this route the hermitage comes first if you turn to the left as you approach Camaldoli. In a clearing are a church and a cluster of

Poppi: castle

small houses with red-tiled roofs which are still used as cells by the monks of a very strict order. The hermitage may be visited but the inmates must not be disturbed. They have a severe routine starting at 1.30 a.m. with prayer and, according to one commentator, they observe total silence. Another says they are permitted to speak at certain times, a third that some of them 'have been incarcerated in solitude for up to fifteen years'. Under such circumstances it is tricky to obtain accurate information; what seems certain is that the contemporary monks are endeavouring to follow their founder, St Romuald, a Benedictine who believed his order was becoming soft and came to Camaldoli in 1012, as an endurance test, in an isolated location about 3000 feet above sea level.

The hermitage church, restored in the eighteenth century, has, reputedly, works by Mino da Fiesole, Andrea della Robbia and Bronzino but we were unable to complete the 4-km walk before the sanctuary closed at 11.15.

The eleventh-century monastery was rebuilt in the thirteenth and restored long after that. It had a hospital and pharmacy attached to it and the monks were certainly less enclosed than their neighbours at the hermitage. Today, monastery and hospital offer a solid barracks-like aspect, but within the thick walls can be found two cloisters at different levels and a church gaudily decorated by, among others, Giorgio Vasari. He was responsible for the Deposition above the altar where figures emanating enormous power triumph over a glare of colour. The ceilings and upper walls employ trompe l'oeil, which I found crude but Christopher thought clever. There is a Madonna and Child resembling a music-hall act and much else that is repellent. I was more attracted to a ceramic of 1960, by one Biancini, of a dozen birdlike apostles in short gowns gazing up at a Christ figure with fishes hanging on one side of him and lambs scampering about on the other. I liked, too, a little red statue of St Romuald, standing on a bank opposite the hospital. It is a formalized sculpture with the head growing from a solid block of stone on which the hands are crossed.

The hospital was used until the last century; the fifteenth-century pharmacy is still trading briskly, now selling perfumes, postcards, herbs, medicinal jars, wine, elixir, pottery and much else. It also maintains a museum displaying pestles and mortars, a wine press, a giant urn, icons, photos of saints and anatomical specimens. Elsewhere in the complex are restaurants, a hotel, a shop selling a vile liqueur brewed by the monks, and another dealing in antiques and books. The monastery is used for conferences of priests and Catholic laymen. On the road to a camping site and picnic tables there is ample room for parking. Another road leads back down the valley to Bibbiena.

Bibbiena is a bustling, crowded town sprawling about a hill much less compactly than neighbouring Poppi, which can be seen clearly from a terrace near its topmost piazza. No attempt has been made to deter traffic and it is only just worth your while to pay a visit, although by the time you have found a parking space in the small square in front of the church of Saints Ippolito e Donato, you may disagree. This church was the private chapel of the Lords of Tarlati, who owned the attached castle. It is difficult to decide where one starts and the other ends and on the frontage between them, to add to the confusion, there is a bar with pin tables. Inside the church is an admired triptych by Bicci di Lorenzo. I didn't get to see it but did experience the della Robbias in the other main church, San Lorenzo. The sheer whiteness of them is in stark contrast to the gloom of the nave. They have typically highly coloured fruity borders and one of them, a Deposition, has rivetingly lovely faces, radiating compassion.

Opposite San Lorenzo is the sixteenth-century Palazzo Dovizi, named after a papal secretary who became a cardinal. He wrote the first extant comedy in Italian – *La Calandria* (1513) – and became known as Bibbiena. His palace, with a largely austere frontage, has had its top-floor loggia curtained in but has suffered greater indignity at street level where a plate-glass window is glitteringly signed THE UNITED COLORS OF BENETTON.

Never mind. The countryside around Bibbiena is all sloping vineyards, interspersed with woods, and the town itself is renowned for its salami.

Next, we climb back into the Apennines by a longer and, for the most part, wider road to another monastery standing at nearly 4000 feet. It has the edge on Camaldoli, being less openly commercial and commanding finer views. It is associated with one of the most favourite of saints – Francis.

It was at La Verna where, on the terrace in front of the various churches and chapels, there is the simplest of tall wooden crosses, silhouetted against the next fold of mountain, that St Francis received his stigmata. You may climb to the precise point where it happened, where he was tempted by Satan, but do not do so unless you are confident of your foothold, or you may crash, as Francis did not, to your death far below.

The ascent to La Verna from Bibbiena (24 km) is through woods with frequent breaks in the trees allowing increasingly magnificent views so, if like me you don't feel a natural attraction to religious sanctuaries, you will be more than adequately compensated by the ride. In fact the monastery itself is an experience even for an unbeliever. First you go through the prosperous small town of Chiusi della Verna, the medieval lord of which gave Francis a lump of mountainside he owned, in return for prayers to be said for his soul. This hereafter life assurance is, in my estimation, no worse than the Catholic church today paying premiums against the risk of child abuse by priests.

Modern Chiusi is popular for second homes and has a public fountain with the word 'Campari' carved on it, though it does not state if this is a shrine for a saint of that name, or if the bitter-tasting aperitif is channelled from a stream associated with an ancient miracle. Not partial to Campari, we soldiered on, high into the National Park of the Casentino, until we reached a spacious car park close to the Corridoio delle Stimmate, where contemporary Franciscans take their constitutionals, and by which we reached the monastery. A monk we met en route did not greet us with 'Buongiorno', because of his vow of silence.

Silence is impressed upon the visitor at all times as you walk towards the hallowed entrance. The admonition is soothing, attuning you to the holy ambience, until that moment when you hear the chatter of waiters in the Pilgrims' Restaurant, the whine of an electric lawn mower or the tolling of a bell. At least none of these sounds is taped.

Winding your way around grim, grey buildings, you make for the wide forecourt where the wooden cross stands. It may be thronged with pilgrims ignoring the tersely worded notices, 'SILENZIO', yet something is achieved. The chatter is at least subdued. There is a hush.

Creep to the wall. Look out over the valley and mountains. You can neither hear nor see a car. There is no aeroplane noise, no raucous sound of magpies squabbling, not even a dog barking. You have truly got away from it all. Fleetingly, I empathized with St Francis and his followers, and thought of those Florentines who rejected the rat race seven centuries ago and founded Monte Senario.

The experience of the church buildings brings you back from your dreams. You are obliged to look at paintings again, and at architecture, to make judgements. Della Robbias mill around you and perhaps you start to think of the man responsible for all this, the merchant's son from Assisi, who fell ill of a fever, had visions, talked to birds and beasts. He founded a religious order, led a blameless though hard life, and died aged forty-four. Would you rather have been Francis or Michelangelo, who was born in the next hill town and led a tempestuous life among popes and paintings, Medicis and marble, for almost nine decades?

Michelangelo was the son of the mayor (*podestà*) of a village 25 km north-west of Sansepolcro, a settlement on what is now an entrancing minor peak in the Alpi di Catenaia. It was the custom of the Florentine overlords to appoint governors who were not natives, so if Buonarroti had belonged to Caprese he would not have been made mayor. But he was a 'foreigner', so he was given the office and Michelangelo was born here on 6 March 1475, a date proven by the records. Born, but not bred, because he was soon sent away to a wet nurse at Settignano. However, Caprese Michelangelo, as it is now known, has become a shrine and should be visited.

Park some way below the summit of the hill and walk up through a winding avenue of conifers to an archway entrance to the remains of a fortress. Here there is now a modern sculpture park, and a museum beside the two-storey house, with outside stone steps, where Michelangelo entered this world. There is not a cot in the room, as there is in the Beethoven birthplace at Bonn; there is nothing, either, in the nature of a nursery. So exercise imagination. Tell yourself that this is where the man who painted the Sistine Chapel ceiling, carved *Moses*, *David* and other

66

masterpieces from chunks of personally selected Carrara marble, wrote sonnets and ate, drank, loved and quarrelled with the greatest of his time, was born.

A guide (no fixed fee) will take you to the first floor of the house where, in two rooms, are some thirty pictures and photos of events in the life of Michelangelo Buonarroti. You are required to examine diligently whatever you are shown, and to express reverence. Try not to skimp the visit. You have a role to play. Having made suitable expressions of appreciation, you will be taken to a room below where there are superb photographs of many of the greatest works, a model of the ubiquitous *David*, another of the *Cupid* (in our National Gallery) and a painting sent in homage from Mexico. You glance up at the ceiling and hope that Adam and Eve, or the Sybil, might be reproduced thereon, and if your imagination is inspired, so they will be. The connection with the master is tenuous, the experience not as vibrant as standing before one of the actual works, but you should feel a frisson of awareness. In any case it is an agreeable place to be. Go out into the sunshine and look at the mountains from a gap in the shrubbery of the sculpture park. You must agree it was a worthy birthplace for a genius.

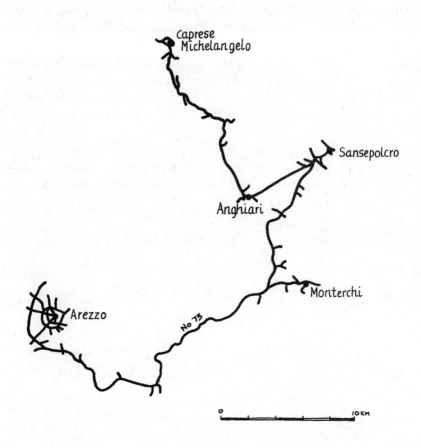

4 Arezzo and Upper Tiber

Anghiari; Sansepolcro; Monterchi; Arezzo

On a narrow spur of the Alpe di Catenaia stands Anghiari overlooking the upper valley of the Tevere, more familiarly known to us as the Tiber. At the top of its principal street, Via Matteotti, the gradient is something like 1 in 3. It is a ski slope of a thoroughfare, running through the town and down into open country where a battle was once fought between the armies of Florence and Milan. It proceeds with veritable Roman straightness to Sansepolcro, eight kilometres away. Walking down it places as much strain on your calf muscles as driving down it does on your brakes. Relief for both is at hand after about two-thirds of the descent, at the Piazza Baldoccio where the rock has been flattened to provide a cobbled surface for a few cars, rather more café tables and the inevitable statue of Garibaldi on which, mysteriously, the dates 1883–1914 are carved. Garibaldi, depicted as a fiery figure pointing towards Rome, died in 1882.

More of Anghiari lies to the south of the Matteotti than to the north, where there is a gentler, more curvaceous road, although it has a hairpin bend or two. When you drive on it you get the full impact of the massive walls supporting the hill town and it looks utterly impregnable. That is window dressing. More seemingly secure fortified towns than this one have proved vulnerable and you do not today, when wandering its maze of streets, have the impression of being encased in a citadel. It is a pleasure to visit because this is not a tourist trap. The coaches go to Sansepolcro and Arezzo. At Anghiari you are likely to be on your own so it can, in some of the more remote corners, be an eerie experience, though seldom for long. At the end of many streets are vistas, and there are always quirks of architecture or ornamentation to offer distraction, plus occasional glimpses, in gaps between buildings. of the alarmingly contiguous Mountains of the Moon (Alpe della Luna) beyond Sansepolcro, and high peaks further south.

From the Piazza Baldoccio there are signs to various churches and museums which are not hard to find, although whether or not they will be open is another matter. The thousand-year-old church of Badia was closed for renovations in 1996 and looked as though it would remain so well into the next century. More likely to be open, although you must ring for admittance, is the state museum in the Taglieschi Palace, housed in twenty rooms on many floors. It was built for Matteo the Dog, a third-generation Taglieschi, about 1437, a date carved on to the facade. The Taglieschi were the richest family in the neighbourhood five hundred years ago but their palace had various other owners up until 1881 when it suffered severe internal disruption which created many new levels and passages. It is partly built around an irregularly shaped courtyard, now glassed over, and entry is free.

Two helpful, charming girls opened the heavy front door, handed out illustrated catalogues in Italian and English, then kept us under surveillance as we roamed the museum. Our perambulation became something of a French farce. As Christopher and I moved separately up short flights of stairs and through rooms with several connecting doors, one or other of the girls would pop into view from an entrance ahead, or look down upon us from a landing. Knowing the layout intimately, and probably using secret passages, they confronted us frequently but without menace. And, indeed, there is little we could have got away with, most of the exhibits being unwieldy or heavy. One of the acolytes stressed that the museum did not own anything by anyone famous, which was not quite true, but pointed out many things of interest, including a sixteenth-century positive table organ from a local church. This attracts musical experts from all over the world. (Positive in this context means 'of fixed position', not portable.) There are paintings, sculptures, church vestments, church bells, a fine stone fireplace, cooking utensils, ovens and all kinds of exhibitable matter, laid out sparingly, in rooms with whitewashed walls and beamed ceilings.

The pride of the collection is a polychrome Virgin by Jacopo della Quercia, the Sienese sculptor responsible for the elaborately carved fountain in the Campo at his native city. The Virgin is touchingly simple, surpassing others on display in the same genre. In contrast, and also in polychrome, is a bright blue nativity from the della Robbia studio (late fifteenth century). In the vestibule we found truncated columns with decorated capitals leaning, unceremoniously, against a wall. Christopher dubbed them 'short-storiated'.

Not far from the Taglieschi is the Piazza Pretorio dominated by another palace, in pale yellow stucco, much bedecked with plaques of the nobility, and a fading fresco. As you explore the network of narrow alleys around it, note the pendant street lamps in wrought iron, sometimes in danger of being masked by bedding hanging out to air, or lines of washing, salutary reminders that this is a living town. It has been one for rather less

70

than nine centuries. I do not know of any great genius who hailed from here but there are plaques on the Via Matteotti to Francesco Nenci, painter, and to Pietro Leopoldo, who must have been celebrated in their day. A little more contemporary civic pride could lead to some restoration of the buildings they inhabited.

Anghiari: Palazzo Pretorio

What a grandstand view those citizens of 1450 had of the battle between Florence and Milan, which left their town in the hands of the former. Leonardo da Vinci was supposed to immortalize the occasion in paint but his work did not last because the technique he used for his fresco was wrong, and it faded.

Three centuries later there was another battle here when the Austrians fought the French, and lost. One hundred and fifty years after that, advancing Allies and retreating Germans made life hell for the residents, something it is easy to forget now when you drive along the peaceful wooded roads in the lush valley of the Scheggia , a tributary of the upper Arno. But we proceed in the opposite direction to Sansepolcro, on a road not quite so determinedly straight as it seemed from high up the Via Matteotti. It lurches slightly to the right to join the main thoroughfare from Arezzo, though the walls remain visible all the way. You should find a parking space outside them without difficulty.

This is a fine town, devoted to Piero della Francesca and pasta. Asked to make a choice, I would plump for Piero but there is no need to play parlour games when you have this rewarding place to explore.

First let's dispose of the pasta.

The town goes back to what we arrogantly call the Dark Ages (AD 500–1000), conveniently overlooking the Dachaus, Hiroshimas and Burma Roads of our own time. Tenth-century pilgrims are thought to have brought relics from the Holy Land and deposited them here – hence the name, Sansepolcro. The actual date of AD 934 is quoted in some books and that is as good a beginning as any, taking us to the verge of the early medieval period when walls were built around the pilgrims' settlement. A chapel sprang up, houses too, a fortress, workplaces, a cathedral. Ghibellines predominated, then the leading families turned Guelph, prior to the pope selling the town to Florence for 25,000 guilders. That was in 1441, not long before Milan was vanquished in that battle beside the Tiber. Pasta production, already established, flourished, becoming the monopoly of the Buitoni family, now a brand name.

By this time Piero della Francesca, born here about 1420, was well into manhood, and it is his paintings which, today, are the town's supreme adornments. And reverently catered for they are, in the Museo Civico, to enter which oldies must pay 7000 lire and others 10,000. It is worth more than the top amount just to walk into the first sparingly decorated chamber where the Piero polyptych (many panels hinged together) of the *Virgin of Mercy* stands in its magnificence. It couldn't be better displayed: the accompanying notes, on a lectern, couldn't be more helpful. It stands away from the wall with no other work of art to distract your gaze on either side. The Virgin, spreading her cloak like a fairy godmother around diminutive, kneeling pilgrims, is that Piero lady with the sulky look whom he often used as a model. Note the glowing golden sky against which she is set, note it again behind the Christ on the cross above her and see how the gold of the haloes merges into the background on all the principal panels, the artist's device for distancing a convention which had probably already become tiresome. Scenes on the predella should be given attention, so should St Sebastian on a panel next to the Virgin's. Martyrdom is well under way and he is resigned to it. On the predella here is the empty tomb with cold-faced women looking astounded – 'Where's he gone?' – against a background of cypresses on a green hill dominated by what is surely the castle of Poppi? There is a satisfying interplay in so much Renaissance art between the paintings and the still familiar landscapes and townscapes.

On the wall opposite the polyptych are the partly restored heads and shoulders of St Giuliano and Santo Agostino, those vivid portraits, with their transfixed eyes, to which I returned again and again. Facing the window, where you may see students crouched on the sill, staring intently through the bars at the paintings which they cannot afford to pay to see, is a screen behind which is an awesome Resurrection. Piero has depicted Jesus, holding a cross of St George flag, climbing from the tomb, staring fanatically straight ahead, while the guards around him sleep, one of them perhaps drunk, his head in his hands.

On the far side of the screen a row of choir stalls stand with marquetry misericords, while on the wall is an Andrea della Robbia with the usual colourful fruit board. The most arresting work here is a Matteo di Giovanni, of the Nativity, a busy canvas with bas-relief barn and figures. A vigorous herdsman, his lunch bag over his staff which he carries on his shoulder like Dick Whittington, and a dog at his feet, marches purposefully towards the crib. Above, jolly angels are playing cornets and seven cherubs on an upper panel are for once looking and behaving seraphically. But, at the predella, where angels make obeisance, there is a gap. More is missing on another triptych – the entire centre-piece, no less, painted by Piero and now in our National Gallery. It should be sent to Sansepolcro at once.

Other paintings are here in abundance, by Pontormo, the della Robbias, Signorelli and less famous names, but after the Pieros they scarcely matter. To be fair to them, they should be the object of a separate visit but I don't believe I could enter this gallery without being drawn to that room of the polyptych, the Resurrection and the two haunting, saintly heads. It is bad luck on the other artists, but they will never know.

In the lobby to the Museo Civico there is a bust of Piero done in 1875: across the road, the Via N. Aggiunti, is a statue beneath two towering chestnuts in a public garden. He stands, imperiously, wearing a long smock, his palette in his left hand. On this same street Piero's birthplace, almost next door to the Palazzo Pretorio, is preserved, stuccoed in light coffee. Steps separate it from the chiesa di San Rocco, a sixteenth-century church which seems to have lost part of its frontage to a neighbouring house. The oratory, lying under it, is approached down steps on the Via Piero della Francesca. You enter by a scene-dock-type door, facing a deconsecrated church (San Francesca Saverio) which looks like a Wesleyan chapel that has grown out of hand. In the oratory is a Resurrection, by Raffaollino del Colle, featuring a Christ who jumps joyfully from the tomb to the astonishment of his guards.

Sansepolcro is a town of many churches but there are none, for me, of outstanding interest architecturally. The chiesa dei Servi di Maria has an odd, four-square, crenellated tower in red brick that is not unattractive, but the interior is gloomily baroque, with plaster crumbling from the walls. The cathedral, built by the Camaldolensian monks in the eleventh century, has been extended and altered many times, yet retains a simple, fitting austerity. There is a much-admired rose alabaster window and I liked the simple frontage with recessed arches in the west door, made of shining, carved, dark wood. Next to it is the small Palazzo dell Laudi, in an arcaded area where there are plaques to various worthies.

In the opposite direction lies the Piazza Torre di Berta but lacking the central tower it once boasted. That was bombed by retreating Nazis. There are some handsome houses bounding the square and even more of them on the Via XX Settembre leading to the eastern walls. Linger on it, admiring the Renaissance mansions, one of which is now a public library, another the Teatro Dante. Note, between the library and the Palazzo Graziana, at no. 127, four high arches keeping the buildings apart and preventing them from falling into the narrow via del Buon Amore. Just before a little square leading to one of the ancient gateways is a turning to the fortezza. Across another road you can see steps rising to an upper storey of the castle. It looks interesting but having climbed the tortuous steps – like tank traps – to a locked gate I assure you the effort is not worth it. You get a better view of the Medici fortress, with its massive, buttressed walls, by walking to the edge of the town.

Sansepolcro has a lot of low towers rising above its roofscape (rather like San Gimignano) and much of the medieval wall is extant. The old part has been pedestrianized and, because some of the streets are unusually wide, it is a pleasure to stroll along them window shopping as well as culture vulturing.

Piero's mother was born at Monterchi, even closer to the Tuscan border than Sansepolcro. We go there next, on our way to Arezzo, to see another fine painting of his, the Madonna del Parto, the Virgin about to

74

Sansepolcro: Palazzo Pubblico

give birth, an exceptional treatment of the Nativity, and one in which the artist again portrays the same woman model, this time looking rather less haughty than at the museum we recently visited. She stands, in a splendid purple robe, slightly opened at the front for obvious reasons, beneath a crimson canopy held apart by two angels who have pulled it back with a theatrical flourish. The angel on Mary's left has a similarly disdainful look but all three ladies (are angels ladies?) are solemnly aware of the significance of the occasion. The painting was formerly in a cemetery chapel, a few miles outside Monterchi, where Kenneth Clark described, with reverence, his feeling of taking part in a pilgrimage to 'one of the few great works of art still relatively inaccessible'. Now we say that of canvases in the Uffizi. The Madonna today occupies a darkened room in a purpose-built civic pavilion – admission 5000 lire.

75

We go to Arezzo, chief city of this eastern part of Tuscany, via the valley of the Certone. It lies in a leg of the Apennines ending at Lake Trasimeno, and was the birthplace of Petrarch, Vasari, Guido of Arezzo (a monk who invented musical notation), the poet Pietro Aretino, Roman statesman Maecenas and several millions of others.

Having passed through nondescript suburbs, park outside the walls and enter by the Porta San Lorentino, leading to the Via San Lorentino, which twice changes its name as it rises steeply towards the cathedral and town hall. If you arrive in the early afternoon you will face a cascade of Fiatry conveying the workforce home to lunch, bobbing merrily over the uneven chunks of stone serving as road surface. It is, for that matter, also the pavement except that there isn't a pavement and, if there were, it would have vehicles parked all over it. This experience can be curiously exhilarating, allied to the comfortable feeling that if all this lot are leaving it will be serenely empty at the top by the time you reach it.

So, pant and puff on, past the duomo and into the Prato Gardens at one end of which, all but hidden among trees, is a forbidding gateway. Through it, turn to your right up a long covered ramp under a roof which leaks (and it rains a lot in Arezzo), until you emerge, past a surprisingly contemporary house, on to a spacious mound of grass and woodland. A wall extends all around it with part of a sentry walk intact. From various points you can view the city, and the mountains and hills almost encircling it, although there is a rich, fertile basin to the north where cereal crops, fruit and vines are grown.

Up here, in what remains of the Medici fortress built by the Sangallos in the sixteenth century, on a site occupied by both Etruscans and Romans, it is tranquil. Probably you are alone, sole observer of vestigial ruins even less inspiring than those in the amphitheatre far below.

Etruscan Arretium was one of the twelve leading cities of the Federation. In Roman times it became celebrated for its Terra sigillata, a pottery with a coral-coloured glaze that became fashionable throughout the empire. An early Christian saint, Donato, was martyred here in the fourth century; at the start of the Middle Ages this was still a free city but, inevitably, it fell under Florentine domination (1384).

Descend from the fortress (the dripping from the roof over the ramp may have ceased; weather recovers miraculously quickly in Italy) through the Prato Gardens, where adults sit and chat, kids play on grass within a circle of umbrella pines, and there is a cumbersome item of statuary in dirty white marble. Primarily, it honours Francesco Petrarch, lyric poet, scholar, possibly priest, whose passion for Laure of Avignon inspired sonnets. His house, not far away, was bombed in World War Two and, rebuilt, is now a centre of Petrarchan studies. His statue survived, with the poet high on one side, separated from frenzied activity in stone, including, Romulus and Remus being suckled by the wolf, an almost flat Madonna and Child, a king being crowned and people swooning and fighting. It has attracted many graffiti.

Across the greensward is the campanile of the cathedral, not added until 1859. It has the slenderness of a rocket and is attached to the duomo by a sliver of house. At the other end is a west front uncompleted until this century, but in between is the vast nave of a Romanesque cathedral begun in the late 1200s. It houses many treasures including stained glass by Guillaume de Marcillat, an exile from France who settled here in the sixteenth century. There is a superbly carved marble shrine to St Donato (c.1369) and an elaborate altar, both by various hands. In a large chapel of consolation, with hundreds of offertory candles ablaze, another ornate altar stands with a classical pediment surmounted by a crown, cherubs and two giant-sized figures holding more candelabra. Above and around are a painted ceiling and two gaudy ceramic panels from the della Robbia workshop, one of a Crucifixion, the other an Annunciation, featuring a smiling God the Father. There are many fading frescoes and other pictures in the cathedral but, above all, there is a Piero della Francesca of Mary Magdalene. She has a halo so it must be assumed that this is after her conversion, although that doesn't stop Piero from depicting her as something of a minx. The manner in which her right hand is holding her cloak, and the slight curl of her lips, has potent sexuality. It is a lovely painting. (Is it that same model again?)

The exterior of the cathedral is plain with a restrained tympanum, a few fluted columns decorated with acanthus leaves and a statue or two. The town hall, opposite, giving a good imitation of the Palazzo Vecchio at Florence, has crenellations indicating support of the emperor rather than the pope. It is an imposing but anonymous building and was not always the town hall; the original, around the corner, and down the Via dei Pileati, is today a public library with a wall smothered in plaques indicative of its former function.

Now we come to the Piazza Grande which, begging Piero's memory, is Arezzo's greatest glory, including as it does the apse and fantastic tower of the parish church, the Vasari loggia, and the Palazzo di Fraternità dei Laici. None of its four sides (and it is not precisely square either) is on the same level as any of the others. Houses with balconies, crenellated towers squeezed amongst them, are on two sides. One faces the noble loggia, the other the rear of the church. Santa Maria della Pieve is built in the Pisan style with a perfectly rounded apse decorated with three tiers of columns beneath a tiled, mushroom roof. The lowest tier is the tallest, without openings between the columns, which are joined in a

Gothic arch. The middle one is about half the height but has twice as many pillars, all open: the top one is the shortest with the number of columns doubled again. Looming over the apse is the fabulous campanile known as 'the tower of 100 openings' – actually there are eighty but that is an entirely justifiable instance of Italian hyperbole. Santa Maria delle Pieve (pieve signifies a parish church) dates from the twelfth century. More about it below. Next to it are the high Gothic Palazzo di Fraternità and the adjoining law courts. They were begun in the late fourteenth century, continued, by Bernardo Rossellino, in the next, when Giovanni di Settignano also chipped in with a loggia beneath the roof. A baroque clock tower was added by Vasari nearly one hundred years later. Then, in the late eighteenth century, the façade beneath the loggia was given a heavy stone facing that does not fit too happily with the lovely palazzo, but is, nevertheless, part of the rich texture of this highly individual piazza.

Arezzo: Piazza Grande with Vasari's loggia

The law courts are joined to Vasari's long, splendid, ground-level loggia where you can sit at café and restaurant tables, beside the red pillars, some of them crumbling. It is quite the best place in Arezzo for lunch environmentally, and the cuisine may also be to your liking. Giorgio Vasari gets a bust at the Via dei Pileati end. It was placed there in 1911, by which time 'the common people', who were excluded from walking along the gallery when it was first erected, were permitted entry. On the bust is an inscription, 'con affete e alterezza' from 'la patrie' ('with affection and pride from his countrymen').

In the piazza itself an antiques fair is held on every first Sunday, except in September when the Saracen Joust takes place, an event on a par with the Palio at Siena for the excitement and rivalry it engenders amongst the citizenry. The fair spreads from the piazza up and around the hill and attracts huge crowds. Before leaving to inspect the frontage of the pieve turn to admire the loggia, as viewed from across the square.

Pass down the alley beside the nave to reach the church frontage, which is difficult to assimilate en masse because the street on which it stands is narrow. You need to be several rooftops away to appreciate the grandeur of three more tiers of columns, in this case in straight lines, above a five-arched entrance. Within, apart from relics of St Donato, there is an altar with a polyptych by Pietro Lorenzetti. This resembles a lavishly adorned battlement with a centrepiece including both an Annunciation and a Madonna and Child. Mary's garments, in bold check, set the pattern for the rich attire of the other characters. The new-born Christ is at least eight years old.

Now make your way across the hillside to another church, San Domenico, a strangely constructed edifice which, from the outside, looks as though half the nave has been removed. A two-hole bell tower clumsily obscures part of it. Inside it is barn-like. At the altar end is a much admired Crucifixion by Cimabue. I find it repellent, a Christ with a bloated stomach. Frescoes, some by the Sienese school, some by the Aretino, are thickly distributed, almost wall to wall. The square the church graces is very pleasing, with trees on two sides and parquet paving overall, some of it covering an original wall of the city.

Here we are close to the house of Giorgio Vasari. He bought it in 1540 or thereabouts, and decorated several rooms himself, before he won fame as an art historian and biographer of painters. He collected Renaissance drawings, portraits and letters, to form an archive which is kept here.

Vasari's house is on the Via XX Settembre. Walk to the lower end of that street, turn right, and you are at the Palazzo Bruni-Ciocchi where the premises are shared by the Museums of Medieval and Modern

Art, open free to oldies. Enter through a courtyard where there are sculptures, some of them heads of Roman horses, removed from the amphitheatre; also columns detached from whatever they once supported, and lined up against a wall. The galleries are on three floors reached by a long flight of steps. The medieval works include paintings by Spinello Aretino (Crucifixions, etc), Balduccio (a Gloria) and Signorelli, none of which appealed to me. There is one huge canvas of saints with their eyes upturned, giving them crazed looks. Vasari is represented by a busy Madonna and Child with great thick thighs. Lots of adoring eyes are focused upon them but a small dog has turned his back on the scene. A benign God the Father (I take it) lies on a foam plastic cloud in a conveniently adjacent heaven. He holds three-pronged instruments (love darts?) and is surrounded by jolly cherubs.

The modern section is something of a relief after so much sacred art of indifferent quality but, by modern this gallery means eighteenth and nineteenth century, with emphasis on narrative painting. The exhibits also include glassware, rather gaudy majolica , small black statues (behind glass), coins, chimney-pieces, ivories and much else that I have found unmemorable in detail.

And so to the church of San Francesco, to the most famous paintings in Arezzo, the frescoes by Piero della Francesca. On our first visit to this city, in 1980, Mavis and I had to buy an umbrella before picking our way through streets smothered in builders' scaffolding to a church similarly encumbered, and also partly protected by sheets of corrugated iron. The interior was stygian and such light as there was did nothing for the frescoes. We came away feeling cheated. Revisiting in 1996, I was delayed by a thunderstorm. Again I entered the hallowed site carrying an umbrella. Again, many of the frescoes were mostly invisible, partly because the apse where Piero painted them was behind high rostrums covered in heavy-duty polythene enclosing restorers, partly because it was impossible to get close enough to those that were on view. The solution, unless you are doggedly oriental and come equipped with powerful binoculars, is to buy postcards or a book. In the latter many reproductions are faint but that cannot be helped. They are sufficiently good to allow you to perceive something of what you are missing.

The frescoes, probably painted between 1452 and 1466, tell the story of the True Cross. There are sixteen panels but they are not all in sequence. The church is late thirteenth century and was built for the Franciscans, and it was they who commissioned Piero. There are many other paintings in the simple interior, which is now decorated with its original austerity after periods when, deconsecrated, it became a barracks. There was also a plan to convert it into a theatre but, eventually the monks returned and, once the frescoes are fully restored and effective lighting has been installed, it will become a joy to visit. The exterior is of rough-hewn stone, which was all that the original brothers could afford.

There are numerous churches in Arezzo but the four I have mentioned suffice for me. Others are SS Annunziata with stained glass by Guillaume de Marcillat; Santa Maria in Gradi (terracotta by Andrea della Robbia); Santa Flora e Lucilla in Badia (high altar designed as a family tomb by Vasari) and, on the outskirts, Santa Maria delle Grazie, a fifteenth-century building, set in verdant acres, with a splendid Renaissance portico.

Finally, there is the archaeological museum constructed in the former Roman amphitheatre. Difficult to find because of poor signposting, it stands next to yet another church, which I ignored.

What remains of the arena is sparse but quite haunting, set in a slightly overgrown meadow, on one side of which is the curving back wall, now part of a three-storey colonnaded museum but once a monastery. To enter, you should buy a ticket from an automatic machine. I had to call for help and it may not have been altogether accidental that I was issued with a ticket marked 'Gratuito', the attendant having consulted my passport and judged me to be on the verge of senility.

The museum is heavily into pots and vases, some Etruscan, some Greek, some post-classical. One, a particular beauty, lovingly reassembled from a myriad of shards, is called the creterie euphronius, and has illustrations of Hercules and the Amazons. There are lots of red Aretino pots and a fine statue of a man wearing a toga , with his arm in a sling. This latter was found in the necropolis here. On the first floor are several mosaics including an attractive one of horses. In a case of assorted odds and ends is something which could be an early backscratcher.

The *Insight Guide* advises that Arezzo need be allocated no more than a day. I think you will find it rewarding for longer.

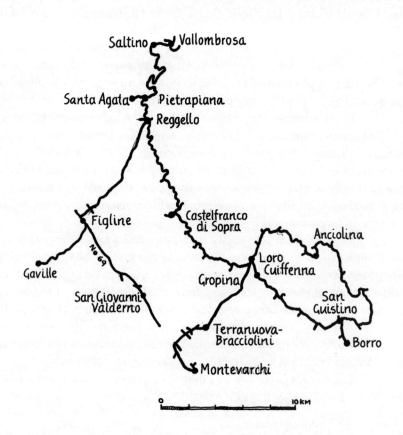

5   Valdarno and Pratomagno

San Giovanni Valdarno; Gaville; Figline; Reggello; Vallombrosa; Castelfranco di Sopra; Loro Ciuffenna; Anciolina; San Giustino; Borro; Gropina; Terranuova-Bracciolini; Montevarchi

San Giovanni Valdarno (north-west of Arezzo), like the bastides of south-west France, was built on the grid system, a pattern found serviceable both for defence and trade. It was imposed on the tiny community here by Florence some time between 1296 and 1300. Over the centuries the walls helped keep the enemy out, but occasionally they were scaled and ownership changed hands. In World War Two the basilica was almost entirely destroyed and by then the castle had long since gone, yet the medieval town remains largely intact and the layout is unaltered. At the centre are two squares divided by one of the most satisfying of all town halls, designed it is said, by the great Arnolfo di Cambio, the first architect of Florence cathedral. After him it is named Palazzo d'Arnolfo. It faces the Piazza Cavour and backs on to the Piazza Masaccio.

Tommaso di Giovanni, known as Masaccio and credited by Vasari as the most innovative painter of his time, was born here in 1401. There is a plaque on his birthplace, now in use as an art gallery exhibiting contemporary works, but none of his limited output – he died aged twenty-seven – is held in the town.

The Palazzo Pretorio (or d'Arnolfo) has an arcaded loggia on all four sides. The frontage is yellow and adorned with about 250 plaques. On the canopied first-floor balcony and under the entrance arcade, they range in date from 1420 to 1772, some are brightly coloured, some grey. The crenellated tower, slightly off centre, is slender and unfussy. And to add to the joy of this delicious structure, inside there is a tourist office manned by dedicated public servants. They exerted themselves enthusiastically on my behalf, making phone calls and each handing me a copy of the admirable, colour-illustrated town guide written in Italian, English and German. It proudly records Masaccio and other native artists, considerately including photographs of works to be seen in Florence and elsewhere.

The front of the palazzo faces a statue of Garibaldi in a small garden, and the parish church of San Giovanni; the rear looks upon the restored basilica of Santa Maria delle Grazie which has a particularly

83

San Giovanni Valdarno: Palazzo Pretorio

colourful della Robbia over the entrance. A third side of the square has a palace and another church – San Lorenzo – with almost unadorned walls, contrasting strikingly with the interior of the basilica. The latter has been rebuilt to its former fifteenth-century state under one huge dome surrounded by nine smaller ones.

The basilica is also an art gallery, housing at least one masterpiece, Fra Angelico's *Annunciation*, formerly hung in the convent of Monte Carlo on the outskirts of the town. It is rapturously lovely, with an angel in exquisite raspberry-red robes and luminous wings, and a Mary, in blue, receiving him in consternation, or even disbelief. The same subject recurs with an even more richly dressed angel and a totally submissive Virgin, by Jacopo del Sellatio. As a change, there is a Tobias and the Angel; by Giovanni di Piamonte, with Tobias holding the fish whose gall he will use to cure his father's blindness. There is also a compelling group of three people staring at the severed head of John the Baptist. This is by another local artist, Giovanni Mannozzi (known as Giovanni di San Giovanni) whose family home may be seen in the Corso Italia, close by Masaccio's.

In the siesta period it is a pleasure to wander the streets of the town and admire the houses of these painters, and others, but, as the community awakes to life after lunch, beware cyclists returning to work, who ride on both sides of streets whichever direction they are taking.

San Giovanni, partly built on land reclaimed from the Arno and, therefore, liable to flooding, has long been a centre of industry. Woolmaking and the manufacture of nails were established early on, while in the nineteenth century glassmaking, ironworking and mining were added. These activities have waned and the population is now less than 20,000, although there are still signs of an industrial presence.

The motorway roars up the right bank of the Arno, partly hidden by great bushes and trees which the Italians use so successfully to mitigate some of the worst of the noise. We will take the left bank on an ordinary road (no. 69) towards Figline Valdarno, but first turning off to reach Gaville. The parish church stands in a small complex, next to an olive grove, in a field across the road from the settlement, huddled on a hillside, it is supposed to serve. It was formerly the pieve for Figline itself, when building started in 1007. Now approaching its millennium, it has been admirably restored to its original simplicity. The exterior is stark, with a gaunt campanile rising above a nave with two aisles, all in unrendered stone. (It once stood beside the Cassia Adrianea where fragments of Roman pottery have been excavated.) Inside, some of the columns dividing the nave and aisles have decorated capitals featuring pelicans and other birds, and a mournful-faced ram.

Joined to the church, at two levels, is the former vicarage round three sides of a courtyard. It is now the Museo della Civiltà Contadina – the Museum of the Peasant – housing a collection, formed over twenty years or more, by Signor Righi Pierluigi, a courteous, somewhat resigned-looking man, who will oversee your visit.

Signor Pierluigi has assembled every imaginable artefact relating to the land and those who work on it, and displays them in an orderly manner. This is no jumble of old tools, furniture, farm machinery, cutlery, bottles and collectors' miscellanea. Everything is categorized and labelled. It may seem to the casual visitor that there is little, if any, difference between the spoons laid out in platoon-like rows, but to the expert they surely have significance... and even if they don't to the expert from the outer world, they do to Signor Pierluigi.

One room is a kitchen, another a bedroom with made-up bed, a third is a shrine with portraits the size of cigarette cards mounted in frames. There are pots, pans, wine vats, scarecrows, pictures of a corn harvest, the paraphernalia of beekeeping, wild flowers pressed behind glass, nails (some, no doubt wrought in San Giovanni) and cartwheels. The prevailing colour is dark brown. There is a musty smell. The floors are cobbled and hazardous.

No matter. This is a serious collection and may become the forerunner of a museum in grander premises, although such a transition could spoil it because it belongs here in the countryside, attached to this ancient church and community. It opens only on Saturdays and festivals but you may be lucky, as we were, to arrive when a coachload of schoolkids was expected. The signore, awaiting them, invited us to look round ahead of them. He also drew our attention to a lemon tree festival which is held annually in the courtyard, and to which curators of other museums of rural life bring specimens.

There is a discreetly placed tin for contributions and you can buy high-quality postcards which make the interior of the museum look like a subject for *Homes and Gardens*.

Figline Valdarno must soon have felt the need for its own parish church. Certainly by the fourteenth century the town had been walled and fortified by Florence. A reconstruction of it, shown on a postcard, indicates that it had four gateways and a dozen towers. It is a small, attractive town for which I have a special affection. Late one August afternoon, after a harrowing drive from Rome through monsoon-type rain, in a situation where I found myself driving recklessly fast for fear of being hit in the rear, we at last reached Figline. The rain had stopped, folk streamed from their houses. We searched for the hotel where we were booked and, dazed from the autostrada experience, I drove into the main piazza down a NO ENTRY. A good-humoured policeman emerged from the crowd,

86

smiled, directed me to the hotel and uttered no word of rebuke.

Nowadays the Piazza Marsilio Ficino is pedestrianized, such is my influence. As at Greve (see Chapter 10) it is irregularly shaped and the houses lining it are of varying height. All are freshly stuccoed in soothing colours, some have pargeting. Most sides are colonnaded, some being beneath the first floors of buildings, others protruding from them. At the northern end is a seventeenth-century loggia where the medieval ospedale was endowed by the ruling Serristori family. (Just outside the town a modern hospital is named after them.) At the opposite end of the piazza is Santa Maria Assunta, though the church of principal interest is San Francesco, lying one block away from the town hall.

San Francesco is fourteenth century, has a two-sided cloister and a fresco at one end featuring a grand, Edwardian-style lady. Inside the church are other frescoes and also trompe l'oeil figures on pillars either side of the altar. They were so convincing that we were fooled by them but that could have been due to the prevailing gloom. Not only is this an ill-lit church but it was raining outside. The frescoes, from what I could see of them, were not exciting apart from an arresting Annunciation.

The town hall resembles a minor Medici fortress, with crenellated tower supporting an ironwork belfry. The tower leans a little but not sufficiently to bring in the coach parties.

From Figline we cross the Arno, then leave it, taking signs to Vallombrosa, but first calling on two Romanesque churches at Cascia and Pietrapiana, both of which places are part of the larger town of Reggello.

San Pietro a Cascia is a simple church with a five-arched loggia complemented by a row of a dozen smaller blind ones beneath the pediment. An opening in the shape of a cross is echoed by a thin actual cross at the apex of an otherwise unembellished, perfectly geometrical frontage. The rough-hewn sandstone campanile stands slightly apart.

Inside, the high nave has arched columns with decorated capitals, most of them with abstract designs, although I noticed two exceptions – a person sitting side-saddle on a horse and another, a male, properly astride, with a child as pillion. Half-way along the nave, on the left, is a fresco of the Annunciation, very faded, by Mariotto di Cristofano, brother-in-law of Masaccio whose *Juvenal* triptych is the church's main treasure. This is Masaccio's first known work and it was commissioned by the Castellani family for their parish church of St Juvenal when the painter was twenty-one and had only six years to live. It was not authenticated until the 1960s and has been here at Cascia only since 1988. Unfortunately poor light and confused labelling make appreciation of the painting difficult. You could be forgiven for overlooking it entirely.

Along with much other loot from central and northern Italy,

Napoleon stole the original bells, of 1247, from this church; the present ones are early nineteenth century.

Reggello gives way to Pietrapiana in what is ribbon development and there, down a lane, reached via a veritable track, is Sant'Agata ad Arfoli, younger and less beautiful than San Pietro but in a charming setting dominated by an ancient cedar hanging protectively over a presbytery. The priest's house is joined by a loggia to the church and campanile, making an agreeable complex. At first it appears that a slice has been taken from the church but this is illusory and due to the fact that from the front view the attached campanile obscures a side chapel. The paintings within are unremarkable. If you have to make a choice, settle for San Pietro a Cascia.

The origin of the monastery at Vallombrosa follows a familiar pattern. A wealthy Florentine, Giovanni Gualberto, having already rejected materialism and made a hermitage here on the slopes of Monte Secchieta in the Pratomagno, founded, in 1038, the Vallombrosan Order. It was based on strict Benedictine principles but that didn't prevent it from becoming, in due course, a major landowner in the region. Gualberto was canonized late in the twelfth century and the monastery prospered until its suppression some seven hundred years later. It is set behind bleak walls, on a heavily wooded hillside where the deciduous trees, planted by the monks, give way to even more densely packed conifers. A visit can be an eerie experience, although today it is not those bent on monasticism who come here. More likely it is holiday-makers and skiers, or those in search of a health cure. Next to the monastery, now used as a forestry school, is a hotel open all the year.

More tourists are catered for at neighbouring Saltino. This makes it an effort to envisage the remoteness and isolation that lured Gualberto, or even the terrain that attracted John Milton who, in *Paradise Lost*, refers to 'thick as leaves in Vallombrosa'. On the approach is a small chapel where, in 1974, I found a plaque commemorating the poet's visit but, returning more than twenty years later, I was unable to locate it.

The monastery is fittingly austere, rather like a barracks except for the thin bell tower rising from its midst. In the church there are frescoes and other paintings depicting the life of the founder. It is rather a sombre place. Probably contemporary Florentine businessmen opting out of the rat race look for somewhere closer to the Equator and rather more worldly.

You can proceed over the Pratomagno to the Casentino, or take a very minor road up to Monte Secchieta (1449 m) but we will return to the Valdarno, passing again through Reggello, aiming for Castelfranco di Sopra, lying on the Sette Ponti (the route of the seven bridges) that extends almost to Arezzo.

Castelfranco is another town built by the Florentines on the grid system. There are many old houses, a medieval gate or two, but nothing architecturally riveting. The central Piazza Victor Emmanuele has a town hall with a few plaques, many banks but no church. In one street running from it is a Teatro Comunale where forthcoming events, in May 1996, included an 'Evening of Alan Ayckbourn', a short version of *The Marriage of Figaro*, and a comedy in the Florentine vernacular.

Outside the walls there was an abbey, Soffena, on the site of a castle built in the Dark Ages. It was suppressed by Grand Duke Leopold I of Tuscany in 1779, and converted into a farm, with the church used as a barn. In the 1960s the government purchased what still remained and restoration began. Cloisters were refurbished and, in the nave, frescoes whitewashed over long before secularization can be seen again. They are thought to be the work of Mariotto di Cristofano and Lorenzo di Bicci, both of whom are known to have worked extensively in these parts. The restoration has been lovingly done, with the unrendered stone of the church contrasting with the stuccoed walls of the monastery buildings but, having gone to the expense of this in a land not exactly lacking in medieval churches, the government should do more to attract paying visitors to it, especially as there is no parking problem. But Badia di San Salvatore a Soffena is poorly signed and, when you do find it, it will probably be closed.

Continue along the Sette Ponti, through fruitful country, passing Montemarciano, where the sixteenth-century oratory, with a fine loggia, was restored in 1954, to Loro Ciuffenna, which is much the most interesting town on this hillside.

The Ciuffenna, a tributary of the Arno, cuts a deep ravine through Loro and is spanned by a medieval bridge with a high-angled devil's arch, and another, more modern, for vehicles. The terrain on which the town is built is so steep and uneven that few dwellings are on the same level. This adds to the picturesque quality but calls for a certain athleticism from pedestrians. Drivers need to be patient because of a one-way system through narrow streets. These are often rendered impassable when deliveries are made to the shops, which themselves are nearly all engagingly old-fashioned, their only concession to this century being the installation of electric light. The church is fourteenth century, with a font, much older, in a kind of oven, and a beamed roof. The organ is behind the altar, beneath a plain stained-glass window, and there is a triptych of the Virgin, by Lorenzo di Bicci, given by the Uffizi.

On the small, sloping piazza are the town hall and the Museo Venturino Venturi devoted to the work of a local sculptor with an international reputation. Venturi, now in his eighties, has returned to live in his native town. There are clumps of sturdy houses both in the shopping area

Loro Ciuffenna: medieval bridge

and below, where the river churns over great slabs of rock. A working mill survives. This is the place from which to observe the intricate terracing and concentric narrow roads and alleys. Here you can see how Loro has evolved over the centuries.

Ciuffenna is an Etruscan word meaning hind. It was added to Loro when the introduction of the postal service in the nineteenth century necessitated precise identification. Roads ascend vertiginously from the town, some going along the west side of the Pratomagno, some rising sharply, then ceasing well below the summit, others scaling it and dropping down into the Casentino. These hills have been inhabited since the earliest recorded times. Traces of Roman pavement have been unearthed in one place, Etruscan name places abound. On the lower slopes fossils of mammoths and elephants have been found. In times of war and disturbance the woods have provided shelter for the hunted, and for resistance fighters. The chestnut forests have always been a source of basic sustenance and the climate is sufficiently temperate for vines, olives, irises and junipers to grow, while, until recently, grain, potatoes, mulberries and other fruit and vegetables flourished. But the 1970s saw heavy depopulation. Farming has declined, old occupations have all but gone. Many houses are now owned by Americans and by Europeans from other countries. The pattern has changed but there are still villagers baking bread and making cheeses that are much sought after by people in the towns.

The roads out of Loro lead to villages and hamlets such as Rocca Ricciarda, Trappoloa, Chiassaia, Anciolina. From the latter one climbs dizzily to the summit, although to reach it you must go on foot by mule track. The views are stupendous, as you would expect. You can see far across the Chianti hills down to Arezzo, and on clear days to the Adriatic.

We have a friend who drives up the Pratomagno not only to buy bread, but to walk. She abandons her car and strides off across the mountain. She rarely meets a soul and, when she does, communication is limited because of the, to her, incomprehensible patois spoken by the natives. I hope she remembers to take a whistle in case she falls.

Loro was where we experienced life in a converted mill close to the river. Le Gualchiere has been made into a number of self-catering apartments set amidst vineyards and orchards, at the foot of a long, narrow, unsurfaced track which played havoc with my car's exhaust unit. It was worth it for the pleasure of meeting Laura and Roberto Boyer who assured us, as the river began to rise ominously, that the climate 'here in May is never like this'. To make amends Laura gave us bottles of their own vintage whenever there was a cloudburst.

There is a choice of road slightly above Anciolina. We will take the one which descends through sweeping pine forests and passes a camp site and football pitch, to rejoin the Sette Ponti near San Giustino.

This town scarcely warrants a stop, although there is a tiny square in the old part with a simple Romanesque church going back to the eleventh century. Its predecessor was built in territory then inhabited by Goths and Longobards. More interesting, two kilometres away, down a road which is no longer part of the Sette Ponti, is the village of Borro, reached over a narrow medieval bridge and a rough stone pathway on which only residents may drive. It is impeccably maintained and conscious of its picturesque qualities. There are houses with window boxes and not a weed to be seen. It overlooks the Lorenaccio valley on two sides but, even in a wet May, I failed to discern any water.

Borro was much fought over by Florence and Arezzo and takes its name from a family that has produced a distinguished mathematician, a poet, an artist in stained glass and an admiral who fought under Nelson. It has become a tentative tourist attraction (and how it will cope if it ever becomes more than that I shudder to imagine) because the resident priest has transformed a small chapel into what he calls Pinocchio's Cave. You enter a darkened room, fumble for a light and are then welcomed by four life-sized figures of musicians playing Mozart. A vast model of a village springs to life. Peasants are seen plying their trades and crafts. Wheels turn, axes rise and fall, as workers toil. There are scenes from the classic Tuscan tale of Pinocchio. Then, suddenly the skies darken, thunder rumbles, lightning flashes, the lights go out, and you are invited to place a contribution 'in the box'.

Across the valley, all but hidden in a wood and under heavy restoration, is a castle that was probably the seat of the Borro family. It became owned in this century by the Dukes of Savoia-Aosta and is still in private hands.

Go north, back to the Sette Ponti again, through San Giustino and along a winding, pretty road cultivated on either side in early summer with irises rioting on banks and walls. There are many signs to the ancient church of Gropina, of the yellow variety denoting an important national monument and, indeed, Scarini's sumptuously illustrated, and thickly documented book on the parish churches of the upper Arno valley describes it as 'the most renowned, admired and frequented church in the province of Arezzo'. If this is so, and the tour operators cotton on to it, there is going to be a major traffic problem on this hillside and parking will have to be provided. If you wish to take your car ignore the first signpost (just round a bend and opposite a grim, greyish pile) because this will soon lead you into the tiny village and you will become a menace. Proceed, instead, to Loro Ciuffenna and take the next sign. When you have wound your way up the steep hill and reached a walled olive grove with an entrance arch, park on the grass verge and walk into Gropina, stopping to admire the profusion of wild flowers and herbs growing out of the stonework.

From the Sette Ponti you will see the church many times, apparently encased in thick woods. This is an illusion. It is surrounded by two or three streets of houses, about thirty in all. The church is documented as having existed in 1016 but there are, allegedly, associations with Charlemagne who gave money to the parent abbey of Nomantola in 780. It stands on the site of an Etruscan temple and there have been numerous interesting finds below the nave. The present church dates from the twelfth century. It has a skeletal low tower, a simple rounded apse and a seemingly low nave. The frontage, seen across a tiny square, is as bleak as the chapel of a mining community in Wales. The glory lies inside, where the unexpectedly tall nave is impressive and almost unadorned except for the capitals of the columns, for which Roman materials *in situ* were used. A double row of columns form the apse which has one central window; the roof is beamed. The exquisitely restored carving reveals, on the capitals, a wolf eating a lamb, piglets being suckled, another wolf with teeth like a palisade; lions, tigers, eagles; acanthus leaves, bunches of grapes; a knight on horseback, a Christ, St Peter and other biblical figures.

Then there is the pulpit, an outstanding, formidable circle of masonry with carvings that vary from saints and a mermaid to abstract geometrical shapes. It is attached to a side pillar and also supported by partly twisted, snake-like, twin central columns. They, in fact, hold the pulpit, not the seriously under-employed caryatids who scarcely touch the plinth above them. Look closely at them; they have the faces of gingerbread men.

Beneath and behind the church is evidence of former buildings. The rear, over a high wall, reveals a perfect Romanesque apse with blind arches at ground level and a small gallery above – if you are tall enough to see.

Return to Loro and take the road to Terranuova-Bracciolini, passing through Penna, where a great outcrop of red rock stands above the fields. Bracciolini was founded, in 1337, on the grid pattern, hence the first part of its name. The second was added in 1862 to honour the humanist philosopher, Poggio Bracciolini. What some call his house, privately owned, is the most attractive feature and stands on the edge of the new town, visible up one of the cross sections behind a large vegetable garden. There is a rough drive, a short hedge, no walls or gate. It has two storeys, plus a squat central tower rising to a pigeon loft under a low, tiled roof. The ground floor is almost half the height of the whole and has eight Gothic arches below a balcony supported by elegantly thin pillars. If it ever becomes a hotel I shall make a point of booking in.

When the walled town was laid out, to protect farmers and encourage trade, neighbouring villages were each allocated a district of their own with a church. The arrangement pertains today. The central piazza is a happy blend of varying styles accommodating one modern apartment block which does not look out of place. The orderliness of Terranuova-Bracciolini is in sharp contrast to the hugger-mugger quality of Loro Ciuffenna, but I know which I would choose.

We now cross the Arno, not to San Giovanni where we started this itinerary, but to its close neighbour, Montevarchi, which, says the official brochure, with 'its elliptical layout, cut by a longitudinal axis, is one of the most curious examples of town planning of the Middle Ages'. I can't say this struck me as I made my way to the main square, Vittoria Veneto, but I expect it is so.

Montevarchi is a busy market town with an academy, founded by Poggio Bracciolini, and a monastery with a fifteenth-century cloister. There are also two churches, at least one of which has a bizarre relic, a receptacle supposed to contain breast milk of the Virgin Mary. That was sufficient to repel me but one of the two, on an approach road to the older

Terranuova-Bracciolini: Casa Bracciolini

94

part, is a pretty yellow, stuccoed, large chapel with a wide loggia on three sides. I much preferred it to the dark and shabby building in the Piazza Varchi, where I suspect the milk is. Next door to it is the inevitable museum of Sacred Art without which few Italian towns can stand on their civic pride. There is also a Museum of Prehistory, rarely open, with 'impressive fossilized remains from the Pliocene period', discovered in this valley. Probably mammoth tusks.

Here, you are close to that convenient motorway which will convey you swiftly to Florence or Arezzo, or help you on your way to your next prosciutto e melone and plate of pasta.

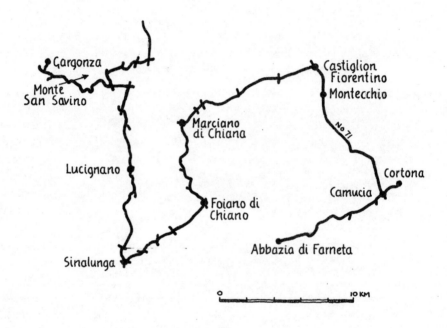

Gargonza

Monte
San Savino

Castiglion
Fiorentino

Montecchio

Marciano
di Chiana

N⁰ 71

Lucignano

Cortona

Camucia

Foiano di
Chiano

Abbazia di Farneta

Sinalunga

0   10 KM

6   Cortona and Val di Chiana

*Monte San Savino; Gargonza; Lucignano; Sinalunga; Foiano; Marciano;
Castiglion Fiorentino; Montecchio; Cortona; Abbazia di Farneta*

The Milan–Rome autostrada runs along the Chiana valley.
Although I do not usually recommend motorways for pleasure, in Italy it is
often sensible to use them sparingly unless you are content to notch up
only one place in the forenoon and one after. The minor roads, frequently
through hilly country, are slow, so a short, sharp stretch of autostrada at
the start and end of the day can add to the experience of an outing by
allowing you to take in two or three more stops. On this route there are
eleven destinations placed in one group. That is for the sake of coherence;
no one in their right mind, even using the motorway, would attempt them
all in one day.

Turning off the south-bound Al, to the west, we come first to
Monte San Savino, the birthplace of Andrea Contucci. Who he? You may
well ask. Well, he was the sculptor Andrea Sansovino who should not be
confused with the more famous architect, Jacopo Sansovino, whose real
name was Tatti. Tatti was about twenty-five years younger than Contucci
and learned his craft from the older man, but after his apprenticeship he
worked mainly in Venice, so he is not part of this book.

In San Savino (not Sovino) Andrea Sansovino is celebrated
throughout the centre of the hill town, from the Porta Fiorentina to the
Porta Roma. On the Piazza Gamurrini, in the rather poky little seventeenth-
century church of Santa Chiara, there is his group of three saints in terracotta; on the gently winding main street there is the Loggia dei Mercanti,
said to have been designed by him (facing the Palazzo Comunale, which is
by Antonio di Sangallo the Elder); in the garden behind the palazzo is a
bust of Andrea and in the church of Sant'Agostino his tomb hangs in the
nave.

It is a shame that the Palazzo Comunale and the loggia glower
at, rather than face, each other. This is due to their height and the narrow-
ness of the street. These two formidable buildings desperately need space
surrounding them but, this being a medieval town, they don't get it.
Sangallo's building is heavy, even ponderous, with a frontage in bulging

97

lumps of dark stone around windows inset and barred at street level. Once inside, there is an instant improvement in a cloistered courtyard with two wells, leading to a simple garden at the end of which, past a wall and down steps, is an open-air theatre. From here you can view both the roofscape of the town and the surrounding country.

Along the street, facing the bust of a poet, Giulio Salvadori, is the church of the Misericordia, very baroque, gloomy and too high. It is also opposite the Torre Civica of the town hall (fourteenth century, with many emblems) which has a bold clock-face.

In the Piazza di Monte is the aforementioned church of Sant'Agostino with a rose window by de Marcillat, whose work we saw at Arezzo. A door in the nave leads to a simple cloister which can also be entered from the street, beside yet another church, once part of a Benedictine monastery. On the Piazza Gamurrini note a house in deep yellow, with caryatids, both legless and armless.

Monte San Savino has Etruscan origins and later became an important fortress on the border between Arezzo and Florence. It was destroyed by the Arretines for its Guelph affiliations but became, at another time, a refuge for both Ghibelline and Guelph exiles. In a later century its Jews were persecuted by the invading French army (1799). Much of the ancient wall remains.

Out on the Siena road, up through the thickly wooded slopes of Monte Pallazzuolo, there is a turning which leads to the thirteenth-century walled village of Gargonza. This fortified settlement is almost hidden among conifers, only its crenellated tower, from which there is a commanding view of the Chiana valley, is visible. The entire complex has been converted into a hotel which lets not only rooms, but houses. The tower has become a restaurant. Few places emanate such an air of exclusiveness. It has also the cachet of having been one of Dante's many hide-outs when he fled from Florence. Everything has been meticulously preserved down to the cobbles on the approach drive. They threaten to break your ankles.

Return to Monte San Savino and take a minor road, roughly parallel to the motorway, to Lucignano, a compact hill town about eight kilometres distant. Enter it by the Porta San Giovanni and either climb by steps, over more cobbles, to the neat town centre, or reach it by describing a semicircle, eventually leading to the multicoloured, rough-stone church sporting tufa columns. It lies above curiously arranged steps, partly convex, partly concave. If you take this second route you will pass La Tavernetta, a trattoria where Christopher and I had good food and wine pleasantly served, and the fourteenth-century castle now the Teatro Rossini. The church has a baroque altar with marble pillars on either side, a crown, a cross, statutory cherubs and an angel wielding an enormous sword, his deity not having informed him about the policy of turning the other cheek.

The town hall, across a square from the church, has a museum housing a gold reliquary known as the Tree of Lucignano, and Sienese paintings from the thirteenth to the fifteenth centuries. It is a dignified, two-storey building, nicely dotted with plaques and having a touch of municipal severity. Next to it is another church with a frontage in horizontal black and white stripes, a recessed doorway with barley-sugar pillars and a rounded arch continuing into a pointed lintel.

Note, as you wander the well-cared-for streets, that the formidable buttresses are multi-purposed. Some are also pathways on the tops of houses, others serve as flower gardens as well as supports.

Lucignano is visually one of the most pleasing of the hill towns. The next one, Sinalunga, is higher, larger and has spilled heavily into the valley that was, for long, so rife with malarial insects that it was little populated by humans.

Lucignano: Palazzo Pretorio and museum

There is no point in lingering in lower Sinalunga, so ascend by a wide, straight road which finally winds up and on to a plateau where the capacious Piazza Garibaldi is partly flanked by three churches, one of which, Collegiata di San Martino, is on the site of an old fortress. The stone from the castle was used in its construction. The church, striking rather than beautiful, presents a severe frontage of four classical columns with minimal decoration, like the picture on a box of bricks for infants. High on the walls of the nave are absurdly small oculi, but the overall appearance is relieved by an octagonal cupola surmounted by a similarly shaped lantern. The interior is typically lofty, with many side chapels where there are paintings, neatly documented, by artists whose names may well be as unfamiliar to you as they are to me. Antonio Nasini occurs several times and there is a highly regarded Madonna and Child by Benvenuto di Giovanni in which angels play zithers on the main canvas, while on the predella below St Sebastian is treated, as usual, like a dartboard. The overall baroquery is mitigated by plain pillars and a bare ceiling. Large marble statues of giants guard the entrances to side chapels. The best feature, soaring above a forest of tall candles rising from the altar like masts in a yacht-packed port, is the organ loft, a curving balcony in front of the instrument itself.

To the rear of the church, down typically narrow, high medieval streets, is the town hall of 1346 with an impeccably symmetrical campanile. At ground level it envelops, just inside the entrance, the original jail. Transgressors were imprisoned in full view of the public. This building alone makes a visit to Sinalunga worthwhile. Garibaldi was held prisoner in the town in 1867, but probably in a less public cell. The piazza named for him is the market square.

Return to the valley, go under the motorway and make for Foiano della Chiana which, by Sinalunga standards, is a mere bump of a hill town. At its modest peak, on the Piazza Cavour, is a yellowish town hall with busts of King Umberto I and a supporter of Savonarola; Garibaldi's statue is just outside the walls.

There are two ancient gateways, sturdily intact but not, architecturally, in the prize-winning class. Nor are the three churches. Modern housing merges neatly with the castle to form a homogeneous whole. The town, in fact, conveys a happy impression of many strands of living history right down to the 1990s. Some fascia boards I observed bore names such as MODA HAIR, FAST FOOD, FUTURE GAMES and, complete with a chessboard sign, CHECKMATE PUB.

Further north, at Marciano della Chiana, the old walls have been even more intricately wedded to later housing, and there is a particularly proud gateway and bell tower bearing the Medici balls beneath

Sinalunga: Palazzo Pretorio

crenellations, and a thin belfry with three little turrets. It is pretty, as distinct from imposing, and leads to a piazza so self-consciously tidy, with freshly painted houses in shades of pale yellow, that it looks like a stage set. The church beyond is large and uninteresting apart from a banner I have not encountered elsewhere, indicating a world beyond religion ... PREGA ... AIUTA ... SORRIDI!!! (Help the suffering).

Marciano: Porta San Giovanni

To the north-east lies Castiglion Fiorentino which stands higher, and is much larger, than the last two places, with a town wall built upon Etruscan and Roman foundations, and an eleventh-century castle.

A hilly main street leads to the town centre, which is enhanced by a loggia with openings providing views of the lower town and of the church of San Giuliano where there are what one guide describes as 'a number of interesting works of art'. I take such comments as a warning that they will not set my adrenalin into top gear, so I didn't bother to tramp down to the Chio valley to make up my own mind. A further excuse was the pouring rain, so I also missed the Chiesa del Gesù, adjoining the collegiate church and said to have 'an ornate Baroque interior and a fresco by Signorelli'. But I loved the view of both churches from the loggia, which itself is overlooked by a third holy building, Sant'Angelo, and the castle. The chapel of Sant'Angelo houses a museum where there are many models of a military nature, emphasizing yet again the strong links between the clergy and the army. The pictures therein should include a Vasari Mother and Child, and another of the same subject by one of the Gaddis, but they were both on temporary loan when I called to an exhibition at Arezzo where, in my estimation, there are already thousands of them. Other paintings, of little merit, still *in situ* showed St Catherine in ecstasy and St Francis receiving the stigmata. There were also some Umbrian Crucifixions painted on wood and a twelfth-century reliquary. The museum is hardly a must but I should add that some think well of it and praise a portrait of St Francis by Margarito of Arezzo which may be the stigmata job. Another church, San Francesco, is at the end of a typically irregular piazza and has a two-tier cloister with fading frescoes, a young palm tree and a tiled roof above a well.

One of the pleasures of visiting these hill towns comes from viewing one from another. At first glance they may seem as alike as any two run-of-the-mill madonne e bambini but, as with the paintings, the more you study the detail the greater the difference.

At Montecchio, just south of Castiglion Fiorentino, impressive ruins of a fourteenth-century castle stand high above the village. A narrow track, partly tarmacked, winds up to it past fields and olive groves, but there is no admittance. It is a dangerous structure; to attempt entry, you are advised, is 'pericoloso'. A pity, this, because inside there was once a small town under the protection of the largest fortress in the area. It belonged to an English mercenary, Sir John Hawkwood who, finding himself out of work during a break in the Hundred Years War, made for Italy, where he fought on behalf of anyone who would pay him. He led the Pisan army against the Florentines, who then deemed it circumspect to offer him employment. Such was his standing that they awarded him this castle and excused him from taxes. When he died he received a state funeral.

The castle remained of strategic importance until the seventeenth century. The main road runs beside the village and leads to Cortona, the principal place on this itinerary. Below it, almost in the valley, is Camucia, while south of that nondescript town, is Melone di Camucia, where you may find a seventh-century tumulus. Christopher and I drove in several directions without locating it and consoled ourselves by remembering that the most interesting objects found in it are now in the archaeological museum at Florence.

We found several other rewarding places in the foothills of Monte San Egidio, on which Cortona stands, not least the lovely, unimproved Romanesque church of San Michele Angelo, its roadside nave wall bulging just slightly outwards. It is eleventh century, and triple apsed, in reddish-grey brick, and it came as a great relief after a surfeit of baroquery elsewhere.

These foothills positively bristle with churches. Santa Maria Nuova, nestling beneath the road, is in Greek-cross style and was remodelled by Vasari, in imitation of another Renaissance church, Madonna del Calcinaio, two miles away. Then there is the convent built to the order of St Francis, in the thirteenth century, where he stayed on his return from Rome, in 1210, when his Order was officially recognized by the Vatican. The original church is extant and the monastery (rebuilt) is now occupied by Capuchins. Also to be seen, if you can find anywhere to park on a particularly narrow side road, is the Tanella di Pitagora, a tomb from a few centuries BC. Michelin states it is Etruscan and circular; Phaidon that it is small and rectangular. Both agree that it is named the Tomb of Pythagoras because of a confusion arising from the fact that the Greek mathematician and philosopher lived at a place far from here called Crotona.

Cortona was described by Archibald Lyall as 'so ancient' it has been called 'the grandmother of Rome'. According to that engaging writer, who did not live to complete his book on Tuscany, the godly Dardanus departed from Cortona to found Troy, 'from which city the pious Aeneas came to Latium', which is a neat encapsulation of a long span of history.

Cortona, more mountain city than hill town, overlooks not only the Chiana valley but also Lake Trasimeno. At its highest point there is a fortress built upon the remains of a thirteenth-century castle, and a much earlier Etruscan settlement whose defences were two miles round and form part of the present wall. Corita, as the Etruscans named it, was probably one of the dozen cities of the Confederacy. The Romans who annexed the city were themselves defeated near here by Hannibal. Cortona has a vivid and incident-packed history.

There is ample parking space outside the walls. Only the residents may – and do – drive into and out of the city. Enter by the Via Guelfa which you may think steep, but wait until you are approaching Santa Margherita. The Guelfa is good practice for that torture to come, so step resolutely up its considerable length and, if you are lucky, enjoy it when it is decorated by blue and yellow flags bearing the motif of a golden lion against fleurs-de-lys. In May, for certain, these banners add colour to drab buildings and perhaps they do in other months as well.

Half-way up the Guelfa is the battered old church of Sant'Agostino, with a cloister in poor repair. At the top is the Piazza della Repubblica, of indefinite shape and usually buzzing with activity. To your left is the Palazzo Comunale, on whose wide steps young people sprawl and chatter. It faces the only level street in Cortona, the Via Nazionale, bordered by noble mansions, some designed, it is said, by Brunelleschi. Another exit is an ample passage to the Piazza Signorelli (market on Saturdays) where a fortified house is now the Museo dell'Accademia Etrusca, and where an equally grand yellow edifice, with a long loggia, proclaims itself Hotel del Granduca. Beside it is a narrower passage to the Piazza del Duomo, a jagged courtyard with a further museum, the Palazzo Pretorio and the cathedral itself.

Cortona: Palazzo Comunale

The duomo is a two-colour-stone enormity, its appearance slightly relieved by the small marble plaques in the simple portico. One is of the city's (or Florence's) lion; the other of St George (or St Michael) standing on the infamous dragon. Basically a Romanesque building, the duomo was much rebuilt in the fifteenth century, despite which columns in the nave are still simply decorated. The side chapels are shallow and there is an enormous risen Christ hurtling down the central aisle with a flag, looking like a marathon runner. Not quite in his path is a statue of Giovanni Battista Tommasi, a local dignitary honoured by the Czar of Russia and other heads of state. The bell tower is sixteenth century but looks older. Giuliano Sangallo was one of the Renaissance architects called in to alter the façade.

Opposite the cathedral is the Museo Diocesano, well laid out on two floors with many rooms. The paintings are not crowded and include several works by Luca Signorelli, a native of the city who returned here after working in Milan, Rome and Florence, where he competed with the foremost of his kind. There is an omnibus canvas of his, embracing the Crucifixion, Deposition and Ascension which has, on the predella, a Last Supper and a Flagellation, against a background of Lake Trasimeno and a city that has to be Cortona. Another signed *Francesco* Signorelli pictures the Ascension with bodiless cherubs hanging like mobiles above Adam and Eve who are active by an apple tree.

The pride of the collection is a Fra Angelico Annunciation even more splendid than those at San Giovanni Valdarno and Florence. The haloes, and the chair on which the Virgin is seated, positively dazzle. The angel is wearing a robe similarly coloured to that at San Giovanni but has more elaborate wings, protruding outside the loggia where he is kneeling, thus affording the artist the opportunity of filling in a background view of figures on a hillock. There is even greater dazzle on one panel of the predella where there are so many saints with haloes that the impression is of a field of sunflowers.

I noted, also, an Aretino (thirteenth century) of Santa Margherita of Cortona about whom François Mauriac wrote an entire book, and whose church high above we shall reach subsequently, and a fourteenth-century fresco by Pietro Aiuti, of the Road to Calvary, with agonized faces looking over shoulders. At the head of the stairs to a basement area are some Gino Severinis, very bold with twentieth-century people in biblical settings. He was something of a latter-day El Greco. Down in the high, wide basement are more frescoes, by Cristofano Gherardi of Sansepolcro. They illustrate Old Testament sacrifices. Powerful stuff.

The Museo del Accademia Etrusca, in the Palazzo Casali, is entered through a tunnel, across a courtyard stacked with masonry and up a flight of broken stone stairs, making no provision for the halt and the lame. So arduous is the going that you can easily fancy you are entering a medieval prison. Once through the door the contrast is startling. You are in a well-lit museum laid out in the current fashion with plenty of floor space for visitor flow. There is so much of it that you could manoeuvre your way about wearing a farthingale without crashing valuable exhibits to the ground. Pride of place is granted to an Etruscan lamp, set under a miniature temple and lit from below. It reveals delicate workmanship. The Etruscans are also represented in several cases containing tiny human figures and a finely carved bronze pig.

Signorelli (again named Francesco, not Luca) is here with a tondo of the Nativity, and the paintings also include a self-portrait by Zoffany, a much-travelled artist, and another by James Northcote, pupil of Reynolds, friend of Hazlitt. And an entire chamber is devoted to Severini who bequeathed canvases, books and much else to his native city. One wall is indicative of his professional debt to Picasso, another has his wife and son depicted as Madonna e Bambino. In a glass case are copies of his books and a photograph of him and four other men, all wearing raincoats and with fags drooping from their lips, looking like a still from a gangster movie.

There are rooms devoted to the Tommasi family (see p. 106) a vast gallery with portraits, some of English nobles, and two giant globes standing in rotundas. Etruscan burial urns are here in profusion, some of them historiated, beside medallions, coins, pottery. There is also an Egyptian section with specimens of funeral papyri.

In the first room of glass display counters there are sixteenth-century ivories of figures on miniature columns confronting each other with droll expressions. The tiny Etruscan figures are like toys. Among them is a small glass cup, whole, except for a slight chip, from the fourth century.

In the Piazza Signorelli I noticed the Gelateria Snoopy, but that apart the American influence was slight.

We walked up to Santa Margherita. I was helped on the way by concentrating on how glad I was not to be a pilgrim on my knees, although I was all but brought to them as I stumbled up the fearsome path. The object of the climb closes at midday, not at 13.00, as the *Green Guide to Tuscany* states, but I didn't mind. I was sure the exercise was good for my calf muscles, if nothing else. Had I gone by car I would have forgone the experience taken for granted by the citizens. I was able to appreciate, albeit slightly, what it is like to live in a precipitously perched house on a mountainside.

On my way up I cheated by taking a breather on one of the streets on a concentric ring of mere slopes. There I came upon the ospedale,

107

in gorgeous yellow ochre. It was tempting to ask for a bed but there is no way of avoiding the final long ascent, whether you take my way from the town centre or you struggle up the Via Margherita, on which, if you are of a pious nature, you may gain inspiration from more Severinis – his stations of the cross which mark the route.

Santa Margherita, when you reach it, by whichever way, is a nineteenth-century church attached to a convent founded by the saint who died six hundred years ago. Margaret, as a girl, was seduced by a noble-man and bore him a son. When he died, violently, his family rejected her, as her own had already. Friends were more charitable and Margaret react-ed by seeking redemption through good works, eventually joining a Franciscan Order. Her son became a friar. She died, a recluse, in 1297. The convent was dedicated to her memory and her tomb, with the body visible, is by the high altar of the church. Why she was canonized is not clarified in my *Dictionary of Saints*.

It was not only Santa Margherita which was closed that mid-week day in May. Most of the other churches had also shut for lunch and in those that were open I found little to interest me. (Why should visiting Tuscany become a matter of dutifully examining church after church? Some are appealing buildings, some are not. Most of them exhibit atrocious paintings badly lit, many have been outrageously baroqued. Just a few have been allowed to remain in their original, simple, elegant state.) There is more to Tuscany than Christian art and architecture, and Cortona con-firms this. Being there succoured my addiction to towns and townscapes uniquely set in ravishing terrain.

Finally, on our way back to the autostrada, comes the wholly delightful triple-apsed Abbazia di Farneta on a hillock, at a bend in the road. Here the attraction is not just the church which does, in this instance, arrest me, but the whole lovely complex of buildings around a courtyard.

All that remains of the ninth-century abbey is a Romanesque church and, beneath it, a much earlier crypt. The church is T-shaped, high and wide, and faced in rough brick, with a west door making use of two Roman columns from villas in the neighbourhood. Inside there are fading frescoes, a few indifferent paintings and a saint in bathing briefs (it may be Christ) flourishing a flag in his left hand, while raising his right in greeting to those who approach the altar.

There are two stairways to the crypt, which was discovered in 1940 by Don Sante Felici. He lives in the house bordering the courtyard, and is founder and curator of the adjoining museum. He has devoted his life to restoring the crypt and assembling the exhibits in the museum.

When Don Felici unearthed the crypt it was full of corpses, snakes and rubbish. It now stands revealed as a ninth-tenth century shrine on the site of a Roman temple. There are many decorated capitals, one bearing the figure of a small horned god.

The museum is an agreeable mishmash of stones, vases, elephant tusks, Singer sewing machines and bed warmers. The latter are signed 'Il preto' and one has an instruction 'Put the priest in your bed'; another 'Paradise for the poor'. They are wooden constructions four to five feet long, on which a bowl of hot embers, or coals, could be placed without setting light to the bed.

There are notice boards with newspaper cuttings about Don Felici and his work. It seems scarcely possible, but the spry, genial little man who shows you round must be Himself, now well into his eighties. I hope he has given thought to the succession.

In one room away from the main museum is a skeleton, probably of a monk, in a glass case. In another are numerous antique bones and, quite incongruously, the smart banner of the Banda Filarmonica which Giuseppe Verdi founded in 1903. No explanation for its presence is given.

Don't miss this singular experience, or fail to savour the placid ambience of the courtyard.

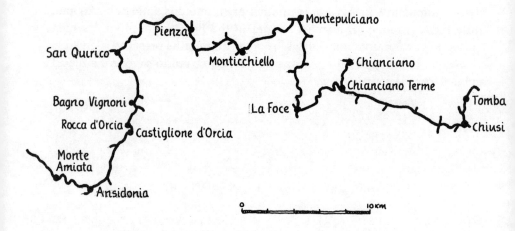

San Quirico
Pienza
Montepulciano
Monticchiello
Chianciano
Chianciano Terme
Bagno Vignoni
La Foce
Tomba
Rocca d'Orcia
Chiusi
Castiglione d'Orcia
Monte
Amiata
Ansidonia

0   10 KM

7   Chiusi and Val d'Orcia

Chiusi; Chianciano Terme; La Foce; Montepulciano; Monticchiello; Pienza; San Quirico d'Orcia; Bagno Vignoni; Castiglione d'Orcia; Rocca d'Orcia; Monte Amiata

In boyhood, one of my favourite poems was Lord Macaulay's 'Horatius' from his *Lays of Ancient Rome*. Horatius was the soldier who defended Rome, while the bridge on which he stood was being destroyed beneath him, against the hordes of Lars Porsena of Clusium.

Clusium was the Etruscan city we now call Chiusi. Its hill is different from others in the region because of its intricate tunnelling system. The Etruscans constructed elaborate underground passages to guarantee a water supply which they drew from below. In later centuries they were used as rubbish dumps but also adapted to take water from a cistern up into the bell tower of the cathedral.

The subterranean passages also led to the tomb of Porsenna (to use the current spelling, not Macaulay's) which Pliny the Elder described as a basement of ninety square metres, in a labyrinth. It was covered in sheets of bronze and topped by pyramids. In the country around Chiusi the tombs of many Etruscans can be visited but you will see nothing like Lars Porsenna's. He was king c. 505 BC. In the following century the Romans had their revenge and vanquished Chiusi, along with other Etruscan strongholds.

The city's next heroic figure was a Roman girl named Mustiola who had converted to Christianity. She refused to marry the Emperor Aurelian because, in her eyes, he was a pagan. This led him to persecute Christians and kill, among others, the deacon who had sheltered Mustiola and her family. In due course she too was put to death in AD 274.

High on the hill are two main squares; one, Piazza XX Settembre, is thought to be the site of the Roman forum, the other, Piazza del Duomo, has the cathedral, campanile and two museums. You should spend at least a morning in and around Chiusi. Ideally, a whole day.

The cathedral di San Secondiano stands on the site of two earlier churches, the first of which was destroyed by the Goths, the second by the Barbarians, a distinction some may question. It was completely rebuilt in the twelfth century, using eighteen Roman columns in the process. Much

111

of it now is a nineteenth-century renovation carried out with painted mosaics in imitation of those found in Byzantine churches.

The exterior of the cathedral is plain, clumsy even. The interior is an improvement, with a high nave where columns support a kind of inner clerestory. The floor has pleasing patterns of marble, the pillars are contrastingly decorated, the mural over the altar depicts the death of Santa Mustiola. If you wish to see her tomb, on the outskirts of town, coaches leave daily for a one-hour tour at 11.00 (charge 6000 lire). The museum, on the spot, is half that price and is mainly interesting for its collection of illuminated manuscripts and for the views from its garden. In the precincts of the duomo are trees rising from gravel, a paved forecourt and an excellent metal memorial to the Resistance, represented by three tragic figures in perpetual agony.

Opposite the cathedral, on the town side in a neo-Greek temple, is the Museo Archeologico which has an overwhelming preponderance of Etruscan tombs. Some are normal length but many are box-shaped (canopi) because they contained funerary ashes only, not entire bodies. All are decorated, usually with a reclining figure on the lid, carrying a candle holder. In each case the sculpture on the tomb was supposed to represent the deceased but not everyone could afford a true likeness. So you could come away with the impression that Clusium was peopled by an inordinate number of identical sextuplets. Decorations on the sides are usually in bas-relief, and sometimes coloured, depicting incidents in Greek mythology such as the death of Oedipus at the hands of his sons and other such familial motifs.

The museum is also rich in vases, some in bucchero ware, a style native to Chiusi, a glazed black, fashionable in the sixth century BC. (They were made from fine clay and powdered charcoal.) In fact, wherever you look there are tombs and pots in endless rows. The shard count, also, is high. But hunt among these ubiquitous offerings and you will discover many delights. On one wall is a mosaic of a boar being hunted, with deer leaping about in the background. And there is a re-creation of a burial cave, in case you do not have time to visit one *in situ*, while among the sarcophagi is a lady comfortably seated in an armchair made for eternity. Make sure you inspect a canopic jar which, typically, has a terracotta head fitted on to the urn containing the ashes. Both stand on a metal-collared chair.

An official of the museum will, on request, guide you in your own vehicle to some of the many tombs situated in the nearby hills. We went, in a procession of cars, to the Tomba della Pellegrina (Pilgrim's Tomb), lying next to an olive grove where the small, prim entrance is under a simple red-brick pediment, behind locked gates. You are ushered into the bowels of the earth to inspect several chambers, some with tombs still in

112

them. Further down the same rural road is the Monk's Tomb (closed for restoration in 1996) and, a larger one, the Lion's Tomb, which has a central round chamber where you may be able to distinguish paintings on the walls. (I couldn't.) We asked the guide why it is called the Lion's Tomb. She laughed and said, 'because it escaped'. This is the only example I know of an Etruscan joke.

When you return to Chiusi, enjoy a walk around the town. The Piazza XX Settembre has what the local brochure calls a 'Tower of Clock' and, at one end, the parish church. Facing the apse of the cathedral is a large orange-coloured building, the Teatro Comunale, built in the 1930s and dedicated to the composer Mascagni. The town hall sports very few crests.

You may climb inside the free-standing campanile of the duomo but be warned, the ascent of 27 m is up unguarded steps, on four sides, with only a handrail against the wall. The belfry dates from the sixteenth century. You may also visit the actual cistern far below, and that is twenty centuries old.

Chiusi lies only just within the borders of Tuscany and is further south than I had intended to go, but it must not be missed.

Cross the Rome autostrada, roughly following the Astrone valley to climb to an altogether more widespread conurbation. This is Chianciano Terme, a spa that has overflowed its hillside and marginalized its ancient precursor, the village of Chianciano Vecchia, mentioned by Horace and known to the Romans as Fontes Clusinae. The ancient town is still there, entered through a brick arch, and it has a recommended museum of religious art, with Sienese paintings and a Madonna in Humility by Lorenzo di Niccolò. Frankly, I don't think it rates a visit.

Chianciano Terme is built on several hills, commands spectacular views and has more clinics than churches. It claims to have the healthiest and wealthiest climate in Tuscany and is famed for the treatment of liver complaints. I admired its broad, tree-shaded boulevards but I didn't look for a parking space. One day I may take the cure because it is not, according to a German I met at an Etruscan tomb, catering only for the rich. He and his wife were staying mezzo-pensione at a four-star hotel for only 200,000 lira a day, whereas Mavis and I were paying, at a two-star establishment in Siena, 314,000.

Eleven kilometres to the south-west is La Foce. Anyone who has read that absorbing diary kept by Iris Origo during World War Two will wish to make a detour to pay homage to a courageous lady. She came of Anglo-Irish-American stock and married the Count Antonio Origo in the 1920s. They bought an estate on land that had been neglected for generations. There they taught the peasants modern farming methods and made

113

them literate. In 1943 they gave refuge to evacuees from the Allied bombing of Milan, sheltered partisans and British prisoners of war on the run, and were forced to entertain German officers who commandeered their home and eventually vandalized it. The last pages of the diary (*War in Val d'Orcia*) record the Countess leading her large band of children, on foot through the woods and open country, amidst the clamour of battle, from La Foce to the comparative safety of Montepulciano. Today the Origo manor has become a hospice but their daughters still live on the estate. There should be not just a plaque but a handsome memorial to the Origos who, in peacetime, were enlightened landowners and farmers and, in wartime, brave and active non-combatants.

Up a gravelled road from La Foce is the castle featured in the diary. Castelluccio, now converted into three apartments, overlooks a quintessential Tuscan view of a meandering road dotted with cypresses climbing to a bare spur. The postcard sells thousands annually.

Enough of rural Tuscany. Let us proceed to Montepulciano, at first on a bumpy, roughly surfaced track, then on a tarmacked road demanding low gear, but taking an altogether less hazardous route than that followed by the Countess and her flock.

Henry James was so overwhelmed by Montepulciano – a name that demands to be sung rather than spoken – and its prodigiously rich, strong wine, that he proved incapable of writing even one coherent paragraph about it. We were more abstemious, although there was nearly an international incident when Christopher ordered bread with his pizza at the open-air Snack Bar Duomo, on the Piazza Grande. My pizza was the best ever, thin, crispy, with easily identifiable elements of meat and veg. I didn't require bread. Christopher did; he's a bread-with-everything man. But not at Montepulciano. The waiter resolutely refused to serve it. He turned his back on us. It reminded me of the song about one meat ball.

It was not, however, a moment for disenchantment. Seated there at tables on the cobbles of that slightly ragged piazza, against a background of palazzi, duomo and Gothic town hall, we savoured what Henry James had missed.

It was the most impressively sited hill town yet. Not as large or as high as Cortona but wonderfully compact and with little on the foothills except the magnificent basilica of San Biagio, Antonio Sangallo the Elder's masterpiece (1529), in the shape of a Greek cross. It has a Bramante-style dome and attached to the gleaming wedding confection of the church is a gorgeous tower with several tiers of architectural jollity. There should have been two towers, closely freestanding, but Sangallo completed only one, rounding it off with a delicate spire. It is a gem but it is far below the city in another world, a vast spread of incomparable country opening beyond it.

114

So I contented myself with admiring it from above; I could not tear myself from the adorable hill town and its tatty cathedral.

The duomo at Montepulciano is disgraceful but it fits. The builders never got around to marble-cladding the great frontage, so it looks, and is, distinctly pock-marked. Inside, the contrast is apparent although it is essentially boring and plain, apart from a glittering altarpiece by Taddeo di Bartolo (1401) and an item of terracotta by Andrea della Robbia. Also, there is a Michelozzo statue of a papal secretary who was particularly important and named Bartolomeo Aragazzi (another cue for an aria). This formerly adorned his tomb, which was destroyed – by Guelph, Ghibbeline or German, I know not. Anyhow, here now the statue stands, in the bleak nave of Montepulciano cathedral, embellishing an interior slightly reminiscent of the Reform Club, Pall Mall.

The bell tower attached to the cathedral has red-brick tiles laid flatly, with rusticated corners up to two-thirds of the height, then two tall openings on each side for the bells, and very slightly pointed roof tiles giving it the edge, in smartness, on the battered frontage of its parent building.

The duomo dominates one side of the Piazza Grande but the other three are visually more exciting. The Palazzo Comunale is another veritable imitation of the masterpiece at Florence. The dizzily high, crenellated tower is centrally positioned. Guelph battlements decorate it, above three rusticated storeys with arched, rounded windows. It is mid fifteenth century, designed by Michelozzo. It lacks plaques almost entirely.

Protruding into the Piazza Grande, next to what is now a music school is the Palazzo Nobili-Tarugi (the elder Antonio again) with deeply recessed arcades and looking slightly menacing. In the right angle between it and the music school is a well which must not be overlooked. It is equipped with two proud ornamented columns joined by a formidable lintel on which hang the hooks for the water bucket. On the upper lateral are carved beasts and birds and a shield bearing the Medici balls. The front wall of the school (also once a palace) is an instructive lesson in the deployment of differing types of stone and brick. Red sandstone mixes with limestone and Roman tiles, evidence of much restoration over many centuries, thus contributing to the pervading atmosphere of this lovely, slightly grotty town centre where the majesty of the past lingers. It was to a house here that Iris Origo led her gallant crocodile in 1944. Since then, many buildings have been refurbished, there is evident prosperity in the numerous wine shops (not to mention the Snack Bar Duomo), yet you have a feeling that turmoil and shooting have only recently abated. Will the post-lunch-time hush of the breadless Piazza Grande suddenly be disrupted by galloping hussars flourishing swords? It is not altogether unlikely.

There was no question of visiting the Museo Civico. The guts of

115

the building had been ripped out and what had happened to the collection of glazed terracotta ware and Etruscan artefacts, or the paintings, 'ranged from the thirteenth–eighteenth centuries', I could not ascertain. The builders had colonized with a vengeance and looked immovable. I asked at the tourist office when the museum would reopen. The clerk shrugged her shoulders elegantly and sold me a postcard of the auditorium of a multi-tiered red-plush theatre. That wasn't open either.

Near the gate at the highest entrance to the city is the Liceo Ginnasio 'Agnolo Poliziano', standing at the end of a thickly shaded drive above a garden. This is a school now occupying the former fortress. Poliziano was a late-fifteenth-century poet, friend of Lorenzo the Magnificent. He was born here. He saved Lorenzo from would-be assassins and, as a reward, was given a villa at Fiesole. His real name was Angelo Ambrogini but he was called Poliziano because of where he was born ... which was Montepulciano ... Never mind. He was a brilliant scholar who translated the *Iliad* into Italian, professor of Greek and Latin at Florence, wrote original works in Latin and, also, the first secular drama in Italian, *Orfeo* (1480). He died aged forty.

Poliziano must have made the streets of Montepulciano ring with his Renaissance spirit; he would have harangued that waiter at the snack bar with Latin tags until served sufficient bread to feed all the pigeons of Tuscany.

Montepulciano provokes such exuberance of thought it renders you on top of the world, which you very nearly are, but contain yourself. There are more things to see.

The Palazzo Contucci, on the east side of the Piazza Grande, is another of that same Sangallo's buildings, although he probably did not complete it. Beneath it are the oldest wine vaults in Montepulciano and if you can gain entry you may taste the vino which was enobled by a pope. Nearby is a school of mosaics, with specimens of work in the courtyard. Across the square, at the town hall, pass through to a terrace and, from a parapet gaze on the great sweeps of farmland, with one thin road running through it, up to foothills and mountains beyond. Then, if it has not already done so, the full enchantment of this country will come home to you. If that is not sufficient there are umpteen other churches, several palazzi, at least one loggia, the house where Poliziano was born and the quite perfect auditorium of the theatre beneath a glittering chandelier. It cannot always be closed.

Henry James missed so much. Open your vino nobile after, not during, your visit.

Retreat from Montepulciano, downhill all the way, and pretend you are aiming for Pienza but then turn off down an unprepossessing road, to reach a smaller hill town, Monticchiello, standing at 546 m, and reached up an avenue of cypresses lined with modern villas.

The walls are almost intact and the keep of a ruined castle stands in private property in an olive grove. Park outside the main gate, where you will probably find elderly inhabitants seated on stone benches. Do they ever tire of the fabulous view, I wonder? (Do they even see it?) Enter the town at the Val di Piano, having noted, just outside the walls, the scrupulously tidy municipal garden next to a café. Walk up towards the church, passing shops whose interiors are mostly hidden behind bead curtains or dark doorways, to the Piazza della Commenda where a gaunt church rises above a concave stone stairway. This is the thirteenth-century pieve with Gothic portal, rose window, many fading frescoes and a Madonna by Pietro Lorenzetti.

The streets weave about in glorious disorder, opening into tiny squares, winding about the hillside, until they peter out by a disused communal washhouse, near a small opening in the walls leading to two rough graves, dated 1942 and 1954. There must be a few others relating to the 'battle of Monticchiello' described by Iris Origo. They would be dated 1944 when partisans came down from Monte Amiata and drove the occupying fascists into the valley, before returning to their hide-out. The same walls withstood attack from the Holy Roman Emperor, Charles V, whose Spanish soldiers succeeded only in knocking the watchtower slightly askew.

The town today is beautifully kept, all buildings in pristine condition, the brickwork scrubbed and gleaming. Outside two houses are small flower gardens under trees. There are pleasant balconies, steps, courtyards, all slightly reminiscent of the Cotswolds, except that the stone is a different colour. In July, in these exquisite surroundings, the inhabitants write and perform their own rustic drama.

Journeying down and across the Orcia valley to reach Pienza makes for further delight. (Actually, the river here is a small tributary.) This is plain farming territory, dotted with isolated buildings, hamlets, clumps of trees, nothing remotely ugly. The road climbs particularly steeply to Pienza, but before making the final ascent, turn off to the left, down a cul-de-sac, to visit the Pieve di Corsignano, the parish church of a small community founded long before a local boy, who made good and became pope, had the town on the hill transformed.

The church, twelfth century, on the site of another four hundred years older, is built in red brick and, on first sight, seems to have a very low nave. This is because it is on a sharp incline. Its uniqueness lies in its attached circular bell tower with six openings. (One of them still boasts a bell.) The main door has carvings on the lintel of a flying sea monster biting

117

the ear of a merman. There are also two women in tutus facing front, one of them nonchalantly strangling, single-handed, another sea monster. Above the door, in a niche, is a saint in a long skirt. You enter by a door in the nave where there are more carvings, nicely restored, of men in procession on horseback, and simple scenes of people in bed. Inside, simplicity and neglect reign equally. The bell tower is accessible at ground level. We were lucky that sunlight silhouetted the surviving bell on a patch of red wall. There was no such illumination in the crypt, nor any evidence that the church is used for services. The altar was undecorated and partly under scaffolding. In the vestry stood an empty bottle of vino santo. Outside an old lady dozed, seated on the uncovered roots of a tree. I don't think our visit disturbed her.

Pienza: Palazzo Pretorio

Pienza, or rather Corsignano as it then was, was the birthplace (1405) of Aeneas Sylvius, a member of the Piccolomini family who became a poet and a diplomat, before being elected pope as Pius II. Once in office, this pope commanded Bernardo Rossellino to design a model city, here on his native soil, which would also serve as a summer retreat for princes of the church. It has survived for more than five centuries but, had Piccolomini studied his accounts more closely, it might not have got very far.

Rossellino, a Florentine, was not loved by all the good folk of Corsignano whose home town he was transforming. One of them leaked to Rome the extent of his overspending but when Pius II next looked in he was so pleased with what he saw that he rewarded Rossellino handsomely. Had he been asked in advance for such exorbitant funding he would have refused, he said, but now that he had seen the new town taking shape he could not do without it.

Try to park below the cathedral where the washing of those who live on the edge of the city may well be draped upon the walls. Climb a steep path with the apse and tower of the duomo dramatically poised ahead of you. Turn a corner at the top and walk straight into the Piazza Pretorio, also called Piazza Pio II. It is one of the few piazzi I know which can claim to be square, which is no accident, because Rossellino was paid to design a city on the grid principle and he certainly began by doing so. There are charming irregularities, though, unsuspected courtyards and alleys that do not conform to planning rigidity.

The Piazza Pretorio is a total success. On it is the travertine white duomo, flanked by the enormous mansion of the Piccolominis. Opposite is another palace (the Lolli) with the ground floor now a bar, next to the more imposing, but shabby, Palazzo Ammannati which was unfinished when Pius died and the money ran out. On the other side of the Lolli is the very slightly prim town hall. It has small loggias on two sides with high arches above decorated capitals. Over these is one tall storey with Gothic windows surmounted by a crenellated bell tower placed at one end. On the fourth side of the piazza is yet another palace harbouring the cathedral museum, where there are Sienese paintings, Flemish tapestries, mitres, a few books of manuscript music and a Madonna della Misericordia with more people protected beneath her voluminous cloak than in any other treatment of the subject I have seen. The prize possession is an item of medieval embroidery, a cloak (or cope) of English origin which reached Pienza via Greece. It is a finely woven garment made up of three semicircles illustrating scenes such as the Annunciation and other sacred subjects, but also including vivid vignettes of hell where devils torment fallen souls by perpetual roasting. Called the Piviale, the craftsmanship of the cope is exquisite.

The Piccolomini palace may also be visited. Enter by a high cloistered courtyard and climb to the first floor for a guided tour of the armoury, bedroom, dining room, library and connecting passages. One room with leather wall furnishings from Cordoba has its original ceiling of 1459. In the library there is a spherical object, made of papier maché, illustrating the working of the universe. It is functional. The apartments are run down and dusty but there is a fine view from the loggia, over the hanging gardens, an effect deliberately contrived by a pope who did not have to grow accustomed to the extravagance and riches of high office. He was born to them.

The interior of the cathedral is light, with a partly patterned ceiling. It slopes rather alarmingly towards the apse, due to subsidence. The paintings include several Madonnas and Child, and a vivid fifteenth-century Assumption with swirling groups of attendant angels around Mary's skirts. The artist was one Vecchietta.

On the other side of the Piccolomini is the chapel of San Francesco. Just inside the door there is a lively, highly coloured grotto sculpture called *Homage to Giotto* by Scarluzzi Puro (1988–9). It features white figures on a volcanic landscape with simple trees such as are found in primitive paintings. Something sacred, possibly the nativity, is taking place in a cave. A little weird but worth some attention.

Beyond the chapel is a modern hotel and restaurant in a mixture of Gothic and Renaissance, with a plain cloister and plastered walls. Perhaps this is where the descendants of the medieval cardinals take their summer break?

This main central street leads to a gateway adorned with a colourful fresco depicting the Piazza Pio. The walls are not complete and the modern town merges with the old on parts of two sides. Many streets have flower-bedecked buildings. The Piazza di Spagna has cafés, some alfresco. Shopkeepers occupy chairs at street corners, going into their emporia only to serve spicy local foods and wines which are easier to buy in Pienza than ordinary everyday produce. Between the walls and the main thoroughfare are shady alleys named Via dell'Amore, Via del Bacio (the kiss), Via Buia (darkness) and Via della Fortuna. They were renamed thus in the nineteenth century to project the notion of an ideal city with lovers' lanes, although it would be hard for lovers to achieve much privacy in them.

A few kilometres to the west is San Quirico d'Orcia, one of the lower hill towns, overlooking the N2, a road which leads to Rome. In the early Middle Ages this was the Via Cassia, the principal thoroughfare joining the eternal city to the north. Frederick Barbarossa, Holy Roman

120

Emperor, who spent much of his reign subduing the peoples of the Italian peninsula, or trying to, received ambassadors from the Pope at San Quirico in 1154. This event is celebrated annually to this day. Why is not clear to me but the townsfolk feel strongly enough about it to make it an excuse for a festival every June. (Like Guy Fawkes Night?)

San Quirico: collegiate church

Enter by the west gate to be confronted by a stunning doorway of the collegiate church, recessed beyond two flights of steps and with a rose window above it. On the south of the nave there are two more, slightly dissimilar, fine doorways. All repay study. Two of them bear carvings of lions, salamanders and mermaids, some of which act as caryatids. On the west door note the pillars leaning on two rams. On the larger of the south-facing portals the lambs and lions are in crumbling red sandstone and need urgent restoration. The church, thirteenth century, is built on the site of a paleo-Christian place of worship of the sixth century. It is in a fine state of preservation and even its baroque tower doesn't spoil its simplicity too much because it is made of similar stone. The interior suffers slightly more from a Renaissance altar but it is easy to forget about it when you see the choir stalls with marquetry backs, by Antonio Barili, depicting various arts

121

and crafts; the small statue of a boy carrying a huge feather (or is it a leaf?); the Sano di Pietro triptych of Madonna and Child, with two saints, and the tomb inlaid to the floor with a bas-relief effigy of Count Henri of Nassau who died here on a journey from Rome. So there is much to admire.

Behind the church are some monastery buildings with a tower incorporating an onion dome, and the battered Palazzo Chigi which was grievously damaged in World War Two. Restoration is still going on fifty years later. It is huge and square, rising to several storeys. Beyond it, along a jolly, straggling street stretches the town, with a couple of piazzas, at least two more churches and a large public garden, all within the walls. Another street leads uphill to the twelve-sided Porta ai Cappuccini, near which an occasional tower of the wall has been converted into a bijou residence.

On the opposite side of town is the Porta Caneti beside the entrance to the Horti Leonini, an octagonal formal garden below an oak wood, and a mound that once held the castle. In the centre of the garden is a statue of Cosimo III who appears to have thrust his sword into his bottom. There is no sign of it protruding anywhere but he does not look bothered. He is sculpted in a Roman tunic, looking sideways at a charming house with balcony and steps, which is part of the wall. At the foot of the mound is a bust of a forlorn-faced chap, with lichen growing over him, standing on a round stone tray. Up where the fortress stood is a wide-open space partly surrounded by a wall with *meurtrières*, so you can experience a bowman's view of the country through slits. A small chunk of low ruin is signed in yellow, Torre del Cassero. There are many paths through the wooded hillside.

Off the road to Rome, where the Orcia meets several other streams, is the turning to Bagno Vignoni, an ancient spa, with thirty-six springs, which has flourished for at least two millennia. Several modern hotels, some of them overlooking a large pond of filthy water supposedly good for treating rheumatism, cater for visitors. At one end is the Loggiata di Santa Caterina commemorating the saint's death, possibly in this very place. Bathing is not permitted in this sulphurous pool. The Russian film, *Nostalgia* was shot here.

From that same road to Rome turn off again to ascend steeply to Castiglione d'Orcia, where you run into a confusion of Roccas. The highest is Rocca Tintinnano, a fortress which commanded the Via Francigena in the ninth century. Huddled around its lower middle parts (whatever I mean) is the utterly captivating village, Rocca d'Orcia. Slightly higher up the mountain is Rocca Aldobrandeschi, a ruined castle of the one-time ruling barons, overlooking Castiglione whose terraces literally uphold it.

You can take your car into Rocca d'Orcia but I beg you not to. In Castiglione there are several places to park while you briefly case the little town, after which there will be ample room for your vehicle at the foot of Rocca Tintinnano, from where there is a choice of two routes, on foot, to Rocca d'Orcia.

Castiglione is one of the most clinging of hill towns with modern apartment blocks tactfully merging with older buildings. The centre of the original settlement is around the Piazza Vecchietta, situated on a cobbled slope, with a fountain, designed for gossipers, its main feature. Below it – some way – is the Pieve San Stefano, proudly displaying its well-preserved apse. Inside, in a locked and gated chapel, is a painting of a simple, soulful Mary gazing at an adoring Jesus wearing a yellow garment, which cheers up the canvas.

There is little else to detain you, except the shy smiles of those residents going about their business, so prepare, at your next parking place, to take a short, single-file walk around the foot of Rocca Tintinnano, with grass and wild plants tickling your ankles as you go. If you don't sprain a ligament you will emerge above Rocca d'Orcia, where you immediately experience a prospect of red-tiled roofs and houses clinging hugger-mugger to the hillside. Everywhere you look there is an entrancing vista: trees, window boxes, flowers and greenery in abundance. Near the top is a half-hearted piazza with a well and restaurant, neither clamouring for attention. There are two bell towers, unattached to churches. Most of the little town has been unobtrusively restored and is simply pretty. It is real, lived in. The Via Chiesa leads deviously to a church, up many, many more steps. The ever-adventurous Christopher climbed them in his indefatigable pursuit of historiated capitals, while I sat and savoured the view.

To return to the car we faced another forbidding gradient, leading us to the fortress on Tintinnano. Or rather to the approach to that fortress – there is no such thing as easy access to a Rocca in these parts. Once again, Christopher was my Man at the Top; he found the museum pathetic and added, ambiguously, that he was glad I had not joined him.

From Castiglione the road writhes upwards to Ansedonia, before descending to Monte Amiata, where the Orcia flows by and there is also a railway. The nomenclature is confusing, the tiny settlement taking the name of the region's highest mountain (1738 m).

On the slopes of Amiata several minerals, including cinnabar – containing mercury – are mined. The Etruscans and Romans worked the deposits but nowadays the mountain is chiefly associated with winter sports. The summit is covered in a forest of chestnuts, beeches and pines; the lower slopes have vines and olives. There are many paths for walkers.

This is our last sighting of the Orcia, which flows due westward into the Ombrone. The country it waters is a part of Tuscany you will not forget.

123

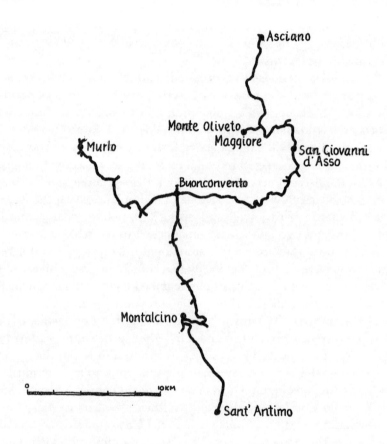

Asciano

Monte Oliveto Maggiore

Murlo

San Giovanni d'Asso

Buonconvento

Montalcino

Sant' Antimo

0   10KM

8   Montalcino and Le Crete

Sant'Antimo; Montalcino; Murlo; Buonconvento; San Giovanni d'Asso; Monte Oliveto Maggiore; Asciano

After leaving the river Orcia proceed meanderingly to Castelnuovo dell'Abate, a little town of limited interest enjoying the reflected glory from what remains of a twelfth-century Cistercian monastery in a field below it.

The abbey church of Sant'Antimo, in its idyllic setting, is a building of quiet perfection, with three small apses below a larger one, a simple nave higher than the aisles which buttress it and a square bell tower joined to it at one end, beside a single cypress reaching almost to the belfry. Clustered about the lower apses are outbuildings. There is all the gravity of a church, coupled with an air of workmanlike business but the abbey it served has long since gone. It is built in the Burgundian Romanesque style and its architecture is a matter for celebration, irrespective of belief.

Inside the main apse is a fine example of a small dome above an ambulatory where there are two frescoes below rounded arches. One is of a young saintly figure wearing his halo like a shepherd's cap. He holds a dart and his eyes have that haunted look of a Piero della Francesca saint. The other is older, more devious of expression and hairy. The fingers of his right hand are raised in attempted piety but they lack conviction. There is also a thirteenth-century polychrome crucifix 'in the Catalan style' according to the notice, and from the same period a Madonna and Child, 'in the Umbrian fashion'. The Christ child represented is wearing pyjamas and looks old enough for secondary school; the Madonna is poker-faced. Nearby there is a Crucifixion with St Sebastian trying to upstage the central figure. But never mind him, it is the masterly architecture, within and without, that makes Sant'Antimo a moving experience. The stone used is a local travertine resembling onyx and alabaster; this gives it a luminosity which is distinctive.

Drive along the hillside and stop just before Montalcino at a lay-by with benches (perfect for a picnic) to take in the exceptional view over the Asso valley. The vista spans 90 degrees and it is fun to pick out places already visited, such as Pienza and San Quirico. In the foreground

125

are patchworks of fields where barley and wheat are growing (although not all the year round!); in the distance are row after row of hills with villages huddled into them. Close by is a suburb of Montalcino propped up by terraces of trees.

Montalcino is dominated by a mighty fortress looking as new and impregnable as it must have appeared to those who saw it when first completed six hundred years ago. It was erected by the Sienese in 1361, about a century after their compatriots, who were Ghibelline, had destroyed its predecessor, along with the rest of the town, following the battle of Montaperti (1260). The Sienese connection has remained strong ever since. When the Florentines captured their city in 1555 the defenders fled to Montalcino, where they held out for four years, before being incorporated into the Medicis' Grand Duchy of Tuscany. A bond was thus formed between the two cities which is remembered today when the men of Montalcino have a place of honour in the Palio procession at Siena.

Montalcino: fortress

The castle, looking as though it is swept and dusted twice a day, has three battlemented towers, two others which have suffered diminution, and a vast inner courtyard where admission is free. There are ad hoc stairways to the towers from the inside and a parapet walk. In times of peril the entire citizenry could shelter here. Now, what remains of the

126

buildings are entered, on payment, via the wine cellars. (Montalcino produces a prestigious, and powerful, red wine, Brunello.)

The town walls, with several gateways, are preserved. The main through-street, Via Ricasoli, leads from opposite the Rocca, on an undulating, slightly curving course to the cathedral and beyond. En route, on the left, is an immaculate Renaissance courtyard behind the offices of the Partito Democratica della Sinistra. (There is a long-standing left-wing political tradition in Montalcino.) Further along, at the Vicolo San Agostino, look back to the castle and, to one side, admire the noble bell towers.

The Museo Civico is soon reached. Its prize exhibits are both from the abbey of Sant'Antimo – a twelfth-century bible and a crucifix of the same period.

The cathedral occupies part of a small eminence of the ridge on which the town is built. It has a dull neo-classical portico, improved by the red-brick columns incorporated into it. The interior is one great marbled hall sweeping up to the altar, itself like the model of a fortress, with a bas-relief temple topped by angels flourishing swordlike candles. The domed apse suggests a honeycomb but I saw no evidence of bees. In the baptistery are carvings from a tenth-century church demolished in 1877.

On a lower level of the ridge is the secular town with an astonishing tower leaping above a three-storeyed town hall that appears to have been sliced down the middle. The main door is in the Piazza Garibaldi which leads to the lower Piazza del Popolo where there is a loggia with plaques. This continues into the Via Mazzini with narrow passages and steeply ramped alleys joining it from above and below. It is lined by houses with Gothic arched windows and overhanging roofs. At the end is a small garden and sign to the church of San Francesco which, along with Sant'Agostino and Sant'Egidio, I took as read because, after Sant'Antimo they seemed superfluous.

On the last Sunday in October Montalcino becomes extravagantly colourful, when the annual Thrush Festival is held. The four quarters of the town stage a procession with participants in historical costume. This is followed by an archery contest and a sumptuous banquet, served in the appropriate setting of the fortress, when something more sustaining than small birds is washed down with Brunello.

Below Montalcino, watered principally by the Ombrone and the Arbia, is the region of Le Crete which reaches south from Siena to the Val d'Orcia. Some of its landscape is stark and volcanic and has been likened to the surface of the moon. Although I have not visited another planet I think the suggestion exaggerated. Certainly Le Crete is less green than much of Tuscany, and it contrasts markedly with the Chianti country north of Siena, but there are many wooded hills and, in summer, the almost bare rocks gleam in the sunlight. It is a varied terrain and ever inviting.

At the confluence of the Arbia and Ombrone is Buonconvento, but before exploring it we will head westwards to a small medieval hill village nowadays renowned only for its museum, housed in the former palace of the bishops of Siena. Murlo was an Etruscan settlement and much of what is on show in the museum relates to that civilization. The most notable exhibit is the reconstructed roof of a patrician's residence, with frieze and statuary. Prominent on it is the figure of a man wearing a stetson, although the Mexican imagery is mitigated by a flat Egyptian-style beard and an oriental face. This was one of many finds from the dig at nearby Poggio Civitate and, for once, the treasures unearthed there have not been carted off to Florence or Rome, but are on display in this tiny place. Murlo, despite this concession, does not put itself out to cater for tourists. Two coaches, and there is a traffic jam in the rough parking space below the walls which, with the houses built into them, have been carefully restored.

The 'Mexican' apart, there is not much of general interest at the museum. It is neatly displayed but consists largely of broken pots.

Back to Buonconvento which lies on the ancient Via Cassia and has had its share of conflict through the ages. The modern road skirts the thirteenth–fourteenth-century red-brick walls enclosing a well-preserved medieval town. The Porta Senese is a noble structure and there are two other gateways also in use. The main street, Via Soccini, has the town hall, the church and the Museum of Sacred Art. The latter holds a number of early Tuscan paintings including a polyptych of the Virgin by Sano di Pietro.

Buonconvento has a place in the history books because it was here that Henry VII of Luxembourg, Holy Roman Emperor, died in August 1313. He was the Ghibellines' last hope and his passing was lamented by Dante (a fervent Guelph in his time), who had hoped he would unify Italy.

By the highest standards of what Tuscany has to offer Buonconvento does not rate, but it is worth a visit for the experience of walking the walls on the inside, through murky tunnels and across courtyards which reveal exits only at the last moment. The town is famed for its truffles.

To the east lies the abbey of Monte Oliveto Maggiore which can be reached direct, or more circuitously, via San Giovanni d'Asso, an attractive small hill town also noted for its truffles, as might be guessed from its air of prosperity. This does not extend at present to its castle, which was in such a parlous state when we were there that we walked through its battered front entrance without knowing that, at the back door, there were

128

signs forbidding entrance and threatening unleashed dogs. We strode up a heavily overgrown ramp to a doorway bearing the symbol of six little bridges, denoting ownership by the Chigi family whose name we encountered at San Quirico. The coat of arms was repeated over a courtyard where we could just see a first-floor loggia. But it was clear that the workmen were in. So we left by a rear opening and passed a small chapel joined to stables with a fine medallion, in terracotta, of a horse's head. Both buildings are joined to the crumbling fortress out of whose walls antirrhinums grow, come from openings where pigeons roosted. Down below, road and single-track railway curve through the valley of the Asso.

From San Giovanni the road winds up and round, through several hamlets, to the abbey, with every bend offering a new view of the dazzling countryside comprised of numerous hills and ridges, some of them denuded of vegetation, that make up this part of the Crete. It was here, in the early fourteenth century when Guelphs and Ghibellines were at each other's throats, that another man of the world, Giovanni Tolomei, a forty-year-old lawyer of Siena, opted, as the founders of Monte Senario in the Mugello had, to renounce the material world of riches, war and plague, and found a religious community in what was then an arid patch of ground forming part of his family domain.

Tolomei, accompanied by two other well-born men of Siena, travelled twenty miles south of the city, inspired by St Bernard of Clairvaux, whose name he adopted in exchange for his own. The men built the first church themselves and planted an olive grove, alternating hard physical work with prayer. When the Black Death struck in 1348 Tolomei returned to Siena to tend plague victims and succumbed to it himself. In due course he was canonized and an abbey was built.

In the development and expansion of the great monastery and church there is implicit irony. Tolomei left Siena and practice of the law, for which he was well rewarded, to build a church on a nearly bare mountain, because he, like St Bernard, believed in the simplicity and austerity of monastic life. In his last thirty years he sought to live according to his principles but the massive complex of buildings now standing on Monte Oliveto, and dedicated to him, exhibit a degree of worldliness that he surely would have abhorred? The once simple church erected in his honour in the fifteenth century was given the baroque treatment with a vengeance. In the grounds are a hotel, a tea garden and a shop selling books, booze (the monks distil their own liqueur), food and religious artefacts.

There is still much to admire if you arrive before the coach parties, or turn up after they have gone on their relentless way. Possibly the solution is to stay at the hotel. This lies behind a drawbridge in a fortified tower which got into the act during particularly desperate times.

Walk to the abbey through a wood, down a winding path passing many small shrines and signposts to sacred places. You come into a clearing to face a handsome enough group of buildings – church, campanile, octagonal dome surmounted by lantern, and monastery, all in red brick, belonging to several different centuries and none of it of outstanding architectural merit. Then you enter the cloisters, where there are frescoes by Signorelli and Sodoma, recording the life of St Benedict, a very early Christian saint whose order the Olivetians embraced. Luca Signorelli tired of this task after only eight panels and the work was completed by Giovanni Sodoma. The many panels, not in chronological order, follow the saint through his entire career in a series of vivid narrative paintings. To get the most from them buy the excellent illustrated guide in four languages. The eccentric use of English employed is easily forgiven for the fun it adds to the experience. What is not fun is the refusal of many visitors to obey instructions to observe silence and forego photography. The rules are not enforced if only because there are no attendants, so the tour leaders harangue in various tongues and some visitors contort themselves in knots to focus their lenses at interesting angles.

From the thronged cloisters you can reach the church and see the superbly carved choir stalls, wonderful examples of marquetry, with subjects ranging from city scenes to a large cat seated on its haunches.

Visiting Monte Oliveto could be – should be – a rewarding experience. It is marred by chattering, camera-clicking and pedantic-voiced guides.

Leave by the road down to Asciano, past bare tufa hills, intermingled with gorse cliffs and gorges. Asciano lies in the Ombrone valley at the junction of many roads. The town itself is not of particular interest, especially when all three museums are closed, as they were to us, but there is a fine Romanesque church standing just beyond the walls.

At the information office a girl strived to be helpful in halting English. Had she allowed Christopher to converse with her in Italian we might have gained some enlightenment, but when you are in the communications business you take a certain pride in showing off your language skills.

We thought the girl said that if we didn't find the Cassioli Museum open we could obtain the key at the Etruscan Museum, but she may have meant the opposite. In any case, she added that if both were shut we should try the town hall. We did that first and were directed to the Cassioli, which was difficult to locate because it is a totally anonymous building. A helpful citizen led us to it. A tiny notice on the door instructed us to apply for entry at the town hall.

So, instead, we searched for the Museum of Sacred Art with

130

little hope that it would be open. It wasn't and there was no indication when, if ever, it would be. It is said to house a polyptych by Ambrogio Lorenzetti, featuring St Michael and the dragon, and many paintings and sculptures of the Sienese school. As we were soon to be in Siena itself we accepted the closure philosophically.

The Cassioli would have added a dimension to our travels because it is exclusively devoted to works by a father and son of that name who spanned a period from 1832 to 1942. The father painted portraits.

The archaeological museum (also closed) is in the church of San Bernardino and has a collection of Etruscan items.

The church of Sant'Agata only looked closed. Having admired the exterior, a typically simple apse and an octagonal dome topped by a neat lantern, both under the shadow of a handsome bell tower, we entered the unadorned interior (eleventh century) and looked at the paintings. There is a fresco, probably by Girolamo del Pacchia, with a Madonna and Child and a devil grabbing at the feet of an angel; and an Assumption with a lively foreground of citizens and soldiers silhouetted against a town. There they all are, beneath clouds billowing and cherubs cavorting, vividly animated.

From Asciano the road wends delightfully uphill and down, through rolling, grazing country, and vast sweeps of land dotted with stark grey rocks, all the way to Siena, beyond which the terrain abruptly changes.

Asciano: Sant'Agata

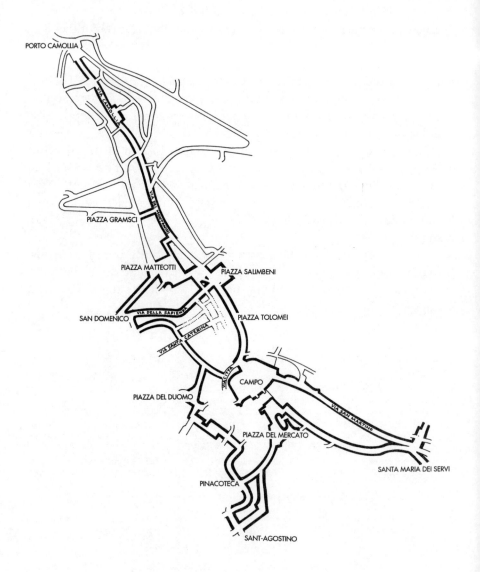

9   Siena

Palazzo Pubblico; Piazza del Campo; San Domenico; Duomo; Pinacoteca; Santa Maria

In most respects Siena must bow to the superiority of Florence. No other Italian city, not even Venice, has as brilliant an array of artistic genius as Florence, although the Sienese school of painting cannot be lightly dismissed. The massive Renaissance palaces of the Medicis and their contemporaries have the edge on the palazzi of Siena; duomo, campanile, baptistery in Florence, though not as fine as at Pisa, outclass Siena's; museum for museum, church for church, gallery for gallery, Florence wins every time, just as she did on the battlefield in 1555. But in one magnificent instance Siena is the undoubted victor. Despite its formidable grandeur, the Palazzo Vecchio and the irregularly shaped piazza in which it stands is no match for Siena's Palazzo Pubblico, with a tower soaring into the stratosphere and the scallop-shaped Piazza del Campo forming an amphitheatre, backed by a crescent in which the centrepiece is the thirteenth-century Palazzo Sansedoni.

The Palazzo Pubblico is breathtaking from every view. The Torre del Mangia, placed to one side with daring effectiveness, is nearly 90 m high, was designed by Lippo Memmi, and built at the very time when Siena's fortunes were weakened by both the Black Death and the bitter rivalry of the city's many warring factions. Inside the city hall the Sienese preoccupation with the mechanics of political leadership was immortalized by Ambrogio Lorenzetti's massive masterpieces, *The Effects of Good and Bad Government*. They adorn two whole walls, or would, but for the ravages of time. Interestingly, the 'Bad Government' frescoes have suffered more from damp, neglect or whatever, than the 'Good', but that must be fortuitous. What remains repays long study because it vividly illustrates life in early fourteenth-century Siena and the surrounding country. It is remarkable, too, for being almost entirely secular; there isn't a cross, a Virgin and Child, a St Sebastian in sight, although the seven deadly sins make an appearance. When you can tear yourself away from these principal offerings, there are many other paintings to see, not least of which is the *Virgin in Majesty* by Simone Martini. It is present thricefold. The original hangs high on a wall, slightly damaged; a photograph of it is displayed at right angles, reaching to the floor so that it may be studied in detail; a third, more brightly coloured version shows how the figures were in the original.

On the facing wall is another Martini of a Sienese general riding a horse, dressed in identical garments, between the two towns he has vanquished. Through the 'Government' room is a vile Massacre of the Innocents by Matteo di Giovanni. It has a particularly villainous Herod and is littered with dead babies drawn with vigour and relish. Elsewhere is a hideously overdecorated chapel behind a grill of intricately complicated ironwork. In other rooms are painted walls and ceilings, and rather too many canvases which should either be cleaned or discarded, although look out for one, of a naval battle, that doesn't fall into either category. Then Lorenzetti crops up again with a rotating Mappa Mundi.

If you have the energy you can climb to the top of the belfry, or make a shorter ascent to the great loggia which looks over the marketplace and the southern side of Siena.

When you have visited the Palazzo Pubblico there is a choice of at least twenty cafés and restaurants on the Campo. By midday they are into serving meals so you should grab a table while you can order only a drink and admire the passing scene. It is probably wiser, and certainly cheaper, to eat elsewhere.

The Campo is where the famous Palio is raced twice a year, in July and August. This is a short, violent contest on horses in which the winner has to circle the Campo three times, riding bareback. There are seventeen wards (contrade) entitled to compete, but the available space reduces this to ten in any one race. The Palio began in the early fourteenth century when the rivalry between the different districts of the city was even more deadly than it is today. The contests are taken extremely seriously and as early as May factions, with banners waving, make processions through the narrow streets swirling their great favours indiscriminately, making way for no one. It is chillingly impressive to watch as the fanatically faced marchers stomp past.

The Campo and the Palio are very much first time round, so we should now take a long itinerary about this historic city, noting its less famous features, although I cannot ignore the cathedral or the church of San Domenico.

I will start outside the walls, beyond the north-western gate, on the road to Florence, in a suburb where there are many hotels, purpose-built contemporary ones, and others in converted mansions. From rooms and terraces at some of them you can pick out the city's greatest landmarks. If you have come to Tuscany by car, you can leave it safely at the hotel and walk, or take a bus, into the centre. I recommend walking. It is a satisfactory way of assimilating the atmosphere of the city gradually, as you pass at first down an ordinary street on the outskirts, with shops, petrol stations, offices, cafés. Then you come to a large section of preserved wall. Immediately within is the Piazza Guido Chigi Saracini and over on the left you can peer out of the city into the deep valley where the railway station (unseen) lies, and where traffic speeds towards inevitable hold-ups as it attempts to skirt the centre. More important, you can look along the walls and appreciate how splendidly sited was the medieval city.

Take the narrow Via Camollia, with high, dark-grey buildings on both sides, interspersed with a few tatty churches and occasional openings, one or more of which may reveal the remains of the fortress, or a modern sports stadium. But stick to the cobbles and tramp your way into the Via dei Montanini, which is semi-pedestrianized and curves its way to the centre without revealing anything much of riveting interest. It is the flavour that counts. All the while you are receiving a strong impression of what it is like to live and work in Siena. You are walking through one or more of the seventeen contrade, the boundaries of which are meaningful to each and every inhabitant. Behind every wall someone is likely to be seething with ambition for his own contrada to win the Palio. To absorb the romance of it all the sun needs to be shining pitilessly down, with the drab, high buildings protecting you from its glare, and probably this will be the case.

Once into the Montanini, you will see one turning into the Piazza Gramsci where, on your return, you can board a bus to take your foot-weary self back to the hotel, and another to the Piazza Matteotti. Take the latter to emerge for a while into the sunshine and to admire the Gothic post office taking up much of one side. It faces a modern hotel which blends in well, and an unnamed, and unopen, church. Siena is packed with churches; there must be almost as many as there are banks. And, in the centre of the piazza, there is a circular bed of flowers surrounded by grass, a rare feature in this city.

Back on the Montanini, on the left is the Istituto Linguistico Europeo, in a crumbling small palazzo with inner courtyards where there are busts of various dignitaries. On to the Piazza Salimbeni which, after the Campo, is the most prestigious in Siena. On three sides of it are palaces today entirely given over to the Monte dei Paschi, a leading Italian bank. It was founded in this city in 1472, and takes its name from the Maremma country in southern Tuscany, formerly part of Sienese territory. It is said that, originally, the produce of the Maremma provided the bankers with their security. Two of the palaces were first constructed in the fifteenth century but the Salimbeni, on the eastern side, was almost totally rebuilt, partly in the Gothic style, in the late nineteenth. The Spannocchi, on the southern side, has stayed basically the same in appearance for five hundred years. The Tantucci, on the northern side, is a century or so later. A monument to Sallustio Bandini (a banker?) stands in the piazza to accommodate the pigeons.

We will return to this street near the end of this itinerary. Now I will take you down the turning opposite the piazza, Via della Sapienza, to the enormous church of San Domenico, with a wide, high nave and no apse. Its rear, rising from a deep ravine, presents a huge, bland wall of flat Gothic windows. It is built in red brick and partly bordered by pine trees. Pilgrims flock to it because it houses the tabernacle of Santa Caterina whose head is preserved, with one great fang in an open mouth. She was one of twenty-five children sired by a dyer, a fact of her life that may well have encouraged her to become a nun and thus avoid the treadmill of constant child-bearing. She had ecstasies and visions, and wrote a treatise on religion. She made genuine attempts to end schisms in the church, spoke out against warfare and, when requested, gave advice to Pope Urban VI, who ignored it. She travelled widely and had a faithful following. As I left the church I heard a young woman exclaim excitedly in English, 'I want to see the head!' to which her companion replied, 'You know the body is in Rome.' Why this should be, when St Catherine is so revered, I do not know.

The interior of San Domenico is likely to be a noisy experience, with tour leaders shouting the odds in many languages. There are frescoes by Sodoma, carvings by Benedetto da Maiano, a triptych by Matteo di Giovanni, and a crucifix painted by Sano di Pietro. I have never felt myself in the mood to appreciate any of them; I prefer the rather austere exterior.

Down a steep hill, where the tables laid for alfresco meals either lurch perilously, or are regulated by one end being foreshortened, is the way to the saint's birthplace – Santuarino Cateriniano. It lies across a courtyard and small car-park, lined on two sides by a double loggia. I find it altogether more appealing than the church, although one of the chapels included in the complex is as gaudy an exercise in baroquery as I found in all Siena. Its effect is mitigated by a painted thirteenth-century crucifix said to be that at which the saint was praying when she received her stigmata. (According to Attwater's *Dictionary of Saints* the occurrence did not actually blemish her, although it caused her pain.)

The sanctuary is on several levels and the original kitchen of the dyer's house is identified. It is now a souvenir shop. Down the road, another steep one, is the oldest fountain in Siena, an elaborate structure, in brick, of 1246. It gives its name to, or takes it from, the Porta Fonte Branda.

In another direction an exceptionally steep hill, which ought to be roped, takes you to the street leading into a small piazza. Here the baptistery of the cathedral weighs heavily on to the paving stones and is partly supported by a flying buttress attached to a house in a neighbouring alley. This is the moment to reflect on the astounding engineering involved in the construction of medieval Siena.

Siena: baptistery

Entry to the baptistery is separate from the cathedral, although it is a part of the whole. In it, apart from paintings, are carvings by Lorenzo Ghiberti on the highly esteemed font, probably by della Quercia. Another panel is by Donatello.

There is a choice of route here to the west front of the cathedral. I recommend the road under the buttress-cum-arch which will deliver you into the Piazza del Duomo without the distraction of the unfinished transept. That can come later. The piazza is bounded by purposeful edifices. Opposite the cathedral steps, and named for them, is the Santa Maria della Scala with an enormous hospital (no longer in use) surrounding the church on three sides. In it many works of art from several centuries are displayed, including a fresco illustrating the work of the hospital. Outside there are benches on which you should certainly find a space to sit and gaze at the remarkable west frontage. It is one of the most intricately designed façades I know. From memory I would say that no architectural feature or conceit has been excluded. It is smothered in statues, gargoyles, pinnacles, finials, mosaics, voussoirs, doors, rose windows, pendentives, mullions, arches, loggias, tracery and numerous styles of brickwork and ornamentation; it must surely comprise a complete illustrated dictionary of architecture. It has been recklessly overdone. Everything has been thrown at it but it defies criticism, so enjoy its luxuriance which at least prepares you for what is inside – if you can get in through the milling throngs. Every single square millimetre of the interior has been worked over. Pevsner, even in his prime, would have quailed at the thought of listing all the paintings, furnishings and ornaments.

You may find it possible to examine some of the remarkable marble floor, laid over two centuries and the work of forty artists on fifty-six panels. Not all of them are on view at any one time; some of them are copies. Get what glimpses you can of the mythological figures and Old Testament statues, then escape to the Libreria Piccolomini.

Entry to the library costs a few thousand lira but it is worth it to escape from the regimented parties of earnest Orientals who crowd the building at most times. You may also be disturbed in the library for a while by a scholarly group, but be patient. Sit them out and study the frescoes and statuary which they have already 'done'.

This is a library, but what you have come to see are the paintings, not the books. The spacious chamber – an oversized side chapel – was decorated in honour of that pope we encountered at Pienza, by his nephew, who was a cardinal. The main series of frescoes records the life of Piccolomini who, before being smoked into the Vatican, was archbishop of Siena. By Bernardino di Betto, an Umbrian known as Pinturicchio, they are extremely vivid and utterly representational, the Renaissance equivalent of modern colour photography for the wide screen. Almost everyone depicted seems to be posing, though many have wistful expressions. This is not to knock them or Pinturicchio. He was recording events in a famous pope's life and anyone present when great events today are being televised is inclined to pose. The frescoes are a fascinating record of a bygone age.

The ceiling is abstract and also highly coloured. On the floor stands a copy of Praxiteles' *Three Graces*, and there is statuary by Donatello and Michelangelo. Below the frescoes, illuminated manuscripts are displayed with their unwieldy pages opened. They are the only books in the library – about one dozen in all.

There is, as indicated, much else to see in this cathedral – not least a rogue's gallery of papal heads beneath the clerestory, but you may find the octagonal marble altar, by the Pisanos and others, roped off, so take yourself back into the piazza and turn the corner to look at the imposing ruin of the cathedral that never was. The Sienese, not content with having built so much of one great place of worship, abandoned work on it and began another, but the Black Death, along with structural problems, intervened. This folly was the result of the Guelph–Ghibelline conflict in which Siena changed sides in a manner that will confuse all but the most clear-headed students of Italian history, if such there be.

In what was intended to be merely an aisle of the second duomo is the museum on three floors. The paintings include a panoramic Maesta by Duccio di Buoninsegna, a contemporary of Giotto, supporting a cast of hundreds. This is displayed in a room with many rows of chairs, thoughtfully provided because the guides like to talk about this exhibit at mind-boggling length. When they have at last finished, the chairs are turned to face the opposite wall where what is left of the reredos, on which the painting was placed, is preserved. Then the oration recommences. But the Virgin is a beautiful painting and should be seen between groups.

The museum has many other paintings and much masonry, including sections of the cathedral frontage sculpted by Giovanni Pisano. And there are rooms bulging with croziers, vestments, candle holders and other clerical high camp. From the end of the third floor you are able to ascend to the narrow top of the unfinished wall of the 'new' cathedral to take in another stupendous view. Even so, I prefer the less panoramic one from a corner back towards the Campo. Here, beside a souvenir shop, turn round and you are confronted by the remarkable sight of the licorice-all-sorts campanile of the first cathedral rising above the nave. It is a servants' entrance view such as you never saw before. In these days when, seemingly, anything can be achieved, apart from social justice, it would be instructive to have this cathedral, and similar buildings, constructed on 'impossible' terrain built in replica on flat ground. How much of the thrill of looking at them would be lost? (I'll give you the answer at Pisa.)

Return to the Piazza del Duomo and turn left at the side of the prefecture to make for the best gallery in Siena, the Pinacoteca, where you are unlikely to be disturbed by guided tours.

The Pinacoteca has been on three floors of the former fourteenth-century Gothic Palazzo Buonsignori since the 1930s. It has by far the largest count of madonne e bambini I have come across, except at Perugia. In some rooms there is no other subject but, thanks to the extraordinary variety and ingenuity of the Sienese masters during four centuries, it does not become tedious. The bambini come in all sizes and most colours. Some are sturdy, upright infants, others lie on pillows at Mary's feet. Most are chubby, some are charming, a few repellent. The Marys are in rich blue and red robes, and often compellingly beautiful. The characters surrounding the famous pair are varied and entirely lifelike – people with grim or adoring faces, people marvelling, people frightened, people disbelieving. The gallery is almost entirely devoted to Christian religious art and I cannot recall ever before having enjoyed the genre so fully. There they all are – Crucifixions, Assumptions, Annunciations, Depositions, Nativities, Adorations, Virgins in Majesty, Virgins in Humility – with all the greatest names in Sienese painting represented, from Duccio, Guido da Siena, Bartolo di Fredi, Simone Martini, Ambrogio and Pietro Lorenzetti (the brothers who both died in the plague), Taddeo di Bartolo, Sano di Pietro to Sodoma. My favourite is an Adoration by Bartolomo di Fredi with dazzling foreground figures and a wonderful city background. Townscapes also come dominantly into Ambrogio Lorenzetti's work here, as much as in the Palazzo Pubblico.

From the Pinacoteca, go south by the Porta Ali'Arco, into the Via San Pietro, until you reach the flaking, rich, yellow church of Sant'Agostino with a colonnaded entrance to what is now a school. In the attached chapel there is a fresco by A. Lorenzetti and works by Martini and Sodoma.

Go down a steep hill, past the Mensa University, into the Via Giovanni Dupre, where the Società Musicale Pietro Mascagni has a house, to reach the Piazza del Mercato, Siena's vast market square lying directly below the Palazzo Pubblico. From one end there is a view of a lush valley but no sign of a river. (The Arbia flowing thinly to the east of the city gives it such waterway as it has.) Prominent on hills either side are Sant'Agostino, from whence we have come, and Santa Maria dei Servi, to which we are bound, on another of those typical Sienese ascents so good for the calf muscles.

From the steps of Santa Maria you have one of the finest views of the city. Inside, the church is all marbled pillars with the apse ceiling

Siena: Palazzo Pubblico and market

attractively decorated by a star motif beneath vaults, and three simple chandeliers hanging from it. The Lorenzetti frescoes here are by Pietro. There is a very large framed Mary in front of the altar by Coppo di Marcovaldo, a Florentine prisoner, and a similar one by Lippo Memmi.

From Santa Maria take the rather gloomy Via San Martino, another typical Sienese street, in which I once found myself trapped in a pedestrianized traffic jam behind a municipal dustcart. It was almost precisely the width of the thoroughfare, and moving at a pace regulated by the operators bringing bins to and from it. I eventually escaped down a side turning into the parallel Via Pantaneto, stumbling over several churches as I made my way. If you take a similar diversion you will be led into the Via Città which runs behind the Campo. It is lined with hotels and shops of all kinds where you can buy pennants of the seventeen contrade for your kids to play at Palio. Or panforte, the sticky local cake like rich, cold, hard Christmas pudding, made of spices, nuts and fruit, guaranteed to remove every stopping in your mouth.

There are steps down to the Campo from the Via Città at several points and, whatever time round it is for you, can you resist a last look at the Palazzo Pubblico, a stupendous building by any standard? And take a final peep, too, at the Fonte Gaia, a copy of the fountain by Jacopo della Quercia, now in the town hall. All over the Campo people sit or lie in the sunshine. It is a venue for locals as well as tourists.

Northwards lies the Piazza Indipendenza with a tatty (and closed) Teatro dei Rozzi in faded yellow, facing a loggia with busts of unnamed fierce gentlemen sporting elaborate mustachios. It seems to commemorate the birth of the Italian nation.

Take the Via Termini to reach the Palazzo Tolomei (with Monte Oliveto associations) now a bank fronting the Via dei Montanini down which we walked from the Florence gate some hours ago. In the Piazza Tolomei there is a column with the she-wolf symbol of Siena, carved by D. Arrighetti. The Tolomei palace dates from the first decade of the fourteenth century, when one of its first visitors was the king of Naples (a Frenchman named Robert of Anjou) who stayed there in 1310. It is still privately owned. In streets nearby, joining the Montanini, are many other Renaissance palaces. They are worth exploring but, probably, you will leave them for a future occasion, along with the church of San Francesco, standing on yet another hill to the east. It houses frescoes by both Lorenzettis. Here St Bernard preached and here Verdi's Requiem was first performed by a choir of four hundred. As a building it is more than usually hybrid. It was begun in 1326 but not finished for 150 years. It was baroqued in the mid seventeenth century and the campanile added over 100 years after. Then, in the late 1800s, it was restored to its Gothic origins. They just

142

cannot leave it alone.

The crowds in Siena can be as intimidating, though not as thick, as in Florence, and the pedestrianization of the centre, apart from taxis and fire engines, works well. But I would never be surprised to learn of angry tourists, squeezed against Renaissance walls, upturning a cab in fury, overlooking the possibility that one, or some, of the passengers might be invalids. If that happens it won't be an oriental group that rebels; they are far too disciplined.

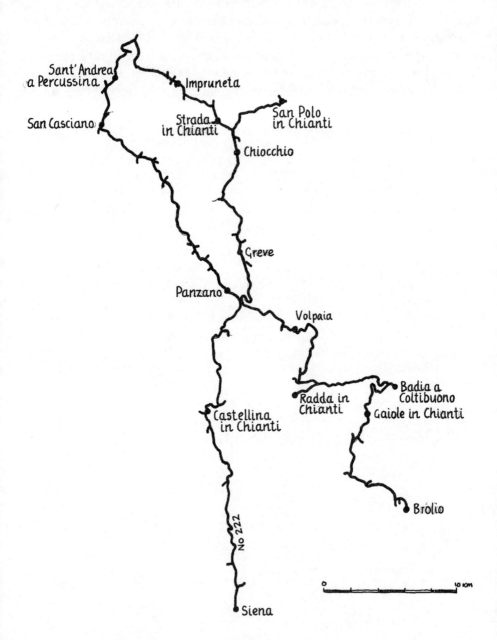

144

10   Chianti Country

Castellina in Chianti; Panzano; San Casciano in Val di Pesa; Impruneta; San Polo in Chianti; Greve in Chianti; Volpaia; Radda in Chianti; Badia a Coltibuono; Gaiole in Chianti; Brolio

The Chianti country, lying between Florence and Siena and covering approximately 800 square miles, is in the centre of Tuscany. Its most famous product is wine, but it is by no means one vast vineyard. It is a region with little flat land and many of its slopes are not easily cultivable, remaining thickly wooded for that reason. Although there are more mountainous parts of Italy, where the native genius for making the most of whatever terrain is available has led to vines being planted on shallow terraces rising vertiginously one above the other, in Chianti the vintage is produced without recourse to this method. Probably there are more chestnuts, pines, cypresses, oaks, olives and other trees than there are vines, but whatever needs to be grown in this region of small population requires arduous labour. Even the ancient Romans failed to straighten the main north–south route between Florence and Siena (today the SS 222). It may look to be lacking in bends on your small-scale Michelin map, but in fact it is continually curvaceous and undulatory.

Historically this was territory that was fought over by the rival cities at its northern and southern extremes. Many of the isolated communities, now peacefully accumulating wealth through the grape, began as fortified hills. When Michelangelo, who invariably accepted more commissions than he could complete in the contracted time, left Rome in a fury because the pope was behind with payments, he stayed for the night on his journey to Tuscany (where other uncompleted works awaited him) not at Siena, but in the old, high part of Poggibonsi, because that was on land belonging to his adopted home, Florence.

Chianti today means wine but in the late fourteenth century, when the Chianti League was formed, the motivation had nothing to do with it. The League was a defensive measure of the Florentines against the Sienese. The principal towns in it were Radda, Castellina and Gaiole, all nowadays major centres of Chianti Classico, labelled with the famous black rooster. After Siena had fallen to Florence, the League was no longer a strategic necessity and its logo was eventually handed down for peaceful

145

commercial use. In fact it is restricted to the environs of these centrally situated towns, although the term Chianti (without the Classico) is permitted in describing wines grown over a much larger area, even as far away as Lucca, Pisa and Ruffina.

The first stop out of Siena, on a tour of this most entrancing region, is Castellina, a long, thin town on a ridge. It is almost worthwhile approaching it from the south-west instead of the south because, as you make your way along a valley there appears, far above, to be a cathedral dominating the skyline. As you get nearer, it resembles more a steel works. In fact it is the wine cooperative, an unsightly hulk of a building but of intrinsic importance.

Castellina itself is more seductive, with a modest castle, a diminutive neo-Gothic modern church with toy-like campanile, a few gently winding streets and one unique feature in its Via delle Volte, a covered way inside the ancient walls. Here, when it was formed, was the first headquarters of the Chianti League. Today, on a street running parallel with the Volte, the Via Ferruccio, is the Palazzo Ugolino, with its Renaissance wine cellars. Around it are many merchants offering tastings and there is an air of prosperity such as is usually found in wine towns. The Via Ferruccio curves gently towards a public park, but before you reach it, turn off for the fifteenth-century fortress, complete with small museum, beside which nestles a three-storey house with a modest balcony. It is shabby, the plaster is flaking, it doesn't really fit in this well-heeled town, but it is typical of that solid style of petit-bourgeois homestead found throughout Italy. It symbolizes survival, showing the scars of centuries of turmoil, and there may or may not be untold wealth beneath its floorboards.

The church nearby, San Salvatore, has a pretty doorway with shrubs and trees in pots on either side of it. In the simple, arched interior the Stations of the Cross are bas-relief ceramic figures. Attached to the apse are two tall walls, possibly the remains of an earlier fortified church. On the edge of the town to the north, making a perfect backdrop when viewed from the centre, is Monte Calvario where there are several Etruscan tombs hidden in the demure hillside.

Road 222 leads towards Panzano, another ex-fortress town of Etruscan origins, but before reaching it there is a turning to San Leolino, a Romanesque parish church described by one guide as being first mentioned in AD 982. It was enlarged in the twelfth and thirteenth centuries and, in the sixteenth, given a portico which rests on five sandstone pillars. In the interior are works by the Sienese school.

Panzano is on two eminences. One holds the busy working town from which a narrow street leads down, then up, to the other, dominated by a plain brick church and squat campanile beside it. Above the

146

door is a ceramic composition that strikes a jarring note. There is little to see in Panzano; it is the views from it that make a visit worthwhile. When you leave, take a cross-country route to San Casciano, along a road that, in 1996, had many 'deformata' stretches, but it was rewarding. It doesn't lead you into actual farmyards, unless you are careless, but it gives you an intimate acquaintance with the land. For many kilometres you see scarcely a building of any sort. You may pass a tractor or two, and even meet another car, but for the most part you are in deep, undisturbed country, from which you emerge to signs of so-called civilization advertising hotels with swimming baths, or gîte-style accommodation.

Climb high above the Elsa valley to reach San Casciano, a rambling town with vestiges of a castle in gardens surrounding private housing, a museum of sacred art in a spruce little chapel (locked, of course) and a well-restored collegiate church entered through the offices of a company providing an ambulance service. The church is baroque inside, Romanesque without. Another building integrated with it is the extant tower of the town's medieval wall. This now houses an import-export agent. So this is a church maintaining true contacts with the outside world. It also has a modest museum of art, exhibiting a painted Crucifixion by Simone Martini; a triptych by Ugolino di Neri (two panels featuring grim-faced saints with, between them, a particularly gentle Mary receiving homage from a midget kneeling at her feet); and a carved stone pulpit of the fourteenth century fixed, impregnably, to a wall.

Facing the old town, at one end, is an enormous red-brick edifice with a courtyard, all gleamingly contemporary. It could easily be a modern fortress but it has the words CREDITO CO-OPERATIVO BANCA DEL CHIANTI FIORENTINO emblazoned on it. Bank it may be, but I bet there's a chapel somewhere inside it, and even some religious paintings. It is a building which successfully contrives to be representative of Chianti in all its manifestations.

North of the town is the village of Sant'Andrea a Percussina, where Niccolò Machiavelli spent some time in exile. Here he wrote *The Prince*, the best-known of his works, in a house now in use as a restaurant. On the premises, inevitably, is a small museum.

Impruneta, the next town, is noted more for the baking of tiles than for wine. Most of it lies on a hillside, about ten miles south of Florence, with the main Piazza Buondelmonti rising steeply from the much-bombed and restored church of Santa Maria. The church, consecrated in 1060, became associated with a legend concerning St Luke and a portrait of the Virgin drawn by him (dated by experts as thirteenth century!). This was found on the site. Some say it was brought here by Romulus, if you please. It is taken in procession to Florence amid prayers, at times of heavy rain, at times of drought, at times of war. It did not, regrettably, protect the church from near total devastation during the German retreat in 1944, although only an expert would know that the five-arched loggia, with a short bell tower on one side and a taller, thinner one rising beside the modestly sized nave, has been heavily restored. The somewhat severe effect of the façade, emphasized by five small, square windows above the arches, is mitigated by a jolly clock tower. On the corner pillars of the loggia there are emblems resembling a headless chicken. The lavishly illustrated free town guide does not explain this symbol.

Impruneta: Santa Maria

Within the church is a museum which opens at irregular hours and certainly not every day. Many exhibits were given by the Medicis and they include a gold crucifix by Ghiberti. There are two private chapels designed by Michelozzo, one of them with della Robbia ceramics, the other displaying the 'St Luke' portrait of the Virgin, which was repainted in 1758 by an Englishman named Ignazio Hugford.

Leading from the piazza is the Via Roma, where there are handsome houses of various periods, also workshops where you can see tiles being processed. Brunelleschi is on record as ordering tiles from Impruneta for use in the construction of Florence cathedral's dome. Terracotta ware from the town decorated many Florentine palaces. Today, all items produced by workshops in the Impruneta consortium bear the guarantee mark of a rosette.

From the Piazza Buondelmonti, after the family who were 'lords of the Manor' for five centuries, there is a tranquil view of the nearby hills studded with pines, vines and a farm complex with a typical battlemented tower. The Buondelmonti clan are also perpetuated in the name of the local olive oil.

Six kilometres south is Strada in Chianti where the church, founded in AD 1000, preserves its triple-arched portico and, at another six to the east, San Polo, renowned for its iris growing. To see the flowers in bloom you must visit in a certain week in May because they droop quickly and anyhow are grown for commercial use. The medicinal properties of the iris were known to the ancient Greeks but the reason they are grown here is cosmetic. Their bulbs are sent to France for making perfume, but it is a dying industry. The driver of a school bus told us the young no longer care for the hard labour involved and the number of people willing to harvest the crop is dwindling. He didn't seem to know what other employment was available.

Rejoin SS 222 again, and make for Greve, a busy market town with a central piazza named, as are so many, after Giacomo Matteotti, the politician who was murdered because he dared to oppose Mussolini, the fascist dictator who allied his country to Hitler's Germany. The piazza is trapezium shaped and lined on two sides by arcaded shops and houses of varying heights, all painted in blending pastel shades, making it one of the most agreeable town centres in Tuscany. At the shorter of the two parallel sides lies a little church with three arches to its loggia; at the other end is the more imposing town hall. Among the many shops behind the arcades is the Libreria la Formicola with a wide selection of novels and guides in English.

The chief exhibits in the church of Santa Croce are a triptych of Madonna and Child by Bicci di Lorenzo and a fourteenth-century fresco of the same subject by Maestro da Greve; in the piazza is a statue to Giovanni di Verrazzano, a mariner who explored the coasts of North America on behalf of François I of France.

Greve is an important centre of the chianti trade and also a major market for extra virgin olive oil, boar sausage and various handicrafts. In the hills around are many wine-producing villages, one of them Castello di Verrazzano, from which the explorer took his name, and to whose Chianti Classico he has returned it.

South, towards Panzano again. Then turn off on a minor road, or track even, to make for the isolated small hill village of Volpaia whose strategic importance in the days of strife between Florence and Siena may be gauged when you see how it commands the vast areas of uninhabited country rolling away from it in all directions. Its castle, begun perhaps one thousand years ago, with a formidable keep in unrendered stone, is now a salesroom bearing the words CASTELLO DI VOLPAIA in gold leaf under a rounded brick pediment. Since 1555, when its function as a fortress ceased, it has been maintained for other purposes. This is an exceptionally well-restored village in which there is little hint of tarting-up. The stone is grey-ish brown with sand colouring; the only modern villa merges with its older neighbours. The overall effect is one of almost provocative anonymity. There are no posters, no advertising of any kind, not so much as a toffee paper blowing in the wind. A narrow alley, partly arched over, leads to the small central piazza. Another leads circuitously away, then back to the same place. In a cramped courtyard an old crone drew aside a curtain to inspect us inspecting her environment. We all looked suitably implacable, no greetings in our eye contacts. The small, gaunt church was closed, a lit-tle café was open, but had no customers. On the wall of the piazza a few young backpackers picnicked in silence.

Volpaia is a tranquil experience. Long may it remain thus.

By comparison, Radda in Chianti, on an altogether higher, more expansive eminence, is a veritable metropolis of bright lights, with suspi-cions of a trading complex in its lower part. Radda became the centre of the Chianti League in 1415, taking over the role from Castellina. Much of the original wall is intact and there are tree-lined ramparts on two sides, one spilling over into an umbrageous public garden. The streets are narrow, cobbled, pedestrianized. There is a small, dignified town hall bearing many plaques and a somewhat drab church towering over it from a higher ridge of the hill. Above the doorway of Santa Maria is a tondo of Mary, Jesus and cherubs; inside the Stations of the Cross are ceramic squares with vivid blue backgrounds. The pulpit, six feet up a wall, is apparently inaccessible.

Radda stands 503 m above sea level, dominating the valleys of the Pesa and Arbia. It is the capital of this part of Chianti, the headquarters of the Consorzio del Gallo Nero, the successor, in wine terms, to the Chianti League. It has an air of quiet authority. After centuries of conflict you feel there is general consensus here to stick together, following a sim-ple function in life, bound into a still remote community. Left alone, the cit-izens will see it through very nicely, thank you.

Almost due east from Radda, except that the road wiggles through forest and up and down hills, is Badia a Coltibuono, where reli-gion once reigned, but it is now the turn of haute cuisine. The blame could lie with Napoleon Bonaparte because it was an edict of his, in 1810, that evicted the monks from the Benedictine monastery and had it converted into a farm.

Radda in Chianti: Palazzo Pretorio

The abbey, which still stands – and so does its massive and rather plain church – was a daughter house of the one at Vallombrosa on the Pratomagna. It was built in the eleventh century. From a crossroads, climb up hairpin bends to a shady car-park beside the austere monastery and church. Unless you have come to take a cookery course at the culinary school which now operates here, the view is everything and not to be scorned. This is one of the most soothing corners of Chianti and deserves to be savoured.

Badia a Coltibuono

When you leave, return to the crossroads, noting a ruin in a nearby field, and take a very steep, wooded road down to Gaiole, a route almost more English than Tuscan, with deciduous trees prevailing. Deep down in a lush valley you come to the smart modern town spreading neatly up meadows formerly tree clad. A stream runs through Gaiole in Chianti, once one of the principal towns of the League, so it must have had strategic importance not now obvious. It seems almost entirely devoted to tourism. There are footpaths to Siena but that would seem an arduous undertaking. If you feel the need of a walk you may settle for the nearby medieval village of Barbischio. On your way south to the huge castle of Brolio, you will pass close to another, that of Meleto, twelfth century, much rehabilitated in the eighteenth, and private property, not open to the public.

Brolio, which you may visit, exemplifies much that is essentially Tuscan. The immediate approach, after a journey through country either uncultivated, or spoilt with loving care, is up a devious road through thick woods. The castle is on a spacious mound, from which there are panoramic views, and stands behind formidable fortifications. Below it, vineyards spread out tidily.

Brolio is of particular significance in Italian history because not only has it been owned by the Ricasoli family for almost a millennium, but one of their number, Baron Bettino Ricasoli, became prime minister after Cavour's untimely death in 1861. In that year Victor Emmanuele II of Savoy was crowned king, and Italy, apart from Venice and Rome (crucial exceptions, admittedly), was unified at last. There is a plaque to commemorate a visit by the king to Brolio, two years later, by which time Ricasoli was between premierships, the average duration being as short in the last century as it has been in this.

Although the Ricasolis have been so long in ownership, the ninth century castle they occupied in 1147 was mostly demolished in 1478, apart from a chapel. The designer of the present castle, following the sacking by the Sienese in 1529, was probably Giuliano di Sangallo. The walls are 450 m long and 14 m high. The Germans, inevitably, were here, and Allied bombing struck Brolio in 1944.

The Ricasolis have always been much concerned with viniculture, caring for their grapes at all times when their land was not being fought over. The same Bettino, known as the 'Iron Baron', when he was not taking a leading part in the Risorgimento, or governing Italy, studied the characteristics of different vines and perfected his own variety. His vintage may be tasted in the cellars by visitors whose tour of the castle and grounds includes the most recent palace, built in Gothic style for Bettino in 1860.

Francesco, the present baron, is the thirty-second in the line. Apart from the Medicis, probably no other family has played so prominent a role in Tuscan, and Italian, history. Certainly none has been a part of it more continuously.

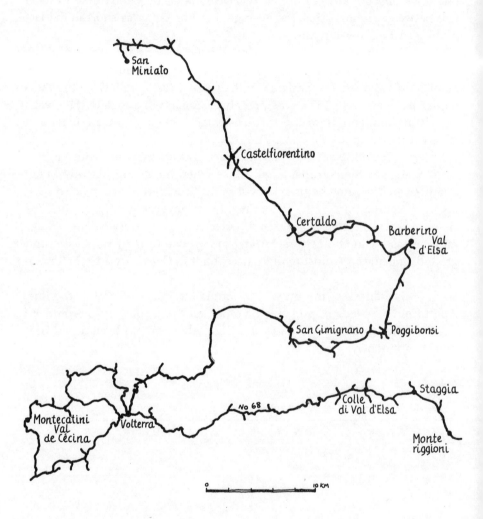

San
Miniato

Castelfiorentino

Certaldo

Barberino
Val
d'Elsa

San Gimignano   Poggibonsi

Staggia

No 68   Colle
di Val d'Elsa

Montecatini
Val
de Cécina   Volterra

Monte
riggioni

0   10 KM

11 West of Chianti

Monteriggioni; Staggia; Colle di Val d'Elsa; Montecatini in Val di Cecina; Volterra; San Gimignano; Poggibonsi; Barberino Val d'Elsa; Certaldo; Castelfiorentino; San Miniato

Seen from the road, Monteriggioni looks like an extensive hill-top fort in good working order. The walls are intact, there are fourteen towers and the eminence on which it stands is just sufficiently high to register strategic significance. It was built by the Sienese at the very beginning of the thirteenth century and was admired by Dante, who waxed fanciful about its wall turreted with giants. It became a Ghibelline outpost against Florence but lost its importance once the Medici city had vanquished its main rival. In its contemporary irrelevance it presents a pretty picture to the passer-by but there is little more to it than a much-restored church with a charming little campanile in different coloured stone.

Monteriggioni: chapel

155

Within the walls it is surprisingly unclaustrophobic. There is a wide cobbled square bordered by a few shops on one side, and a modest hotel with large vegetable garden. Residents may drive their cars through the gates; visitors must remain without. So you park in a field, part of territory said to be the site of Etruscan tombs. One shopkeeper confirmed this, another said they no longer exist *in situ* but are exhibited in the National Museum of East Berlin. Having experienced Chiusi, and with Volterra to come, we did not go in search of them.

Slightly to the north is Staggia, where not nearly as much medieval wall is extant but what there is has been incorporated into homes of later dates on either side of it. One tower is occupied up to three storeys and in this section there is a public way behind the low battlement.

Staggia has a ruined castle, although parts of it have been patched up with modern plate-glass windows. It is not open to the public. In the small central piazza are the church, with a near-contemporary tower, possibly of concrete, and the Museo del Pollaiuolo, open only on Saturdays. The museum is said to have a work by Antonio Pollaiuolo, the Florentine goldsmith and sculptor who took up painting late in life under the guidance of his brother Pietro. Vasari does not mention a Staggia connection for either of them.

Colle di Val d'Elsa is in a different league from Monteriggioni and Staggia, although this is not apparent until you have emerged from its ragged and busy industrial lower part, Colle Bassa, where a redeeming feature is a neat piazza with a thirteenth-century church holding paintings by Ghirlandaio and others. The old part, owned by the bishops of Volterra until the twelfth century, is built on two spurs of rock joined by a bridge. It has many palazzi of the fourteenth to sixteenth centuries, some well preserved, others flaking, many just grimy.

Enter at the west end, or by the hospital near the brow of the hill. The streets are much wider than in many old towns but there is ample space outside the walls for parking. One of several intact gateways, at the end of the bridge, leads to the oldest quarter where, at the far end of the main street, there are plaques on the birthplaces of architect Arnolfo di Cambio and poet, Lorenzo Lippi. Arnolfo is credited with part-design of the carved pulpit in the cavernous cathedral. (I cannot trace any connection between the poet and the painters who also bore his name.) On the same rectangular square is the town hall and the archaeological museum.

The pavements in Colle are laid out in varying colours of stone; the buildings are mostly red brick. There are shops selling the local cristallo (a major industry in Colle Bassa) and a number of restaurants and hotels. From the Piazza Canonica, and other points on the upper level, steps and ramps lead to lower terraces. The bridge joining the two sections of the old

156

Colle di Val d'Elsa: entry to the old town

town has seats on its pavements commanding views over Colle Bassa and
beyond. There is also a civic museum and another devoted to sacred art. I
was not too disappointed to find them closed.

The singularity of Colle cannot be appreciated without the help
of an aerial photograph. This reveals the density of the tightly packed red-
roofed buildings lying, snakelike, on the ridges.

The road to Volterra is all bends and hills. Be prepared for a
slow journey, especially if you find yourself behind one of the many coaches bound for the most famous of the ancient Etruscan cities, or a giant truck
conveying supplies to it. If this happens do not fret. The countryside you

pass through is under-populated, endlessly fascinating, sometimes sensational, with many bare rocky crags. From whichever direction you approach Volterra you are aware of a massive, impending presence. No other hill town is quite like it. For the moment, however, we will not stop but, when the centro is signed, fork left and descend the hill, with many more hairpin bends, before plunging off across farmland on what is often little more than a track.

The object is Montecatini in Val di Cecina. Here again is a splendidly sited hill town where the older part is neatly divided from the new by a through-road. The new is spruce, all smart villas and apartments, a town fit for twentieth-century man and his luxurious needs; the old offers the usual heart-pounding climb to yet another castle of the bishops of Volterra, through a glorious maze of thoroughfares, off which narrow alleys fork, into a small uneven piazza. The Giuseppe Garibaldi, as it is named, has a Pisan-style Romanesque church standing at an angle of 30 degrees from the small colonnaded town hall, on the roof of which is a glass pyramid reminiscent of that controversial one at the Louvre. There is a bas-relief plaque on the town hall to one Ferdinando Porciani who saved many lives on liberation day, 2 July 1944, and another to King Emmanuele II, noting his accession at precisely 11.55 on 14 March 1861. There's history for you.

Go through a covered passage to a lower, prettier square, Piazza Belforti, where the houses have window-boxes contributing much-needed colour. One, high up, has a rounded brick well. Others have diminutive entranceways down three or four well-worn steps, not exactly helpful to young mothers with prams or old grandmothers with arthritis. The dwellings here emphasize the benefits of the new town on the other hillside. As you descend, turn away from the view for a moment to inspect an alleyway, Vicolo del Fornaccio, leading deviously to a crush of dwellings, which are probably not desirable as second homes but may still be in demand by those natives who cannot afford the 'new' hillside.

Before we went up to the old town Christopher noted that the hill road is called Via XX Settembre, a name frequently encountered on our travels. Pointing at the street sign, he asked an elderly resident what it meant. She took the enquiry literally and replied, 'The twentieth of the month of September, Signor.' 'But what', he persisted, 'is the historical significance of the date?' She shrugged her shoulders. She knew nothing of history. She pointed upwards. 'There is centro storico,' she said and turned her back on us.

In fact, the twentieth of September was the day in 1870 when Rome, despite papal opposition, became an integral part of Italy and the country was at last unified, except for Venezia and the tiny enclave of the

Vatican. For the next fifty years no pope left the Vatican for fear he would not be permitted to return. I dare say the lady, to whom the date 20 September meant nothing, is a practising Roman Catholic.

We left Montecatini by another rough road to join a main artery from the coast to Volterra. There was little to be seen on it apart from a posh hotel. We revelled in the spaciousness. We might, alternatively, have retraced our route to the other main road and taken a different, second approach to Volterra. Had we done so we would have faced Le Balze, where great chunks of cliff have fallen, making crevasses engulfing ancient Etruscan tombs and endangering a monastery long since abandoned. Augustus Hare named it 'an arid and ghastly desert'. The church of San Giusto fell into the gorge but the faith that moves mountains also builds upon them, so the enormous hulk of church we see today is its successor, where we witnessed a service being held in honour of its saint. It stands at the top of a long meadow with wide steps marked by four columns bearing statues of prelates and popes. We walked from it to the Balze, where a small section of the Etruscan wall survives, next to a camp site poised above the weird volcanic landscape below. Wild flowers grew in profusion around us – poppies, honeysuckle, gorse. They offered some comfort in this inhospitable terrain which I left without reluctance, strains of Mussorgsky ringing in my ears.

Even allowing for the impact of first seeing Cortona and Montepulciano, you can hardly fail to be bowled over by Volterra, whether first, second, third or fourth time round. There never was a more obvious site for a defensive settlement. The only point not in its favour is that the rock on which it is built is being gradually eroded through the action of water on the bottom strata of clay. The sandstone fills the gap but neither early man, nor the Etruscans, knew about this and the latter made it one of their principal cities, one which ruled over vast stretches of country far to the north and south.

Allow Volterra to gradually overwhelm you.

Enter by the Porta San Francesca, after leaving Le Balze (and also parting from your vehicle). Climb slowly up the Via San Lino, hemmed in somewhat by the tall, dark buildings, including the church of San Francesco with a fresco cycle about the story of the Holy Cross, until you reach the Piazza dei Priori. This 'square' is not as irregularly shaped as many but sufficiently so to take the eye into unsuspected crannies and, eventually, to lure you on down a comparatively narrow exit. First, feast your senses on the quiet Gothic grandeur of so much that is there. High above is the crenellated tower of the Palazzo Pretorio, known as the Piglet's Tower because of a porcine carving above a window. The town hall is be-plaqued inside and out and has a courtyard with a large well.

Le Balze: San Giusto

On the east side of the square are the Palazzo dei Priori, with an ancient tower embedded in it, and other palaces. Next to the town hall is the apse of the cathedral and an almost hidden back entrance. There are banks, shops and cafés too, but there ought to be more than one restaurant with tables alfresco. This is a piazza for lingering in but you may have to resort to sitting on a low wall at the rear of the duomo in order to savour it all at leisure.

The cathedral faces a smaller piazza across from its detached, octagonal baptistery where there is a high altar by Mino da Fiesole. He was also responsible for the ciborium (canopy) in the cathedral. The frontage of the cathedral, which does not rate with Pisa, Florence or Siena, is heavy, relieved by mosaic decorations on the pediment but rather mundane. The interior is dark, apart from a gaudy ceiling, and dripping with unmemorable paintings. There are more of them in a long side chapel but you don't come to Volterra for the paintings. It is primarily an architectural and open-air experience.

So, leave the gloomy cathedral, go into the Via Roma (where there is an entrance to a Museum of Sacred Art) leading into the Via Buonparenti where a high arch joins two elegantly tall mini-mansions of the thirteenth century facing each other across the street. Soon, in the Via dei Sarti, you reach the Pinacoteca occupying the Palazzo Minucci-Solaini, and more paintings. Away with them, and with us, to pass by the Renaissance Palazzo Viti, which has a theatre in its courtyard.

Continue your perambulation along similar streets, mostly pedestrianized, until you reach a small area of greenery at the Piazza XX Settembre where you can tell any ignorant residents who wish to know what that was all about. Just beyond it is the Museo Etrusco Guarnacci, which we will certainly visit because it displays a collection of all things Etruscan in the region. Its five-star item is the renowned statue, encased in glass, of a painfully thin boy. At first glance you think it must be by Giacometti; certainly it influenced him. It stands in the centre of one room to be admired from all directions.

The museum boasts hundreds of Etruscan tombs, some of them superbly carved with themes and scenes, military, romantic, pastoral, allegorical. On the top floor are Greek tombs which were more refined and, throughout the building, vases and pots of all sizes proliferate. You cannot have a museum without pots. In fact, a brisk visit from a bull directed at certain rooms would make a beneficial clearance. There are also busts, tools, cooking utensils, jewels, lamps, rings, emblems, all the bric-à-brac of a great civilization. But there is too much of it. When you have endured all you can, go into the unweeded garden where the pots are urn-sized, in stone, and sit on a bench in the shade.

Once revived, take a stroll down to the thirteenth-century Porta di Docciola with its attendant oblong fountain of the same period. There is an earlier gate, Porta all'Arco, on the other side of the hill and this is genuine Etruscan, as are some of the walls which covered a more extensive area than the later, medieval, defences. You should walk around them for at least part of the way and take in the Roman theatre on the northern side. Inevitably Etruscan Velathri gave way to imperial Rome but the conquerors are not greatly in evidence.

Then take another rest in the Parco Archeologico on the great swathe of grass which rises up to the fortress, now used as a prison. The older part is twelfth century but there is a later square endpiece with four round towers. This was thrown up at the command of Lorenzo the Magnificent, who had previously besieged the city.

Volterra has been famous since Etruscan times for its alabaster, which was used by the ancients to make funerary urns. The industry was revived in the eighteenth century and the city is now an international centre for the production of a mineral whose by-products are on sale in every street.

The rivers Cecina and Era meet below Volterra but you see little of them. We caught a glimpse of one as we drove towards San Gimignano, after following a recklessly driven trailer down and round the mountain on a road unsuitable for overtaking, though allowance should be made for the Volterran spirit.

I was thinking what a pity it is, in these days of ubiquitous high-rises, that the medieval skyscraper town of Tuscany has become diminished. Then, as we turned a corner, there was a sight which made us both exclaim, like stereotype American tourists, 'Wow-Ow!'

San Gimignano is as dramatic as ever in its impact. Is even the New York skyline, seen from the Atlantic, more impressive than this four-teenth-century burgh with thirteen of its original seventy-six towers remaining proud and aloof above its walls?

Not only are the walls and towers extant, but many of the houses and churches also. The city entered a time warp after the Black Death (1348) had decimated the population. Soon after, it became a vassal of its great neighbour and, in this instance, the conquering Florentines neglected to destroy what they had annexed. But San Gimignano lost its silk trade and its road seemed no longer to lead to Rome. It became a backwater until this century, when it has revived, not only as a tourist venue high on any operator's itinerary, but also as a wine-producing centre.

The rows of medieval buildings are often almost solid with just occasional gaps between them leading to murky alleys. We sat enjoying a snack on the Via San Matteo. Opposite was a mere crack of an opening made even narrower by a buttress shoring up the building on one side. The city refuse cart, driven by a brisk woman in slacks and shirt, veered towards it. As I was about to shout a warning she pulled away from the inadequate aperture then, almost immediately, a boy on a Vespa swerved theatrically and disappeared into it like the White Rabbit.

San Gimignano is very much first time round but visiting it again after a twenty-year gap I found it entrancing. Were those solid towers status symbols, erected by rich merchants each determined to go one better than his neighbour? Or were they used, as has been suggested, to store the crocuses from which a special yellow dye was made? And were some of them linked for defensive reasons? Those that remain are scattered, unaligned, except for a group close to the duomo where they stand together, of unequal height, like columns on a graph.

Needless to say, there are many churches. Most of them can be ignored but time should be found for Sant'Agostino, conveniently placed if you have parked below the walls by the Via Ghiacciaia. It is simple, severe thirteenth-century Romanesque/Gothic, and has frescoes by Benozzo Gozzoli portraying, in seventeen panels, the life of Saint Augustine.

Frescoes also feature in the collegiata, which is as much an art gallery as a church, although it could do with improved and permanent lighting. In the north aisle the frescoes are by Bartolo di Fredi; in the south, by Barna da Siena. If you are fortunate they may be lit for you by coins inserted by guides. Or you may count yourself lucky to be there between tours when something resembling silence can be enjoyed. More frescoes, by Ghirlandaio, are in the chapel commemorating Santa Serafina di Ciardi, a local girl who died paralysed, at the age of fifteen. On the day of her death flowers descended on to her bed without the assistance of human hands, and all the bells in the towers and churches pealed of their own accord. Why this should have sanctified the poor lass is hard for an unbeliever to understand. Forster refers to the incident in *Where Angels Fear to Tread*, some of the action of which takes place in San Gimignano, thinly disguised as Monteriano.

There are more paintings in the Museo Civico, which may be entered from the courtyard of the Palazzo del Podestà, although it seems to have become augmented with the Museums of Etruscan and Sacred Arts. I am convinced, from memory, and from my notebook, that all the items mentioned below I found in rooms first entered from this courtyard, which also has access to the Torre Grossa, but other books consulted place the latter in two museums off the charming, small Piazza Luigi Pecori. Yet some of the paintings they place in the Museo Civico I certainly saw in what I entered as the Museum of Sacred Art and amongst them were a pair of Filippino Lippis of the Annunciation, framed in two tondi, with a much larger unattributed canvas of an Assumption between them. In the right-hand tondo Mary has a sorrowful face and looks down, quite overcome, into the folds of her richly coloured robes. Her halo is pale as a jellyfish and all but invisible. The angel in the other tondo is quivering with the importance of the news he has to impart. In the Assumption, Mary has her feet on the heads of cherubs and is surrounded by a frame of putti heads without bodies.

163

There is a Taddeo di Bartolo of a saint holding a model of San Gimignano partly under the folds of his cloak. Devils feature as large black insects, so presumably this has plague associations. Some paintings are captioned, some are not. A few of those that are have the signs lying freely on the floor. Beneath all the fading frescoes in one room is a canvas, behind glass, on an easel, of a shepherdess and sheep, dated 1897.

In the Sala Dante is a modern statuette of a mother and child, perhaps representing one-parent families. Also there was a very large Maesta with eleven saints on each side of Mary. I think this was the one by the Sienese Lippo Memmi, as restored by Gozzoli, but it may have been the Pinturicchio of the same subject. Again, lack of signing.

Did I visit these museums during a period of transition? Instead of closing for months or years on end, as they do in France, was a great reorganization afoot whilst the galleries remained open?

The Piazza Luigi Pecori mentioned above has herring-bone tiling as pavement. Note the little Gothic houses, rather run down, in one corner behind the well. Nearby is the Piazza Cisterna with two high towers and, between them, an almost contemporary building with a top-floor, glassed-over, loggia that harmonizes well.

Finally, as at Volterra, take a walk around the walls.

The road to Poggibonsi goes through gently undulating territory, for the most part across vineyards and farming land. Poggibonsi, which sounds like the name of a prize fighter, is a thriving commercial/industrial town but, earlier, it was an important link in the Florentine defences. In 1270 Guido di Monforte razed it to the ground, demolishing its ancient castle two kilometres up a hill overlooking the Elsa. Two centuries later Lorenzo the Magnificent ordered the building of another, larger one, but the conquest of Siena in the next century took away the necessity for completing it. The ruins of this, the Rocca di Poggio Imperiale, loom over the town where the small old part centres around the Piazza Cavour. Here are the town hall, on a corner site, its upper walls bearing coats of arms, its ground floor a drogheria, and a collegiate church. The latter was rebuilt in the nineteenth century and restored again after the severe bombing of World War Two, but Poggibonsi is really not a must.

Take the S2 for Barberino Val d'Elsa, lying on a spur of hill between the two river valleys, the other being the Pesa. This allows for extravagantly wide views all round. Two gates remain to the small fortified town and the buildings, lining the main street running between them, are all in good nick. Immediately inside the Porta Sienese, on the left, is a Renaissance house with a heavily corbelled first floor. The street is named Via Francesco da Barberino after a lawyer-poet-philosopher who was born here in the 1400s. A plaque was raised to him five centuries later but doesn't give his precise dates. The small central Piazza Barberini has a low loggia on one building facing a modest two-storeyed town hall with eye windows in its attic floor, a spruce and cheerful municipal headquarters with the customary plaques. Behind it, down the hillside, the much-restored church has a proud double stone stairway to its unremarkable frontage and stands next to a smart house in whose high-walled garden is a lone palm tree.

Certaldo: castle

Just beyond a bank where, beneath trees, a small market is held, is the road to Certaldo. It is all hairpin bends through olive groves and vines, and goes through the hamlet of Petrognano, just past which is Santa Maria a Bagnano, a domed church all but hidden in a small copse.

At Certaldo descend into the valley of the Agliena which here joins the Elsa. You are immediately enveloped in a sprawling modern town of no distinction. Persevere through it until you see signs for Certaldo Alto situated, as you might expect, on the hill far above. You can reach it from the main street of the new town and become a nuisance when you get there, or you can approach it from the back door by driving up a foothill, then traversing farmland, before doubling back on a rough track to an even rougher car-park below the castle walls. Walk around them until there is an entrance into the town where Boccaccio may have been born, and where he certainly died and is heavily commemorated. His house, bombed in World War Two, has been restored and is now a national centre for the study of his work. There is a large library containing numerous editions of the *Decameron* in dozens of languages, and a collection of more than five hundred fourteenth-century drawings. The latter are displayed periodically in the utterly captivating Palazzo Pretorio, forming part of the castle at the top of the main street. (See previous page.)

One wall of the room where Boccaccio died is covered by a painting of him seated at his desk and wearing a kind of cowl covering head, neck and chest. Entry to the house is free but if you attempt to leave without tipping the caretaker she will flourish a fistful of banknotes and give a shrill wail that can be silenced in one way only.

Boccaccio's tomb is in the nave of SS Jacopo e Filippo, a gloomy church redeemed by a most striking two-tiered cloister of unusual shape. The four sides are of different lengths and the longer two are not parallel.

The chief glory of Certaldo, a town that is all in red brick, is the pretorial palace which, until the end of the thirteenth century, was owned and inhabited by the lords Alberti of Prato. It displays all the attributes of a fine castle, coupled with both domesticity and municipality. It is sited, as all self-respecting fortresses should be, on the brow of a hill. It is crenellated, has robust buttresses and massive curtain walls. It also encompasses a chapel with frescoes but has no drawbridge, only a ramp of steps above a lower flight facing a curious tiled, open-fronted structure, a cross between a washhouse and a bicycle shed.

The municipal quality comes from the plaques post-dating the Albertis, who submitted to the Florentines earlier than some other independents. Many plaques are coloured and there is one of much piquancy, surmounted by the white ceramic head of an infant who died, aged one, in 1499.

Inside, the architectural treat continues. Go through a covered lobby into an unroofed courtyard bordered by loggias and stairways. Galleries lead from it; the chapel of SS Tommaso e Prospero is attached. Paintings spread over the vaulting and walls, and you are permitted to walk about the many rooms, some of which may display temporary exhibitions. When we were there the subject in one of them was DIABOLIK, celebrating a Batman-style character from television. It seemed entirely inappropriate until you mused upon the possibility of medieval equivalents of Batman haunting the building.

From Certaldo there are trekking, mountain-bike and horse-riding routes around the countryside, organized by Dolce Campagna Antiche Mura. Ask about them at the palazzo or, down in the new town, at the tourist office.

Ten kilometres to the north is Castelfiorentino, where the contrast between old and new is less marked because the hill is lower and there is nothing as distinguished as the Certaldo fortress. The town is notable for its small communal arts centre where fifteenth-century frescoes by Benozzo Gozzoli are hung. This is not often open. The best day seems to be Sunday, when they can be viewed both in the morning and the afternoon – except in August. The church of Santa Verdiana has a jolly, symmetrical, eighteenth-century frontage. According to the Phaidon guide its treasure is a Madonna and Child by Cimabue, few of whose works have been confidently authenticated. The illustration in the book features a particularly large and somewhat sullen child, with one hand pushing into Mary's left cheek immediately below her eye. Mary's hands are very thin, long and horny, as in a Cimabue included in Berenson, but I cannot find a reference anywhere else, nor have I been able to enter the church.

You need not be much of a linguist to appreciate that San Miniato al Tedesco has German associations. This impressive hill town above the lower Arno valley was the seat of the representative of the Holy Roman Empire whose first effective emperor, after Charlemagne, was Otto I in 962. During the time of the preceding unholy Roman empire it had been a military station under Augustus. In the twelfth century, Matilda of Tuscany, a native of the town who had married a Bavarian named Guelph, willed the territory to Rome. She had always been a devout and militant Catholic and had even gone into battle personally on behalf of the pope, but her bequest ignited the Guelph–Ghibelline fracas.

The Holy Roman Empire was back in charge at San Miniato later in the century, which was when Frederick II, Barbarossa's grandson, whose uneasy alliance with the Vatican was followed by rivalry for the same lands, built a great tower. Its successor, restored after World War Two, dominates the landscape today with twin columns reminiscent of

Battersea power station. Below it stands the cathedral incorporating another tower, once part of the fortress, a Museum of Sacred Art, a domed sanctuary, a Franciscan church with attached convent, the bishop's palace and a hotel which was once the residence of the imperial vicars of the Holy Roman Empire. The castle is associated with the tale told by Dante about Frederick II's bad behaviour to his adviser, Piero della Vigna, whom he imprisoned and blinded, driving him to commit suicide here.

The brick frontage of the duomo is decorated with ceramic saucers. The interior is baroque with marbled pillars. The organ pipes are behind the altar with the keyboard far away below and in front of it. There is a tomb to Jacopo Bonaparte Miniat, 'Philosopher, Poet, Historian'. His significance is otherwise shrouded in obscurity. No dates are given.

The Diocesan Museum attached to the cathedral was locked on both occasions we visited San Miniato. A priest in the bishop's palace assured me it was open, but his conviction faltered when another would-be visitor confirmed my finding. At the information office a clerk attempted to phone the custodian but got no reply. I defaced a neat notice on the door, giving the opening times, with the words 'Sempre Chiuso'. The treasures said to be on display include works by Verrocchio, Filippo Lippi and others.

We did gain admission to the Santuario del Crocifisso, a formidable baroque temple erected in thanksgiving for the town being spared the plague, and also to the church of San Francesco whose origins are in the ninth century. It has a hint of Romanesque in its west door, which has been much altered. The interior is light and high, with no columns and the main item of interest is a modern carved wooden pulpit by Razello Lupo. One panel shows St Francis getting the bird in a big way. A cloister with a garden of box hedges and palm trees is attached to the church.

Lying below the cathedral is the Piazza Repubblica, the concave side of which is known as the Palazzo del Seminario where aphorisms and frescoes are emblazoned on the upper part. The lower part was formerly a medieval shopping street and has been nicely restored.

In the rather cramped town, facing a small piazza is the church of San Domenico. It has a strangely patterned brick frontage with a colourful painting on the portico, giving relief to an otherwise drab exterior. Inside, in a chapel close to the altar, are some early frescoes one of which intrigued me. It shows Mary in bed, having given birth, about to receive what looks like a bowl of goldfish. The newly born Jesus is already sitting up and being nursed at a table beside the bed. Next to the church is a three-storeyed cloister in yellow and green. Along the street is the admirably restored Palazzo Grifoni (sixteenth century).

San Miniato has a truffle festival in October. It also has Napoleonic connections. Bonaparte House in the Palazzo Maioli was the

168

home of Filippo, the priest in the family, who was visited by his eminent relative in 1796. But there are those who insist that Napoleon's mainland family came from elsewhere.

Don't visit San Miniato on a Tuesday if you wish to find a parking space near the cathedral. The market takes over the hillside.

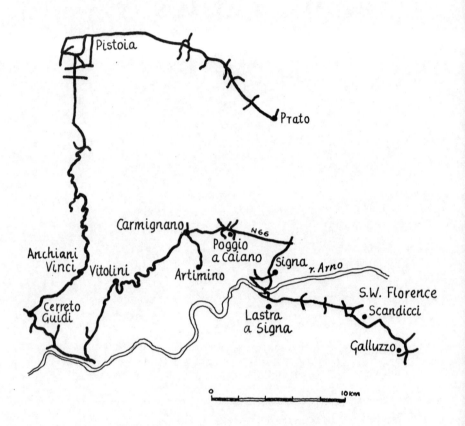

12   South and West of Florence

Galluzzo; Poggio a Caiano; Artimino; Cerreto Guidi; Vinci; Pistoia; Prato

Close to where the Via Cassia is crossed by the Milan–Rome autostrada stands the charterhouse of Florence, Certosa del Galluzzo, on the sacred hill where the fourteenth-century banker, Niccolò Acciaiuoli, had a monastery constructed for the Carthusians. He intended to live in a house in the same complex but died before this could be built.

Little of the original building remains but this is an imposing pile standing above lush greenery concealing, at its centre, a particularly spacious cloister. To see that and the formidable collection of paintings it is worth enduring a guided tour, even though you may have to wait at least half an hour before it starts. The time can be spent in the well-stocked shop where various liqueurs, perfumes, books, crucifixes, postcards, slabs of trappist chocolate and even egg timers are on sale. There is also a bar. We were served by an Eritrean lay brother who enjoyed practising his English. The monks here have had a typically turbulent time over the centuries, having been suppressed on several occasions. The present regime is Cistercian, the Carthusians having left for ever in 1957.

On our first visit I maintained that we could not wait thirty minutes before embarking on the tour and whisked Christopher away. On our second, it was a day without further commitments. We dallied until an African monk was ready to guide us in a party of only four, the other two being a German couple. For the first part of the tour the monk thought we were all Germans and addressed us in Italian; then he overheard something I said to Christopher and asked if he might use English which, of course, the Germans also understood.

According to notes I had made we should have come almost at once to what would have been Acciaiuoli's accommodation, up a long, bare stairway. In the first hall there are five frescoes which I particularly wished to see. Our monk led us instead to a chapel where we admired the choir stalls and marquetry thereon. In the Colloquium next door we were informed that here the monks were permitted to gather once a week to speak, and shown the stained glass of 1560. I tried to relax and told myself we would get to the Pontormos in due course.

We then went to several small cloisters for the use of laymen and, after that, into the big one, familiar from a photograph. Somehow the reality disappointed. It was expansive but not impressive, contributing further to my belief that the camera can indeed lie. The ornamentation of the cloister includes sixty-six busts by Giovanni della Robbia of saints expressing surprise, dismay, apprehension, anguish and other emotions. There are eighteen well-appointed cells, each with a bedroom, living room, bathroom and, at a lower level, a garden. The furnishing is sparse but the accommodation is not cramped. The cells are still in use. (I have stayed in worse hotels.)

We were taken to the charter hall where there is a marble tomb of Bishop Leonardo by Francesco di Giuliano da Sangallo. The prelate lies on a realistically carved pillow, wearing a benign smile. The door to this room has early sixteenth-century carvings by a hermit who took twenty years over the work.

Finally, we saw the refectory, overlarge, I thought, for so small a community. Silence was the rule there for all but one brother who read passages aloud from the Bible at a pulpit near the ceiling.

By then all four of us were wondering when we would be shown the paintings. One of the Germans actually asked. The monk was genuinely contrite. A concert which was to be televised was being set up. If we had come yesterday we could have seen the Pontormos and other paintings; if we came tomorrow, they would be on view. Today it was not possible.

So I can report on the paintings at this Certosa only from illustrations in the guide also on sale in the monastery shop.

The Pontormos, originally in the main cloister, are apparently in a state of extreme decomposition, partly due to humidity, but it should be possible to appreciate something of their quality. Pontormo is categorized by art historians as a mannerist, a term which can be used pejoratively. It would be correct to say of these frescoes that the figures in them are posed; everyone is acting and reacting but that does not make them unacceptable to me. Pontormo's paintings are certainly different from those of many of his contemporaries as we shall see at other places on this itinerary.

At the Certosa, in better condition, is a portrait of Acciaiuoli standing in a workmanlike stance with one hand on a sword, his right arm akimbo, his head in profile. Another canvas portrays the interrupted domesticity of a Carthusian brother, seated in front of a substantial meal, when a cherubic emissary of the Lord appears through the wall, hailing him cheerfully. In the church there is an enormous fresco by one Bernardino Poccetti, of the ascent of St Bruno, who founded the Carthusian

172

Order. It has immense detail, with a vast crowd of priests and congregation gathered round the catafalque of the saint, who is also seen rising upwards through the church. Christ, surrounded by angels, is suspended on a piece of stone in midair, beside the clerestory, receiving him. It is a riveting item of sixteenth-century fantasy, teeming with action.

The town of Galluzzo is now a suburb of Florence. From it runs an enjoyably rural route, along narrow, curving lanes, to Scanducci where there is no need to linger. Go through it to get to Poggio a Caiano and the first Medici villa on this itinerary.

This villa dominates a shabby town, from a low hill, where it is partly counterbalanced by a typical church with an elegantly thin spire. The walls surrounding the villa are heavy and plain, the entrance over cobbles is uninviting. Once past the lodge, where you pay for admission, you are translated from the seediness of the town to a kind of splendour, from which you can imagine the glory departing on dark grey clouds hung with cherubs yearning, if not for retirement, then at least for a fresh pair of wings.

Poggio a Caiano: Villa Medici

The radiance has gone from this hefty item by Giuliano da Sangallo, as commissioned by Lorenzo the Magnificent in 1485. Alright, so it stands in umbrageous grounds with two noble yew trees in the front garden, and down a slope from one side are formal flower beds and a huge hothouse for lemons. Walks trail away from the rear into the woods, giving an impression of endless country, but the villa itself, for all that it has colonnades on four sides, is in a category distinctly inferior to the châteaux of the Loire, English country houses, and castles on the Rhine.

If the Medici had concentrated their riches on fewer second homes of finer quality they would have done better by posterity. However, they provided employment for artisans and artists, and here we have enormous areas of inner wall painted by Andrea del Sarto, Allori and, in one instance, Pontormo. The della Robbias, as always, are in evidence and, as is equally customary in a Medici establishment, there are no signs or notes about anything. One of the numerous foundations based in Italy, or some great museum with funds (if any such nowadays exists) should launch a project to label succinctly, authoritatively, CLEARLY, and in several languages, the paintings, sculptures and bric-à-brac housed in the numerous abodes once owned by the Medici.

This one, at Poggio, concentrates on emphasizing the liaison between Francesco I, Grand Duke of Tuscany, and Bianca Cappello, his second wife and former mistress. Both were poisoned here (1587) presumably by agents of their sometime partners who had already bitten the dust. It is a squalid tale of little interest. The interior of their erstwhile residence, with its murky, crypt-like ground floor, private theatre and vast billiards room, is worth examining for the frescoes, wallpapers and ceilings. I particularly liked a Pontormo, a jolly, arc-shaped painting with a central tondo almost covered by a curtain. It clings tenaciously to the wall without damage from damp, and illustrates the story of the Italian deities, Vertumnus and Pomona. They, as gods, protected gardens, whenever Vertumnus, disguised in some outlandish gear, wasn't pursuing the lady. Here some mild pretence at harvesting is apparent, but the overall impression is of maidens and cherubs provocatively posed on walls and ground. The gods also double as peasants. Are they the two figures with a baleful dog standing between them, or are they getting up to something behind the curtains? It is a painting to prompt curiosity, probably easier to understand if you know your Ovid because it is based on a tale in *Metamorphosis*.

In the dining room, redecorated in the nineteenth century for Vittorio Emmanuele II, there is a group of figures on the ceiling, including the first Cosimo, undoubtedly based on the Pontormo portrait in the Uffizi. The robe he wears is almost exactly the same colour but perhaps, in the manner of some royalty, he always wore that. Most of the frescoes are in

174

delicate pastel shades.

The exterior of the house, to be fair, is not unhandsome. A double staircase leads to the first-floor portico which has a frieze in the della Robbia style. A copy of it is displayed in a room close to the royal bedchamber. Here you can study the detail, such as the baby Jove being suckled by a goat, Adam and Eve, and some beehives.

Most of the ceilings are painted, or rather overpainted. The one in the billiards room contrives to look like a vine in early growth. In the room where Blanca Cappello died a stone staircase mysteriously enters part of it, then disappears into an adjoining chamber. Poggio has its surprises.

Go on to Artimino, where another smaller Medici pad of the sixteenth century is set amidst rolling hills, far from small-town squalor. The villa was built by Buontalenti in 1594 for the Grand Duke Ferdinando I who, like most of his kind, had to have something new. Hand-me-downs were not the fashion. The siting is marvellous and the actual villa is on the Adam scale, undoubtedly verging on the palatial but small enough to be homely, given the odd touch of eccentricity. This is achieved by a roof covered in decorated chimneys bearing cowls topped by dolls'-house-style structures. The house, now occupied by the Gruppa Zurigo, has otherwise little to offer apart from an outside baronial staircase and a small archaeological museum run by the Comune di Carmignano, the town at the foot of the hill.

Outside the gates is a hotel where it must be peaceful to stay; on a neighbouring hillside – a splendid, straight, tree-lined avenue between them – is a village with a church far below it in a cluster of conifers. The church was partly constructed from the remains of Etruscan buildings and dates from 1107.

At Carmignano there is a fine Visitation, by Pontormo, in the chapel of San Michele. Mary and her cousin Elizabeth (mother of John the Baptist) greet each other affectionately in the presence of two other women who stare unblinkingly past them.

There is yet another Medici homestead, in this case their idea of a mere hunting lodge, at Cerreto Guidi, north of Empoli, although I doubt it is worth a detour unless you have a lot of time to spare. It is reached through winding country roads between vineyards. It calls itself a villa, and was also built by Buontalenti, in this case to the order of Cosimo I. Of course, it is larger than a hunting lodge and, indeed, roomy enough for a family of six or eight, but there is nothing arrogant or grandiose about it. The chief attraction (and annoyance) is a picture gallery of Medici portraits, including wives and offspring. Most of them, surprise, surprise, are not captioned, and there is little available information about them. One that is identifiable is of Paolo Orsini, who murdered his wife Isabella when he discovered she had been unfaithful. The Medici believed in keeping their skeletons out of the cupboard. Another, which is named, is one of Cosimo I. Many are very good portraits indeed. There is a pleasant small garden behind the villa which crowns the hill where a castle once stood. The prosperous wine town clusters around it.

If you decide to ignore Cerreto, go straight to Vinci, approaching it through heavenly, quintessential Tuscan countryside, all olives, vines, cypresses. Leonardo wasn't actually born here but the town has adopted him. The great man was the illegitimate son of a Florentine notary, San Pietro, who had property in Anchiano, about three kilometres uphill to the north. There a maidservant gave birth to one of the world's foremost geniuses. The event may, or may not, have taken place in the two-roomed cottage hung with souvenirs and linked with other buildings. There is a simple brick memorial to Leonardo and a bust by Francesco Wildt (1939), as well as a *table d'orientation* pointing to those places most associated with the man: Florence, Rome, Venice, Mantua, Milan, Amboise. On the walls are quotes from panegyrics by Goethe, Delacroix, Berenson, Kenneth Clark, etc. Beside the door is an emblem said to be the coat of arms of the Pietro family. Somehow it doesn't quite all ring true but it is a lovely, peaceful place.

The official brochure for Vinci names it 'Leonardo's Home Town'. At least he was baptized here in the church of Santa Croce and the place has certainly become his monument. The ancient castle of the Counts Guidi houses the Museo Vinciano, complete with Biblioteca Leonardo, and soon there will be another celebrating the great man as a painter. Inevitably, there are shops, cafés, hotels bearing his name and the library within the castle is also a centre for study and research on his life and works.

The museum, opened in 1953, has a collection of fascinating models made from drawings in Leonardo's notebooks. They include a flying machine, an early helicopter, devices for measuring humidity and the force of wind, and quickly constructable bridges for military use. In the room where the flying machine has been assembled, partly suspended from the ceiling, partly on the floor, there is a della Robbia-style frieze with a holy bambino who seems to be signalling approval of the invention. So much for the old lady who asked, if God intended us to fly, why did he give us the railways? I didn't notice a locomotive but there are an auto-cart, a paddle boat and all manner of scientific instruments, as well as drawings.

Vinci, apart from the Leonardo connection, is a charming hillside town with Etruscan and Roman associations. Florence annexed it in 1254 and it became a frontier post which was attacked in the next century by Pisa, using a force including the English mercenary, Sir John Hawkwood. The surrounding country is exquisite. Enjoy it as you drive slowly up and over Monte Albano to reach Pistoia.

Medieval Pistoia, rebuilt after total destruction at the hands of the Longobards in AD 400, became a free city whose status was challenged by both Florence and Lucca. Florence, inevitably, won. The previously walled city is now surrounded by industrial suburbs enclosing the irregularly shaped central piazza, one of the best in all Tuscany, which has withstood the troubles of many centuries. You can park fairly close to it on wasteland that once held factories. On a baking June day, clad as for the beach, in shirt, shorts and little else, we were greeted by a cheerful woman attendant encased in a steel ticket office situated in full sunlight. We could park all day, she said, for 3000 lire but must pay in advance. Her English was good, so was the omen. As we made for the centro storico I noted two fragments of wall, one opposite a small hotel on a corner boldly signed HOTEL PICCOLO RITZ.

Soon, on our right, we came to a long expanse of Pisan black-and-white ecclesiastical architecture adorned with plenty of blind columns on two levels of the nave. This is the church of San Giovanni Fuorcivitas. It was once attached by an archway to the neighbouring oratory – also in licorice allsort – now deconsecrated and harbouring a bar beneath a finely vaulted roof. The interior of San Giovanni is a nondescript high barn with standard stained glass. There is a thirteenth-century altar by a pupil of Nicola Pisano, a Visitation by Luca della Robbia and a few fading frescoes, as well as a Virgin by Taddeo Gaddi. I derived more visual satisfaction from the five-storey merchant's house, with top-level open loggia, facing the church. It is one of many that proudly line Pistoian streets, although not all of them are authentically Renaissance. One, next to the bishop's palace, has a bold frieze around its midriff suggestive of age, but dates only from 1898.

Next to the house facing San Giovanni is an alley, Via del Cacio, leading to the Piazza della Sala where there is a cheerful fruit and veg market with haphazardly placed stalls. Freshly painted high houses rise above it; in its midst is a well with a sculpted crouching lion and cubs. Another lane leads to the noble centre-piece, the Piazza del Duomo, which is, in effect, also the Piazza Pretorio. Every building in this geometrical conundrum of a square is magnificent in its own way. They include the cathedral, campanile, bishop's palace, governor's palace, the baptistery, the town hall, several banks and a tower commemorating a Roman conspirator who was tracked down and slaughtered here. And if that is not sufficient, the flagstones are dotted with sculptures by Marino Marini. Wherever you look the eye is carried up, down, along, to a new focal point of excitement.

177

Pistoia: duomo

Let us move gently about this piazza starting at the fourteenth-century Palazzo Pretorio with its great Gothic windows and a courtyard, smothered in plaques, where judges sat in session on a stone bench and where, high on a stuccoed wall of fairly modern appearance, a della Robbia (I don't know which one) tondo happily blends with its surroundings, as does the palace as a whole. This surely is good. Not everything can be preserved but what is new can be appropriate without jarring.

To the right of the old town hall is the octagonal baptistery by Andrea Pisano. It has an immensely high dome beneath which stands a giant font while, over the doorway beneath the tympanum, are bas-reliefs of the life of St John including the inevitable appearance of Salome serving up his head on a platter. Much of the baptistery is marbled, in the prevailing dark green and white.

178

Cross to the bishop's palace (Palazzo dei Vescovi) where there is an information office, and also the entrance to the cathedral museum, said to be rich in church vestments and silver plate, in addition to items of Roman wall and Etruscan burial tombs which you may, or may not, wish to compare with those you have seen in a lot of other museums. I was relieved to find it closed for lunch and compensated for what I had lost by admiring the façade of the palace, which is all elegance, as it were, from the waist upwards. There is a central layer of Gothic arches divided by uprights decorated with sculpture, partly concealing a loggia and, above that, a bland tier of mullioned windows. But at ground level, once it has got over being an information office, it becomes a bank partly concealed by odd-shaped pieces of Pisan licorice allsort. The effect of the whole façade I can only liken to the product of a mating between a bird of refined plumage and a magpie.

Between the palace and the campanile (another architectural hybrid warranting long study) is the comparatively diminutive cathedral looking as though it has been lowered gingerly into the available space with no more than a millimetre to spare. It is not to be taken seriously in an ecclesiastical or architectural sense; it is fun and should be enjoyed. There are three arches on spindly columns either side of the narrow entrance that is glorified by an Andrea della Robbia rounded pediment. The pillars protrude from a thin arcade under a tiled roof, above which are two tiers of blind loggias and a triangular pediment with a tiny cross. From the outside, Pistoia cathedral is the equivalent of a large parish church. Inside, it goes on and on, below a fairly simple timbered ceiling with abstract designs. The nave is wide and flanked by decorated, though not historiated, columns. The altar of the main church glitters, so do the painted walls and dome above them. There is an extensive crypt at two levels, one with carved sarcophagi.

Just inside the della Robbia door, facing the font, is an elaborate carving illustrating the life of St John the Baptist, with Salome and her grim offering served up again. Then there is the much revered chapel of San Jacopo, behind bars hindering appreciation of the silver altar. This intricate work includes more than six hundred figures carved over three centuries by successions of silversmiths. It portrays the life of Jesus as well as St James, but is named for the latter. (Ask for the sacristan, who may light it for you and even unlock the chapel doors.)

The cathedral, called San Zeno after an African who became bishop of Verona and was an admired orator, is the product of many periods on the site of an early church that was burned down in the twelfth century. The red-brick lower part of the tower probably survived the conflagration. Above that it is Pisan in style for three tiers, before giving way to a pointed turret, lantern, and bell tower of much later date.

Pass along the outside of the cathedral nave from the back of the campanile to reach the Palazzo del Comune (mostly fourteenth century). This is both town hall and civic museum, concealed behind a deep colonnade fronted by five open arches. The museum, on three floors, displays a great range of Tuscan and Umbrian paintings from the thirteenth to the sixteenth centuries.

Between the heavily imposing sedate palazzo and what is known as the Catiline Tower is a lower building with tables outside, where you may sit and have a drink. It is called a café and has no cultural or historical significance. Placed there, you can relax and let your eyes roam over the piazza, noting to your right two bland yellow palaces immaculately maintained. They are banks. Facing the far end of the last one, on a corner site, is a typical house with first-floor stone balcony. Above it seems to be another balcony. Is it trompe l'oeil, or not? You decide.

As you leave the piazza, pass the medieval tower (commemorating Lucius Catilina, conspirator against the Roman state who perished here after being pursued by those whom he sought to topple) to reach the enchantingly decorated Ospedale del Ceppo where Giovanni della Robbia was allowed to let rip on the portico above the arcaded entrance. The figures on this frieze, set against a typically rich blue background, are engaged in acts of mercy towards the needy. Some appear jolly in their good works, others severe. The arches of this pretty loggia also bear six tondi from the same workshop which have the usual preponderance of bright fruit around their borders. If all the della Robbias in Tuscany were to fade or be removed, how they would be missed. At times their ubiquity can be irksome but I wouldn't be without them.

The hospital, founded in 1277, is now a pre-natal clinic and administrative offices. A few blocks away is the church of Sant'Andrea, traces of which go back to the eighth century, I am told, but I cannot advise which particular sections they are, or even if they are above ground. In any case, despite the west frontage dressed in green and white marble, and the simple Romanesque nave with a carved wooden ceiling, I have eyes for only one object in Sant'Andrea, and that is the superb stone pulpit by Giovanni Pisano. It is hexagonal with five marble panels representing the Annunciation and Nativity (together on one), the Adoration of the Magi, the Crucifixion, the Massacre of the Innocents and the Day of Judgement. The astonishing craftsmanship which breathed life into the often minute figures led me to feed 500-lire coins into the lighting system until my companion had run out of them. This is a work of thrilling genius. The sixth side of the pulpit was for access, although the steps are no longer there. A rather unwieldy item of church furnishing, it is transformed into high art by the intensity of Pisano's work, which is supported on seven dark-red marble pillars. Two of them stand on lions lying on lesser beasts, one is held up by birds, and one by an ancient bearded man. The other three reach to the floor unencumbered. Compare the carving of the beasts with that on the panels above.

A church in total contrast to Sant'Andrea is that of the Madonna dell'Umiltà, a round, domed oratory reached through an oblong sacristy. Outside, all crude, unadorned brickwork, inside it is impeccably maintained early baroque, suggesting anything but humility. A notice claims it as the most beautiful church in Pistoia. The style of the dome is Brunelleschi's but it is, of course, much later and was actually the work of a local carpenter/architect named Ventura Vitoni who left Vasari to complete it. The original plan was by Giuliano da Sangallo.

There are many other churches in Pistoia, including the deconsecrated Chiesa del Tau, with fourteenth-century frescoes, next to the palace of the same name, now the Fondazio Marino Marini. There is also San Bartolomeo in Panzano. Panzano means marsh and that is where the original eighth-century abbey church was built, outside the walls of the city. It sounds perverse, but perhaps there was no alternative terrain at the time. The later building, much of it extant, is twelfth-century Pisan, topped by seventeenth-century work of no great moment. You may come across it as you wander through this lovable, prosperous town where so much delights the eye.

Midway between Pistoia and Florence, most of it to the west of the river Bisenzio, lies Prato, now one of the most highly populated cities of central Italy. For many centuries it has been associated with the textile industry and a foremost citizen was Francesco Datini (1330–1410), a merchant and a banker, who may have invented bills of exchange. He left a wealth of documentation of his business dealings which enabled Iris Origo to write his biography, *The Merchant of Prato*, giving valuable insight into trading methods pertaining in the period immediately before the Renaissance. Datini was also a benefactor to his city, leaving much of his wealth to the poor partly because he had no legitimate children and partly because his friend and notary urged him to cease thinking so much of worldly things and attend to his immortal soul. He is commemorated in a statue in the small Piazza del Comune and in his palace in the Via Rinaldesca, where his archives are kept.

Better known than Datini are the painters Filippo and Filippino Lippi, father and son. The son was born in Prato in 1457. His mother was a nun in the convent where his father was chaplain. Lippi senior (Filippo) entered the ministry as a boy, became a slave in Africa after being captured by pirates on the high seas, gained his release by exploiting his talent as an artist, never took the laws of the church seriously and finally married his nun with the permission of the pope. The works of father and son are well represented in Prato.

The central square, Piazza del Comune, is ludicrously confined for the magnitude of the buildings enclosing it, whereas the Piazza del Duomo rambles amorphously and is distinguished only by the cathedral itself which enjoys a unique feature in a rounded, open-air pulpit by Michelozzo, with sculpted decorations by Donatello. From it is displayed, on certain high feast days of the church, the holy girdle believed by some to have been given to Doubting Thomas the Apostle by the Virgin Mary herself. It came here in the twelfth century from Jerusalem, brought by a Prato man who had been given it as part of his Palestinian wife's dowry. The wife died on the journey home and the grieving man kept the girdle hidden, only to be found out by interfering angels who disturbed his bed under which it was kept. To get a good night's sleep he handed it over to the cathedral. As a story, apart from credibility, it lacks narrative compulsion, but in the Middle Ages the church liked to propagate such miraculous tales and they were believed. For most of the time the girdle is kept locked in a chapel to which there are only two keys. It lies behind formidable iron railings which prevent not only entry but also a clear view of the frescoes by Agnolo Gaddi (late fourteenth century). There are others, however, by Filippo Lippi, in the choir.

Beside the black-columned nave are many chapels and a stone pulpit by Mino da Fiesole and Antonio Rossellino (late fifteenth century). The interior is dark and I left with some relief to go to the adjoining museum, where there is an ancient crypt with pre-Christian flooring, carved sarcophagi and frescoes, some of them faded. At ground level are two small chambers off a half-cloister. Here may be found the originals of the Donatello adornments for the exterior pulpit. There is also a Filippo Lippi of St Jerome who led the team which translated the Bible from Hebrew and Greek into Latin. It is a fine painting with disciples and handicapped people mourning Jerome's death and, above them, saints climbing steep hills, while others ascend even higher, giving an impression of lively dancing, as they swirl aloft enhanced by their haloes. In contrast, there is a forbidding angel in flight by Carlo Dolci, a seventeenth-century Florentine. The angel has expressive hands but that is all.

At the Civic Museum, a partly Gothic, partly Renaissance palace, with appealing stonework, incorporating some Roman bricks and a baroque façade bell tower, you are instantly into the Mother and Child syndrome. There is no escaping it on either floor, although the subject is given variety by a Filippino Lippi featuring a bevy of disarming cherubs and another by his father, showing a doleful Mary with equally cast-down

Prato: duomo

saints at either side of her. A clutch of midget-sized worshippers are at her feet and one of them, we are told, resembles Francesco Datini. The subject is also treated in bas-relief sculpture by Benedetto da Maiano, and that I preferred to the others. Both mother and child look loving and beautiful, and the Christ is a real baby. Best of all exhibits is an unsigned nymph kneeling on a pedestal, in the centre of a room.

Datini's personal palace may be seen in the Via Rinaldesca. It was here, almost five hundred years after the merchant's death, that the enormous cache of documents relating to his life and work was found stashed away under a staircase. They are now kept elsewhere in the palace and may be inspected by scholars. The building is extremely well preserved and the exterior is almost overwhelming, with its emblems, painted walls, Gothic-arched loggia and grilled windows at ground level. It positively oozes wealth. Nearby in the Via Luigi Pecci is a smaller Renaissance house which has become a museum of contemporary art.

Prato has a Castello dell'Imperatore built by the Emperor Frederick II in the mid thirteenth century. It is like a large toy, with four great walls intact and a fitted lawn inside them. Next to it is the church of Santa Maria delle Carceri, started by Giuliano da Sangallo but never completed. Other churches of note in the city are San Francesco, where Datini is buried, and San Domenico, which has a fifteenth-century cloister. I didn't visit either because they were closed. Instead I went to the Piazza Il Mercatali where the stretching and dyeing of cloth was done in the Middle Ages. Here I admired the differing shades of cream and yellow on the houses and hotels. Then I wandered vaguely, hoping to come across the Piazza San Marco, where there is said to be a Henry Moore, and keeping half an eye open for the Museum of Tapestry. I failed to find either but enjoyed noting odd names on shop fronts, such as, REPLAY COUNTRY STORE (blue jeans, overalls, classy shirts), MAGIC MOMENTS (I'm not sure what they were) and THE END (fashion, of course).

Prato: Palazzo Pretorio, housing the Civic Museum

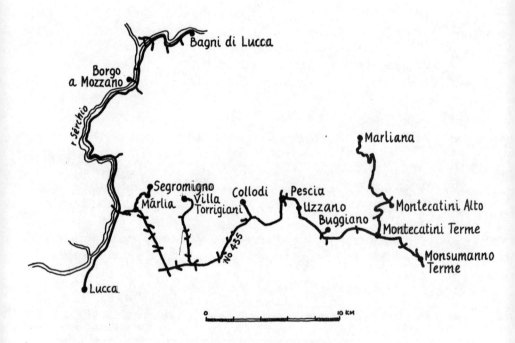

13   Lucca and Environs

Monsummano Terme; Montecatini Terme e Alto; Pescia; Collodi; Villa Mansi;
Villa Torrigiani; Bagni di Lucca; Borgo a Mozzano; Lucca

West of Pistoia, you are soon into spa country with
Monsummano Terme and Montecatini Terme on opposite sides of the
autostrada. Monsummano, to the south, specializes in respiratory disor-
ders, gout and arthritis. For treatment it is necessary to descend the bowels
of the earth into a deep cave with stalactites and stalagmites. Here, steam
pours from the rockface or rises from the water – I am not sure which
because it is an experience I have avoided – and confers benefits partly
derived from sweating in extreme heat.

Taking the cure is popular with Italians, who go on family holi-
days whether or not they are ill to enjoy the amenities of a spa in luxurious
surroundings.

Montecatini Terme, on the north of the motorway, has been a
health resort since the fourteenth century, and long before that the curative
properties in its waters were known to the Romans. It is now on the international circuit, ranking with the like of Baden-Baden. All the attendant
services are here – golf courses, swimming pools and, in this instance, a
museum of modern art. The latter is in the Viale Diaz, where you can take
time off from the Renaissance to admire a fresco by Annigoni, if you can
find the gallery. I drove around for a while in a traffic jam looking for it,
then chanced upon the road to Montecatini Alto and took that. It can also
be reached by funicular, which is probably a better bet because parking
space at the top is extremely limited.

Walk to the Piazza Giuseppe Giusti, named after a poet who
was born here, and whose house you will pass when you pant up to the
church. The piazza has several cafés in a tranquil setting on a comparatively gentle gradient. At the top end is the preposterously pretentious theatre,
battlemented, turreted, a piccolo castle exuding innate theatricality. It is
now a bar and pizzeria.

It is a gruelling haul up to the church, where terrible things
have been done to a basically Romanesque building. This is not at first
apparent when you pass an enormous free-standing campanile,

187

complemented by a lesser building which was the keep of the castle. But, once inside, you will notice historiated capitals on columns mostly concealed beneath crude baroque pillars erected around them. Apart from this atrocity there is nothing worth remarking. Outside, once more, observe the ancient brickwork of the nave from a path round the fortifications where you should look out for a cypress that has grown out of the defensive wall. Outwards, then upwards, because, having broken through the stone laterally and literally, it has righted itself to a truly straight and proud position.

There are two hills at Montecatini Alto. The other is equally steep and bears a squat clock tower, an anonymous chapel, a hotel and houses, from one of which, to my delight, came the sound of Puccini on hi-fi. A tenor belted out arias into the warm, early evening air, joined by a householder who appeared on his balcony and sang quite unselfconsciously. (Perhaps he had been a butcher's boy in his day? See p. 19.)

Should you still be hankering after views, go up into the Pistoian hills, from Montecatini to Marliana, on what one writer has named 'a breath-taking, hair-raising drive'. There is a campanile to be climbed, the ruins of a castle and an incomparable panorama of much of northern Tuscany.

Pescia, a town renowned for its daily flower market and biennial horticultural exhibitions, is a calmer experience. It can be reached directly, from Montecatini through an eighteenth-century gateway displaying the Medici arms, or via the little hill town of Uzzano, after perhaps taking a short detour to another village, Buggiano. Here there is an attractive Palazzo del Podestà with well-preserved frescoes, massive oak beams and a generous collection of plaques. No need to drive up and into Uzzano; the view from below tells all.

Pescia lies beside the river of the same name. On the right bank is the wide Piazza Mazzini, a wonky parallelogram where the Saturday market is held. There are tall terraces of buildings of varying heights, but the focal point is the twelfth-century Palazzo dei Vicari, filling most of the top end and one corner. It has a high, noble tower, a stone Madonna and Child and a variety of medallions. At the opposite end is one of the smallest churches I have encountered, the Madonna of the Piazza. It is all vestibule, with a wooden ceiling. Elderly crones slipped in and out of it, like mice.

The governor's palace is higher up the hillside and now holds a permanent collection of early nineteenth-century plaster casts, called gipsoteca, by Libero Andreotti. He was a local sculptor. Nearby is the civic museum known as the Magnani Collection, after another worthy citizen. The atmosphere is dingy, the presentation orderly. Two curators rose eagerly to greet us and one of them indicated what he claimed was a

Giotto. One of the few paintings labelled, it bore the artist's name: 'The Master of St Cecilia'. There are also what are described as two Dürers. We were sceptical about them, too. There are several rooms with books, rifles, portraits, the robe and cape of a magistrate and a spinet on which stands a bust of the Pescian composer, Giovanni Pacini.

Across the river is the cathedral, a ninth-century ex-parish church of which the medieval tower remains. The best of the many paintings is a 20C. portrait of Sant'Allucia da Pescia by Romano Stefanelli. It is hung above a gold-rimmed casket containing the skull and bones of the saint. Up river from this undistinguished duomo is the church of San Francesco with a series of frescoes by Bonaventura Berlinghieri which are thought to be the earliest portrayals of St Francis. In another nearby church, Sant'Antonio Abate, there is a thirteenth-century wooden Deposition of some quality and, above the altar, a picture of Pescia as a walled city. Possibly it was more interesting when it was like that.

In the neighbouring valley is Collodi, famed for its Pinocchio associations. Carlo Lorenzini took as nom-de-plume the name of the village and wrote the popular story about the wooden puppet who came to life, in the kitchen of the Villa Garzoni where his father was employed. His masterpiece is celebrated permanently in the Parco di Pinocchio which is laid out with statues of characters from the book and mosaics illustrating the story by Venturino Venturi. Follow a trail which will take you into the cavernous jaws of a shark and provide other shock therapies. Adult tastes are catered for in the spectacular Garzoni Gardens, rising sumptuously in terraces beside the villa, into a thickly wooded hillside. They are hard work but worth the effort. The villa, when we visited it in 1986, was run down, although we were allowed to wander in unsupervised. The kitchens were particularly interesting and, against the rules, I photographed the crumbling plasterwork of a still-occupied wing. It had a beautiful convex façade broken by a protruding bay, below a short, octagonal clock tower with lantern, ironwork weather vane and cross. In 1997 the villa was firmly closed for restoration.

Between Pescia and Lucca, on the hills to the north of the road, are several villas which, for a change, do not have Medici connections. The gardens and grounds of at least three of them are open to the public but only two of the houses may be visited. The best, of those I saw, is the Villa Mansi at Segromigno, where the gardens are informal in the English fashion. There are flower beds backed by avenues of high hedges, a thick bamboo wood at one end is bordered by palm trees and a large pond with stone balustrades is fed by a stream running from a small garden dedicated to the dog. There are many paths and walks, a great deal of sculpture dotted amongst them, and a stunning first view of the house as you emerge from a copse by a syringa tree.

There, across a sweep of lawn, it stands, elegantly symmetrical, with a monumental staircase to the deep piano nobile behind three arches. There is statuary on the frontage at every level, in every niche, and the colour is uniform yellow and brown. Stone dogs guard the tops of the staircase and there are busts, as well as statues, at the back of the loggia where two little balconies appear at mezzanine level. It is unashamedly theatrical.

The decoration of the central hall is flamboyant, covering all available space with indifferent paintings but in three at least of the smaller chambers the murals are delightful and often humorous. They are not crowded, having more white background than detail, but that detail is capricious and singular. In one room there is a circus motif with a man, standing upon an elephant's back, holding a parrot. There are miniatures and strange semi-human figures, mermaids and men with serpentine legs. It must have been fun lying in bed observing them.

Not far away, by the village of Camigliano, is a more ornate version of Mansi, the Villa Torrigiani. This much-converted manor house looks its best from the grand avenue of cypresses, some very old, before you reach the gateway. It still looks good from just inside the wall, where you pay your 12,000 lire. You must not approach it directly across the spacious lawn but come upon it, up a gravel drive, from the side. Then it looks faintly ridiculous in close-up with a prodigious number of statues, on balconies, in niches, on pedestals, reaching towards the roof, *on* the roof ... You expect to see them hanging from the windows, clinging to the parapet. It is unrestrained and the colour of the frontage is also worrying. The yellow is wrong and doesn't suit the shades of grey and brown, or the several styles of brick and stone. Yet it is eye-catching and, in its way, impressive, although the print of how it was before a major face-lift in the seventeenth-century makes one yearn for what has been lost.

The interior – guided tour – covers the entire ground floor, starting and concluding in the great central chamber where the decorations set the tone for the whole. The frescoes, in pastel shades, are a pleasure but pictorially the portraits and photographs of the various owners are of greater interest. The Santini family, which married into the Torrigiani, has owned it for at least three centuries and resisted pressure from Napoleon's sister, when she was Grand Duchess of Lucca, to hand it over to her. Nonetheless, Bonaparte slept here and you are shown not only the room, but the bed. The counterpane is prettily woven with camellias, from which the village derives its name. There are several bedrooms on this lower floor because it was cooler here in summer than up above. Some beds have elaborate awnings not just for the sake of pandering to aristocratic grandeur but to stop insects falling from the ceiling on to the sleepers.

190

The estate was designed by LeNôtre in the fifteenth century, but altered when the fashion for English gardens came in. There are beds and beds of marigolds, salvias, geraniums, a fish pond, a grotto dei venti with dome and cupola, statues to Bacchus and Eolo and hidden water jets. Also two prominent notices warning of the dangers inherent in the stone steps and deep pond.

The setting, against another great sweep of grass and the encroaching foothills of the Apennines, is very satisfying.

Go on to the Villa Reale, close to Marlia, and badly signed, only if you can spare the time. The seventeenth-century house, not open to the public, is plain, but in the gardens is a delectable small open-air theatre made of yew trees and bushes with stage, wings, stalls, balconies, footlights, podium. Upstage stand three terracotta figures from the commedia dell'arte. Paganini once performed here and occasional concerts are still given. Below it, in what could be termed the 'foyer', is one of several fountains using 'natural pressure'. There is also a lemon garden with ornamental lake and swans.

Lucca, where this itinerary ends, lies beside the River Serchio on what was formerly marshland ('luk' in ancient Ligurian). Up the valley are numerous small farming communities, some perched on land that is never naturally flat for more than a few metres. We stayed once at a converted farmhouse hemmed in by hills with a few clearings large enough for the odd uneven meadow. The contours of the land, for miles around, change abruptly and often. Driving to and from it, one moment we would find ourselves on a narrow ridge, incredibly accommodating a small bar with shop attached, the next we would be descending, by sharp bends, into small, dense woods. Then we would come upon an unmarked crossroads, perhaps flanked by a few vines, while around the corner would be a sprawling, undulating olive grove. Once we walked through farmyards and fields down towards the river, passing isolated homesteads with ferociously barking dogs, tethered, mercifully. Then we heard birdsong. That was comforting until we saw from whence it came. On the wall of the farmhouse next to ours, in mingy little cages, birds were clawing the wire frames, singing their hearts out for freedom.

It can be idyllic staying in the hills around Lucca. I think of another super holiday home with every luxury, two miles up a mountainside and with a view of the Arno basin around Pisa, but others proved acceptable only in small doses. Rusticity can be a refreshing change, but not without hot and cold running water, constant electricity and a well-equipped kitchen. I am not the stuff of which explorers are made. The comfort of a good hotel, with room service, is bliss after roughing it in a converted three-hundred-year-old barn.

In the nineteenth century you would have found luxury at Bagni di Lucca, 27 kilometres up the Serchio. The lower part of this now unfashionable spa is shrouded in heavily wooded riparian territory, more than a mite gloomy, but the upper part, on an escarpment above the river, boasts a theatre and restaurants, and allows daylight to penetrate it.

Bagni di Lucca had a brief heyday as a spa in the nineteenth century and its healing waters had been known about since the Middle Ages. Byron, Shelley, Elizabeth Barrett Browning came here for the cure, but none was a good advert. Seated at an alfresco table in a restaurant in the upper part, in 1991, it was not difficult to understand why the English had found it an agreeable watering place. It is still partly in business, with steam-vapour grottoes operational, and it is almost certainly cheaper than Monsummano Terme.

Downstream is Borgo a Mozzano, remarkable for its Devil's Bridge of the twelfth century, or earlier, a magical construction with one exquisitely curving high arch centrally poised, and several lower ones of varying spans. It is exceptionally beautiful in this setting in a valley of upper Tuscany, silhouetted against the dark hills.

Lucca has an illustrious but less tempestuous history than most Tuscan cities, a quality that becomes apparent when, on arrival, you promenade gently round the Passeggiata delle Mura, and that should be your immediate objective. This wide outer wall above grassy slopes intended for the moat was not completed until the late seventeenth century and has never been used in active defence, although, in 1822, its presence prevented serious flooding. Beyond it is a ring road, which keeps the worst of the traffic out of the centre, and well within it was the Roman wall once enclosing the small ancient city.

The walk should be a tranquil experience – the distance is about four kilometres – although you may encounter a vehicle or two at certain points. The object of it is to familiarize yourself with the chief landmarks and get the feel of Lucca. You will pick out the duomo, the churches of San Michele and San Frediano, the tower of the Casa di Guinigi, the Palazzo Pfanner, the National Museum, not to mention the coach terminal, and it is worth knowing where that is. The walk is quite the most pleasant introduction possible to a city bursting with life and interest and, moreover, one that can be enjoyed unfrenetically. The unused defence system was deliberately transformed into something resembling parkland in the last century, so, where the cannons once stood, you can spread out a picnic on genuine green belt between old Lucca and newer suburbs.

There is ample parking space outside the walls and once you are down in the city you can walk without fear of being mown down –

192

except by bicycles. About them you just have to relax, hoping that the riders' skills in person-avoidance prevail.

In Lucca there is much to see at various levels of interest. Enter at the Piazza Santa Maria (historically there were four gateways, now there are five) and filter into the Via Fillungo through a couple of narrow alleys. Immediately you are confronted by the choice between catching up on your culture and window shopping. Soon, on your left, there is an opening leading to the oval area, bordered by houses, on the actual site of the Roman amphitheatre. The lane by which you enter it may be the very passage through which lions, or gladiators, came into the arena. The satisfaction of being here now is still that of a spectator, but the scene is peaceful and were you the emperor your task would be to give thumbs up to the architecture which, outwardly at least, is urban domestic at its best. The individual units of the curving terraces are of varying heights but none is above five storeys. The roofscape is a mixture of penthouses, chimneys, television aerials, with red tiles ruling over all. The frontages are painted in pastel shades, one or two need replastering. The elliptical shape is that of the original arena.

Lucca: Piazza dell'Anfiteatro

The Roman colony was founded in about 180 BC, more than a century before Julius Caesar, Pompey and Crassus, the triumvirate who ruled for five years, met here. Caesar saw Pompey off to Spain and Crassus to Syria, himself retaining the consulship of Gaul which was the nearest of the three to Rome. As we know, that did not finally prevent a clash between Pompey and himself.

Off the Fillungo, on the opposite side, is an exit which widens to include the frontage of San Frediano, a church which faces the wrong way, by the usual Christian practice, because what you would imagine is the west door is, in fact, the east. St Frediano was bishop of Lucca in the sixth century. He built the first church here and was canonized, not for that labour but for damming the River Serchio. The present church succeeded his in the twelfth century and the Byzantine-style mosaic of the Ascension on the wall above the east door dates from then. It is rather gaudy and in no way prepares you for the two greatest churches of Lucca. San Frediano is utterly different in appearance from them because it is not built in Pisan-Romanesque. Stone used on the façade, and inside for columns, probably came from the dismantled amphitheatre. In one side chapel there is a carved stone triptych of the Madonna and Child by Jacopo della Quercia; in another there are frescoes by Amico Aspertini, one of them telling the story of how the Volto Santo came to Lucca. (More about that when we get to the cathedral.) The twelfth-century Romanesque font has the life of Moses sculpted on its sides. From the interior rises an elaborate centrepiece like a wedding cake prized apart by a gallery of pillars.

The bell tower has a feature occurring elsewhere in Lucca. The openings increase in number with the height, so the bottom has a single aperture for one archer, while at the top (sixth) level there are four mullioned spaces and above that the tower is battlemented. The apse of the church approximates more to Pisan-Romanesque, with a first tier of columns and blind arches.

Near the church, best seen from the Passeggiata, is the Palazzo Pfanner with high loggias at two levels and a garden strewn with statuary. The building was begun in the late seventeenth century for the Moriconi family, merchants who sold it to the Contronis, who enlarged it and kept it in the family until 1860, when it was bought by a Swiss brewer, Felice Pfanner. His descendants are still the owners. You are permitted to climb the partly covered grand staircase to the first floor but you may not go inside. Admission is chiefly to the garden where the main feature is an avenue, bordered by sculpted figures of gods and goddesses, ending at a worn wooden gate under the wall of the Passeggiata. On either side of this gate are two more statues, one of them of a goddess who is either about to blow out her own brains, or is applying a hair dryer to her head. The

194

avenue is interrupted by a circular fountain with more statuary.

Return to the cyclist perils of the Fillungo. Near the end, on the left, are the Torre Civica delle Ore, a handsome thirteenth-century clock tower, rising from the street front, and the deconsecrated Romanesque church of San Cristoforo, where a rose window causes colourful lighting effects.

At the end of the Fillungo turn right into the Piazza San Michele and settle yourself at a café to enjoy, at leisure, its stunning church.

The façade of San Michele in Foro is one of the most arresting architectural sights in all Tuscany. It is entirely formal, yet totally exuberant with only one noticeable deviation from the strictest symmetry. (That is a corner statue of the Virgin, with golden spikes.) It contains its Romanesque simplicity in a riot of decorated columns above which are friezes, mostly of monsters or more benign animals. On the capitals are beasts, heads of saints and soldiers, and abstract emblems. The columns are by no means uniform but conform to a scheme. Some are plain, some have sculpted figures, others have vivid patterns in their marble. There are four tiers of them above the strikingly high, plain, arcaded ground level, which has three doorways. The second tier slopes with the roof of the nave; the two above it are only seven columns wide and topped by a figure of St Michael. At each end of the pediment is an angel on a tiny temple playing a cornet. It is a façade of sheer exhilaration.

If you don't wish to spoil the effect of the entrancing frontage, standing on the site of the Roman forum, take the interior of the church as seen. It is both stark and dark. Through the murk a Madonna by Andrea della Robbia may be discerned, and a panel of saints by Filippino Lippi. The church was intended to match its façade in height but funds ran out.

Go past the over-grand Palazzo Pretorio, the Piazza Napoleone (generously still named for him), the opera house in the small Piazza del Giglio and the church of SS Giovanni e Reparata, to reach the duomo, where the façade is very nearly as stupendous at that of San Michele and the interior is much more rewarding. The façade, not quite perfectly symmetrical, by Guidetto da Como, is one tier shorter than the other. It partly conceals a noble portico where the lintel and surrounds are by Nicola Pisano. There are also bas-reliefs illustrating the life of St Martin of Tours, the one who shared his cloak with a beggar. His name was chosen for the building when it was merely a parish church of the eleventh century, on the site of another seven hundred years older. It was much rebuilt long after that, but the façade and campanile (note the defensive openings, as at San Frediano) are thirteenth century. It would be a criminal act to attempt to 'improve' them. The beasts sculpted on the façade represent the fight between good and evil which would have been immediately apparent to the majority of citizens who, in the Middle Ages, were illiterate. Every carving, like every painting, told a story. It is good to be reminded that what we admire solely as art had a practical purpose.

The interior is gloomy but you should be able to make something of the roof of the very high nave decorated with brilliant blue, abstract motifs. Probably the paintings are not quite as dark as they seem, but equally probably they would benefit from cleaning. One of them, a Last Supper by Tintoretto, is outstanding. A 200-lire coin will light it for a minute; if you are short of change wait for the meter to be fed by a group leader. It is a painting packed with activity, showing the apostles leaning across the table at each other in vigorous exchanges. Mary Magdalene slumps on steps at the bottom right-hand corner. Above Christ, at a table which the artist has drawn obliquely, almost vertically, is a great glow of glory, with angels milling around at the top of the canvas.

There is statuary by della Quercia and Civitali, the latter being responsible for the Tempietto del Volto Santo protecting the eleventh-century wooden crucifix that is Lucca's foremost religious relic. The story goes that Nicodemus, the Pharisee who helped to bury Christ, carved it from memory and that centuries later it was washed up on the Tuscan shore at Luni. The citizens of Luni regarded it as their treasure trove but the Lucchese made claim to it. A bishop (of Lucca, as it happens) was asked to arbitrate, which he did by placing the crucifix on a cart and bidding the mule pulling it to go where God intended. The animal took it to Lucca. Archibald Lyall says it was a Byzantine cross of much later date and made of cedar wood. The Lucchese will have none of that, always supposing that they have actually read Mr Lyall's excellent guide, and they are backed by the faithful of other parts of Tuscany, who come annually, on 13 September, to see the relic paraded through the city.

The cathedral museum is now in the church of SS Giovanni e Reparato. A major exhibit is the early-fifteenth-century tomb, known as *Ilaria del Carretto,* by Jacopo della Quercia. It shows, in effigy, the young second wife of Paolo Guinigi whose Gothic house beyond the medieval walls is now the Museo Nationale. Paolo Guinigi ruled Lucca, well though despotically, from 1400-30. He was one of a network of merchants and bankers who were agents and scouts for the pope, helping to ferry information and tithes to Rome.

Guinigi's name also belongs to the crenellated brick tower from which oak trees sprout maturely like umbrellas. It can be visited but, if you have to make a choice, plump for the museum, which is strong in archaeology, marquetry, Romanesque sculpture and Etruscan jewellery. It also takes pride in its collection of works by indigenous artists. The other major museum is the Pinacoteca on a corresponding site at the other side of the

Lucca: Torre Guinigi, Piazza dei Mercanti

city, occupying the Palazzo Mansi.

    The Pinacoteca stands behind heavy doors in a high Luccan street. Visitors are admitted on the half-hour several times a day for a tour that is not guided but is accompanied. It provides an opportunity of inspecting the interior of what I take to be a typical town mansion. Many of the rooms are heavily hung with boldly pictorial tapestries and there is what is called a Conjugal Chamber where an enormous canopied bed lies behind a gilded arch supported by caryatids. The overpowering effect is partly mitigated by a pleasantly patterned floral counterpane and wall. Subsequent bedrooms become calmer but, on another floor, the walls and ceilings have violent representations of the elements.

The many paintings include two recently restored. One is an anonymous exquisite thirteenth-century Madonna and Child painted on wood, beautifully composed with the Virgin leaning to one side, her long thin fingers and hand at right angles beneath the child's (also long) left hand. Up in a corner is St Ann in a tiny triangle. The other, by Giovanni Stradano, is an imposing St Martin on horseback in process of cutting up his cloak. There are many portraits of members of the Mansi family and two of Puccini. A Pontormo of a smart young man is difficult to see because of reflection; a Veronese high on a wall is all but invisible.

On the ground floor, where a large hansom cab stands behind the massive doors, several rooms are devoted to costumes, with ladies' gowns sparingly displayed, each one in its own glass cage.

Another museum is devoted to Giacomo Puccini, who was born in Lucca. You can pay for a guided tour of the premises, close to San Michele, where the happy event took place. In an adjoining piazza there is a statue of the composer smoking a cigar. Also born in Lucca was Luigi Boccherini. He doesn't have a museum but his works, and others by native composers, are performed at the Sagra Musicale Lucchese, held twice yearly in spring and summer.

Amongst the churches I have not mentioned there are at least seventeen within the walls alone. They must offer something to the connoisseur but attempting to visit all of them might provoke some violent reaction. I suggest taking in those upon which you happen to stumble during your peregrinations. Santa Maria della Rosa incorporates a section of Roman city wall; San Giusto combines the more extrovert Luccan style with the more formal Pisan-Romanesque; San Pietro Somaldi has a jolly doorway; San Francesco has Boccherini's tomb and San Paolino is, for a change, Renaissance, despite harbouring a pre-Christian sarcophagus. That will do. And the same goes for palaces, of which there are an inordinate number. Enjoy them as wallpaper as you stroll about, assimilating the flavour of Lucca, a city, you may be surprised to learn, that relies very much on agriculture for its prosperity, and especially on olive oil of the extra virgin variety. In the past, industry was important – the city was noted for its cutlery – but today the emphasis has returned to what comes from the land.

Historically, Lucca was the one Tuscan city which outployed Florence. Although occasionally under submission to Pisa, across a low mountain range (now penetrated by road tunnel) it was, for most of the time, an independent state or duchy, having at one stage Volterra, Pistoia and Sarzana within its territory. Its borders were extended by Castruccio Castracani, who was held in high repute by Machiavelli. He once defeated a massive army of Guelphs, captured a Florentine chariot and gave thousands of prisoners a feast in a piazza, before despatching them to prison. He had style but, unfortunately for his compatriots, he contracted malaria, which was the end of him and of Luccan supremacy.

But not of independence. Once free from Pisa, Lucca remained outside the Medici Grand Duchy until Napoleon Bonaparte stormed into Italy and gave the city to his sister Elisa Baciocchi. She was promoted to princess and it was during her tenure that the Piazza Napoleone was laid out. Here may be seen the statue of Maria Theresa, a Spanish Bourbon to whom the Congress of Vienna awarded the Duchy. In 1847, for a brief spell, it was joined to the grander Duchy of Tuscany at last, but by then all Medici influence had gone and in 1860 it became part of the almost unified state of Italy.

If you stay in or near Lucca, use it as a base from which to visit other northern Tuscan cities, particularly Florence. Take a coach from Lucca to Florence and you are free of parking problems, with the added advantage that on the return journey, after slogging it about the capital of the Renaissance for several hours, you can enjoy a doze on the autostrada.

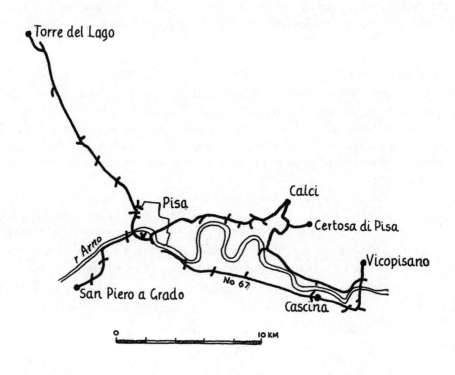

Torre del Lago

Pisa

Calci

Certosa di Pisa

Vicopisano

r Arno

San Piero a Grado

No 67

Cascina

10 KM

14   Pisa and Environs

Pisa; Torre del Lago; Calci; Certosa di Pisa; Vicopisano; San Piero a Grado

Those who come to Pisa only because they have heard of the astonishing tilt of its tower may not be interested in knowing more of its history. Next time rounders will like to be reminded that it was once a maritime power dominating the western Mediterranean, sending argosies to its colonies in the Balearics, Elba, Corsica, Sardinia, and despatching its fleet to drive the Saracens out of Sicily.

Pisa was probably the first place in Tuscany known to anyone apart from its indigenous tribes or the Villanovans who settled it. The Greeks established a trading post here around the seventh century BC. Half a millennium on it became of vital importance to the Romans, so much so that when the River Arno, which with its then tributary the Serchio flowed into the lagoon, silted up, the Emperor Augustus founded a new port at what we call Leghorn. The Italians call it Livorno, the Romans named it Portus Pisanus.

Long after the Roman empire had disintegrated the Pisans held supremacy of the seas as an independent power, until one of its city state rivals, Genova, sank its fleet at the battle of Meloria in 1284. Following this disaster Pisa gradually lost its empire, was conquered by the Viscontis of Milan and sold by them to Florence in 1406. The Pisans accepted this only after a long, bitter fight because they were Ghibellines, under the Holy Roman Empire, and their independence had been upheld by both Henry IV and Barbarossa. The Florentines, like the Genovese, were Guelphs, supporters of the pope.

During the centuries of its pre-eminence Pisa has been endowed with the most exquisite complex of ecclesiastical buildings ever imagined, erected on a great swathe of lawn where, even today, at the height of the tourist season, the grass remains green throughout the summer.

The fabled centre of Pisa was almost entirely saved in the terrible German retreat of 1944. It might still be spared if the owners of the stalls, bulging with rubbishy souvenirs, lying on the perimeter of the Piazza dei Miracoli, were ordered to another site beside a main coach park, but even if that were to happen the crowds would still be enormous. Admission by ticket, limited to so many hundred a day, might work, although that would be certain to inspire a racket and would also be hard on genuine worshippers.

What should be remembered is that these beautiful buildings would not be here but for the success of Pisan commerce. You could call them the acceptable face of capitalism; the sinking of the fleet at Meloria and the sacking of Palermo being the reverse, for those on the losing side. This is not the place to take that argument further; better to feel grateful that the chances of war left the best of the complex unscathed. What were lost were all too many of the frescoes in the Camposanto, the adjoining cloister and cemetery, although even there it was not as bad as it seemed at first. When restoration began the under-drawings were revealed. When a fresco is painted on to a clean base speed is essential because it dries rapidly. There is little or no time for second thoughts, so painters learned to work from drawings already made. These are now on show in the Museo delle Sinopie which occupies the thirteenth-century hospice.

One of Pisa's most famous sons was Galileo, the astronomer who upset the considered opinion of the time by believing and saying that not only does the earth rotate on its own axis, but that it moves round the sun at the same time. Such political incorrectness brought him before the Inquisition and forced him into retirement. His life and work are as well known as his native city, where the celebrated leaning tower was brought into his scientific studies.

The leaning tower is as first time round as the Taj Mahal and Niagara Falls only because of its dramatic tilt caused by subsidence soon after building commenced in 1173. It has gone on leaning, fractionally more all the time, and nowadays visitors are not permitted to undergo the queasy experience of climbing its unprotected arcades. Forget the lean, the tower is a serenely lovely building and still would be if it were upright. It is also part of a wondrous complex. If you have never done so, try to spend a night in Pisa to experience these buildings late in the day when the crowds have departed and you may sit on the steps by the apse of the duomo and gaze up at the tower. When you can tear yourself away, walk to the great west frontage of the cathedral and drink that in for a while, then turn round and repeat the ritual facing the baptistery. There is no need here to say more about these familiar structures. I have known them for more than thirty years and never tire of seeing them.

However, for this visit we should concentrate on the other sights of Pisa, beginning with the Piazza dei Cavalieri where the republic was born nearly six hundred years ago. It then looked very different because Cosimo I, long after Florence had assumed power, had Vasari redesign it, partly for the benefit of the Knights of St Stephen, whose particular crusade was directed against piracy in the Mediterranean. Their church of Santo Stefano (1569) alongside their palace, now part of the university, is decorated with the Medici balls and many busts. Vasari also refashioned the clock house, including in it what remained of the tower where the admiral in charge of that fated Pisan fleet was incarcerated. He, along with his wretched family, were condemned to starve there. There are attractive buildings on all sides of the piazza and, inevitably, a statue of Cosimo, outside his former palace. He stands with his right foot on what appears to be a crocodile. He is often rendered ludicrous by the presence of a pigeon on his bald pate.

Walk to the Arno on the Via Curtatone e Montanara, where you will find an entrance to the School of Jurisprudence leading to a charming courtyard. Here galleries are dotted with busts of famous Pisan scholars, all in deep yellow ochre.

Proceed to the river and admire its graceful curve. Of the numerous churches away from the Piazza Campo dei Miracoli, the most celebrated is Santa Maria della Spina, an item of sheer wedding cake set beside the Arno in a position higher than when it was built in the early 1300s. It was then placed too close to the water and became, over the centuries, undermined by damp. So, in 1871 it was painstakingly demolished, stone by stone, finial by finial, gable by gable, and reconstructed many feet higher. It is a gorgeous little building in pink marble housing a Madonna and Child by Nicola Pisano, whose workshop was responsible for most of the statuary. It is unfortunate that for feast days it is fitted with fairy lights. The effect is regrettably vulgar and the practice should be discontinued. The church takes its name from the thorns in Christ's crown, one of which was a relic here.

Santa Maria stands beside the Lungarno Gambacorti where the river bends. It is one of six sections of the embankment, each named differently, but prefixed Lungarno. Enhancing this riparian scene are many of the palaces of Pisa, some with literary associations. (Byron wrote parts of *Don Juan* in one of them.) They are individually decorated, although not as richly as the palazzi lining the Grand Canal in Venice. They contribute much to the essential quality of romance which pervades the setting. Lean on one of the bridges. Give yourself to it. Pisa is good for the spirit here, along the Arno, just as it is in the field of miracles.

At one end of the Lungarno Mediceo is the Museo Nazionale di San Matteo, occupying a former monastery. Much of it, very properly, is devoted to Pisan painting and sculpture, with religious subjects, of course,

Pisa: Santa Maria della Spina

predominating. I regret to record that from a visit in 1991 very little remains in my memory. As a museum it did not bowl me over in the way that the Pinacoteca at Siena did and I have not been able to revisit it.

The other museum, attached to the cathedral, contains items from the buildings in the Piazza dei Miracoli, superb sculptures from the baptistery, by the Pisanos, Nicola and Giovanni, for instance, and the cathedral pulpit by Guglielmo which made way for a later one by the abovementioned Giovanni. In fact this is a copy because Guglielmo's original went to Sardinia to another cathedral. The museum is also a repository for items formerly in other Pisan churches, things Egyptian, Etruscan and Roman, mainly of archaeological interest. There are documents of Pisan history, Roman milestones and a Madonna and Child in ivory by G. Pisano.

Not far away, at the end of the Via Santa Caterina, is the church of the same name with a pretty Pisan frontage above two ugly blind arches. Note the supporting houses in a yellow wash, one of them at right angles. They give the church a precinctual air.

Pisa also has Botanical Gardens, a haven of peace at the centre, attractive shopping streets, many palaces and fine houses. It ceased to be a port long ago but on the south side of the Arno estuary there is a marina with miles of sands. Memories of maritime greatness are revived when it is Pisa's turn to host the Historical Regatta, an event shared with Genova, Amalfi and Venice. June is the month for this and other celebrations centred upon the Arno, some to honour the city's patron saint, Rainier, about whom I am unable to discover anything more.

On the north bank of the Arno a vast pine forest stretches over what was once Medici property and is now largely a national nature park. Beyond, beside the western bank of Lake Masaciuccoli is a house, built upon the ruins of an early watchtower, where Puccini lived and composed. The community that has grown up there and, in effect, become part of extended Viareggio, is called Torre del Lago. The Villa Puccini is now a museum. There is a statue of him in a public garden outside, where he is posed, standing somewhat flamboyantly, smoking, and wearing a large-brimmed trilby. The lakeside restaurant is a pleasant lunching place, with a view of mountains across the water. The museum is a hotchpotch of Puccini memorabilia that is strictly for devotees only. Ownership of the villa has been contested for twenty years during which time its condition has deteriorated alarmingly, but Puccini's granddaughter last year launched an appeal to restore both it and the birthplace in Lucca.

East of Pisa, beyond where the Arno performs extravagant loops, is a charterhouse founded in the late fourteenth century. It is approached through the small town of Calci, where there is an eleventh-century church with a crumbling tower and a once handsome west frontage. Here St Catherine, according to one source, met the English mercenary Sir John Hawkwood, engaging his services on behalf of the church militant. She was certainly a saint to involve herself in material matters, and she is known to have corresponded with Hawkwood. Calci, at the foot of Monte Pisano, on a site that does not suggest any strategic significance, has nonetheless attracted all rulers of this territory since the Etruscans.

The Certosa stands aloof from Calci by a kilometre or two. It is now mainly seventeenth century, an enormous complex of buildings providing for only fifteen monks who had their own suites, although most of them did not get their own graves, because they were buried in the earth where they quickly decomposed and added to the sulphurous nature of the soil.

205

A large rectangular forecourt with gateway and lawns is the visitor's introduction to the monastery itself. On one side is a double gallery housing the Museo di Storia Nature e del Territorie, a department of Pisa University. The right-hand wall has bas-relief statues in stony settings beside highly decorated gates. Facing you is a three-storey ecclesiastical mansion with sixteen bays on either side of a monumental grand staircase. There are two lesser arched entrances symmetrically placed, with pediments high above them, on which clockfaces permanently record the hour of 11.25.

The guided tour, which lasts an hour, begins with a lecture about the monks' routine in the somewhat cramped quarters of the pharmacy. Once into the main building you are all but overpowered by the frescoes on walls and ceilings. The chapel is so vividly decorated that you would think it bound to distract from the contemplative approach to life. The colours are joyful but the painting mediocre. There is a marble altar below some effective trompe l'oeil and an extraordinary throne with cherubs' heads at the end of each arm rest.

Every monk had, as well as an en suite apartment, his own chapel with marble floors in abstract patterns – squares, diamonds, octagons, rectangles, cubes, and so on, in black, grey and white. The walls of these chapels are more calmly decorated than the main church and culminate in one that might have come out of a sample book for Regency wallpapers. And there are panels of biblical scenes which do not shout at you.

The cloister is so large that it must have been possible for all fifteen monks to walk and meditate without ever encountering a colleague. The centre enclosed what is virtually a small wood surrounding a huge monumental fountain.

The Certosa today emanates an atmosphere of calm prosperity.

The lower Arno valley is heavily industrialized and crisscrossed with motorways and other roads, many of them on long, low bridges skimming over fields. Not a pretty sight, not in keeping with the image of alluring Tuscany. A small haven, south of Pisa, is found down a straight avenue of thick lime trees at the little town of Vicopisano. Here there is a delectable Romanesque church with a low frontage on which there are simple carvings, on one cornerstone, of three characters, all looking like cartoons of Alec Guinness, about to dismember one of their number. Be sure to observe the side of the nave which has a graceful slope; try to blot out the clock tower of much later date. Inside there is a moving Deposition carved in wood. The Stations of the Cross have been grouped into two lots of seven in double rows and are simple plaques. The columns are interestingly varied, so are the historiations.

The seventeenth-century town hall, in a pink wash, has many

white medallions and is joined to a medieval tower. It looks out on a garden where there is a construction made up of many stone balls, perhaps celebrating several Medici at once. Up a steep hill is the keep of the former castle whose walls may have been built by Brunelleschi.

The town stands below Monte Pisano where the hill is topped with a single line of trees, like sentinels.

A final act of patience is required if you are to end this Tuscan odyssey on a truly uplifting note. You must return to Pisa along unlovely highways and navigate towards the Marina, passing through drab, semi-industrial suburbs until you come upon the superb Romanesque church of San Piero a Grado, four kilometres south-west of the city. It is unique in that it has four apses (three of them at the same end) and no frontage, just two long stretches of nave. Its origin lies in the arrival of St Peter from Rome at a quayside here. There has been a church here since the fourth century and parts of the apses of that, and its successor, have been excavated. The present building was begun in the tenth century and finished in the following. The tower was destroyed by the Germans in 1944 because they believed it would be a valuable look-out point for the Allies. Only a small portion of it has been rebuilt.

San Piero a Grado: basilica

The brickwork, inside and out, reflects many building periods and materials. The colours are too numerous to mention – brick, stone and the ceramic saucers seen at San Miniato, in the Morescan style, blend to make a marvellous composition. The columns have different styles with foliated capitals topped by a row, on either side of the central aisle, of about eighty early popes. Above them are murals, late twelfth–early thirteenth century, by Deodati Orlandi of Lucca. Some are in a good state of restoration. The altar is below the single, later, apse, and is a plain stone table with marble top. Behind it is the simplest of wooden thrones. To one side is a fresco of, perhaps, St Peter.

Well-prepared hand-outs in English, French, German are free and helpful, adding to one's appreciation of this exquisite building which encapsulates much of what you will have experienced of Tuscany. Do not deny yourself the warmth of feeling romantic about this marvellous church, which has survived the vicissitudes of many centuries of warfare. It is the likes of San Piero which make Tuscany so appealing; what you may feel in your bones is there in its stones, and I say that as an uncompromising unbeliever in the faith it represents.

Bibliography

A complete bibliography of works about Tuscany and the Renaissance would fill a book longer than this one. Here I will mention a few which I found helpful, enjoyable, informative or all three.

Bartlett, Vernon, *A Tuscan Retreat*, Chatto & Windus, London, 1955.

Berenson, Bernard, *Italian Painters of the Renaissance*, Phaidon Press, London, 1952.

Borsook, Eve, *The Companion Guide to Florence*, Fontana Books, London, 1973.

Bull, George, *Michelangelo: A Bibliography*, Viking, London, 1995.

Fabbri, Don Basilio, *Loro Ciuffenna e Pratomagna*, Loro Ciuffenna, 1996.

Hale, J.R. Hale (ed.), *Dictionary of the Italian Renaissance*, Thames & Hudson, London, 1995.

Hearder, H. and Waley, D.P. (eds), *A Short History of Italy*, Cambridge University Press, 1963.

Insight Guide, *Tuscany*, A.P.A. Publications, London, 1993.

James, Henry, *Italian Hours*, Penguin Books, London, 1995.

Lyall, Archibald, *The Companion Guide to Tuscany*, Collins, London, 1973.

McCarthy, Mary, *The Stones of Florence*, Heinemann, London, 1959.

Michelin, *Tuscany, the Green Guide*, Michelin, London, 1996.

Murray, Peter and Linda, *The Art of the Renaissance*, Thames & Hudson, London, 1963.

Origo, Iris, *The Merchant of Prato*, Penguin Books, London, 1992.

Origo, Iris, *War in Val d'Orcia*, Century Hutchinson, London, 1985.

Phaidon, *Florence and Tuscany: Cultural Guide*, Phaidon Press, London, 1986.

Scarini, Alfio, *Romanesque Pievi of the Upper Arno Valley*, Grafiche Calosci, Cortona, 1990.

Vasari, Giorgio, *Lives of the Artists*, (trans. George Bull), 2 vols, Penguin, London, 1965, 1987.

I also consulted dictionaries of architecture, art, history and saints, in addition to numerous handbooks and brochures to galleries, museums, palaces, institutions, churches, cathedrals, abbeys and private collections.

Appendix

Glossary of some architectural terms used in the text

Ambulatory – a semicircular or polygonal aisle enclosing an apse or straight-ended sanctuary

Baldacchino – a canopy over a throne, altar, doorway, etc.

Bas-relief – a carved relief projecting only slightly from its background

Campanile – a bell tower, usually separate from the main building

Capital – the head or crowning feature of a column

Choir – the part of a church where the service is sung

Clerestory – the upper stage of the main walls of a church above the aisle roofs, pierced by windows

Corbel – a projecting block, usually of stone, supporting a beam or other horizontal member

Finial – slim, vertical ornamental crowner to a roof or other feature

Historiated – Decorated with flowers or animals.

Lantern – a circular or polygonal turret with windows or openings above a dome or roof

Loggia – a gallery or room open on one or more sides, sometimes pillared

Meurtrière – vertical slit, usually in a castle tower or wall, through which to shoot arrows

Misericord – a bracket on the underside of a hinged choir stall for leaning against, when turned up, during long standing services

Oculi – circular openings in a wall or at the apex of a dome

Pargeting – exterior plastering of a timber-framed building

Pendentive – a concave spandrel leading from the angle of the two walls to the base of a circular dome

Piano nobile – the main floor of a house, containing the receptions rooms

Predella – painted panels below the principal scene or scenes on an altar-piece

Putti – plump naked cupids or angels in Renaissance and baroque paintings and sculpture

Reredos – a decorated wall or screen, usually of wood or stone, behind an altar

Rotunda – a round, especially domed, building or hall

211

Rustication – masonry cut in massive blocks, separated from each other by deep joints

Stela – an upright stone slab or tablet

Tondo – a circular painting or carving in relief

Tufa – the commonest Roman building stone, formed from volcanic dust

Tumulus – a mound covering an ancient burial or tomb

Tympanum – the area between the lintel of a doorway and the arch above it

Voussoir – a brick or wedge-shaped stone forming one of the units of an arch

Index of People and Places

Places are shown in upper case.
Rivers are listed in one group.
Bold numbers indicate main entry.
Dates of birth and death are given where known.
HRE denotes Holy Roman Empire

Ian Norrie, born in Southborough, Kent, in 1927 was a journalist at Eastbourne before becoming a bookseller. From 1956 to 1988 his main occupation was as manager, then proprietor, of Hampstead's High Hill Bookshop but he has also written and edited many books, contributed reviews and articles to newspapers and magazines, and dabbled in publishing. He was Secretary and, later, Chairman of the Society of Bookmen and served on the Executive Council of the National Book League (now Book Trust) for thirteen years, and on the management committee of the Booker Prize for three. He and Mavis, his wife, have two daughters and four grandchildren. They live in Barnet, Hertfordshire.

Michael Floyd, born in Somerset, in 1923, was an architect who qualified in 1950 after war service with Bomber Command had interrupted his studies. He was in private practice for thirty years and was a member of the Society of Architect Artists with whom he has exhibited at the RIBA. He contributed appreciations of the architecture of Hampstead, the City and Westminster to symposiums published by the High Hill Press during the 1960s. Until his death in December 1997, he lived in London.

Ian and Michael collaborated on NEXT TIME ROUND IN PROVENCE which is now in its second impression and NEXT TIME ROUND IN THE DORDOGNE, both available from Aurum Press.